Transnational Actors and Stories of European Integration

Clash of Narratives

Edited by
Wolfram Kaiser and Richard McMahon

Routledge
Taylor & Francis Group

LONDON AND NEW YORK

First published 2019
by Routledge
2 Park Square, Milton Park, Abingdon, Oxon, OX14 4RN, UK

and by Routledge
52 Vanderbilt Avenue, New York, NY 10017, USA

First issued in paperback 2020

Routledge is an imprint of the Taylor & Francis Group, an informa business

British Library Cataloguing-in-Publication Data
A catalogue record for this book is available from the British Library

ISBN 13: 978-0-367-58305-7 (pbk)
ISBN 13: 978-0-367-08646-6 (hbk)

Typeset in Myriad Pro
by codeMantra

Publisher's Note
The publisher accepts responsibility for any inconsistencies that may have arisen during the conversion of this book from journal articles to book chapters, namely the possible inclusion of journal terminology.

Disclaimer
Every effort has been made to contact copyright holders for their permission to reprint material in this book. The publishers would be grateful to hear from any copyright holder who is not here acknowledged and will undertake to rectify any errors or omissions in future editions of this book.

MIX
Paper from
responsible sources
FSC™ C013985

Printed in the United Kingdom
by Henry Ling Limited

Transnational Actors and Stories of European Integration

This book makes a major contribution to understanding European politics and identity. It examines how politicians, cultural elites, and other actors fight over Europe's future with words and stories, telling narratives about European integration in different political, social, and cultural contexts. The chapters explore how actors formulate stories to make sense of Europe's past and contemporary challenges and to legitimise their own positions and preferences. The contributors explore themes ranging from divisive stories about the European Union (EU), mobilised in institutional reform referendums, to the top-down deployment of legitimising narratives by EU institutions, religiously inspired apocalyptic narratives of European unity, and stories about nations and Europe told by museums and academics. Combined, the chapters of this book are essential reading for everyone interested in Europe's common past and contemporary challenges and the EU's highly contested nature in times of apparently increasing disintegration.

Wolfram Kaiser is a Professor of European Studies at the University of Portsmouth, UK. He has published widely on contemporary European history and politics including *Writing the Rules for Europe* (with J. Schot) and *International Organizations and Environmental Protection* (edited with J.H. Meyer).

Richard McMahon lectures on EU politics at University College London. He has written widely on European political identities, including in the context of European integration, and in a monograph entitled *The Races of Europe: Construction of National Identities in the Social Sciences, 1839–1939*.

Contents

Citation Information

The chapters in this book were originally published in *National Identities*, volume 19, issue 2 (June 2017). When citing this material, please use the original page numbering for each article, as follows:

Chapter 1
Narrating European integration: transnational actors and stories
Wolfram Kaiser and Richard McMahon
National Identities, volume 19, issue 2 (June 2017) pp. 149–160

Chapter 2
Different narratives, one area without internal frontiers: why EU institutions cannot agree on the refugee crisis
Adina Maricut
National Identities, volume 19, issue 2 (June 2017) pp. 161–177

Chapter 3
The Promethean role of Europe: changing narratives of the political and scholarly left
Nikola Petrović
National Identities, volume 19, issue 2 (June 2017) pp. 179–197

Chapter 4
Almost the same stories: narrative patterns in EU treaty referendums
Wolf J. Schünemann
National Identities, volume 19, issue 2 (June 2017) pp. 199–214

Chapter 5
One narrative or several? Politics, cultural elites, and citizens in constructing a 'New Narrative for Europe'
Wolfram Kaiser
National Identities, volume 19, issue 2 (June 2017) pp. 215–230

Chapter 6
Progress, democracy, efficiency: normative narratives in political science EU studies
Richard McMahon
National Identities, volume 19, issue 2 (June 2017) pp. 231–249

Chapter 7

European Union or Kingdom of the Antichrist? Protestant apocalyptic narratives and European unity

Brent F. Nelsen and James L. Guth

National Identities, volume 19, issue 2 (June 2017) pp. 251–267

Chapter 8

Post-communist invocation of Europe: memorial museums' narratives and the Europeanization of memory

Ljiljana Radonić

National Identities, volume 19, issue 2 (June 2017) pp. 269–288

For any permission-related enquiries please visit:
http://www.tandfonline.com/page/help/permissions

Notes on Contributors

James L. Guth has taught at Furman University, Greenville, USA since 1973. He has served as the Chair of the University Faculty and of the Politics and International Affairs Department as well as on many faculty committees and task forces. His recent work has assessed the impact of religion on the electoral process and on public policy in the Clinton, Bush, and Obama administrations.

Wolfram Kaiser is a Professor of European Studies at the University of Portsmouth, UK. His main research interests are contemporary European history and politics, especially European integration and the European Union (EU), and Europe's international relations past and present.

Adina Maricut is a Postdoctoral Researcher at the Hertie School of Governance, Berlin, Germany. Her research interests lie in the area of EU institutional decision-making, with a focus on political accountability in EU economic governance and institutional behaviour in the field of justice and home affairs.

Richard McMahon lectures in EU Politics at University College London. Previously, he worked as a Brussels-based journalist of EU affairs and taught at University College Cork, Birkbeck and the universities of Bath, Portsmouth, Chichester and Siegen. He has written widely on European political identities.

Brent F. Nelsen is an American Political Science Professor at Furman University, Greenville, USA. He has held positions on the Board of Directors of the Corporation for Public Broadcasting, Washington, D.C., USA and was the Republican Candidate for State Superintendent of Education for South Carolina in 2010.

Nikola Petrović is a Research Associate at the Institute for Social Research in Zagreb, Croatia. His research interests include sociology of science, research of ideologies and European studies.

Ljiljana Radonić is a member of the research staff in the Institute of Culture Studies and Theatre History at the Austrian Academy of Sciences, Vienna, Austria. Her research interests include memory politics in Central and South East Europe, memory theory with a focus on World War II and the communist era, theory of anti-Semitism, psychoanalysis as a theory of society, and critical gender studies.

Wolf J. Schünemann is an Assistant Professor of Political Science at Hildesheim University, Germany. He does research and teaching in the fields of international relations, European integration, and Internet governance. He serves as a Spokesperson of the subgroup "Politics and the Internet," established under the umbrella of the German Political Science Association.

Narrating European integration: transnational actors and stories

Wolfram Kaiser and Richard McMahon

ABSTRACT
This article introduces the special issue on narrating European integration. Narratives, or stories, are a key mechanism for constructing individual and collective identities, and other politically important elements of discourse. The articles in this special issue go beyond most existing work on narratives. First, they examine the actors and networks, ranging from EU institutions to political parties and social groups, which create, foster and disseminate narratives. Second, they address major narratives and sets of narrating actors of at least a partly transnational nature. Third, the authors transgress disciplinary boundaries, drawing on contemporary history, sociology, political science and cultural studies.

This special issue explores narratives of European integration, broadly conceived, in politics, society, and culture. It contributes to the growing literature on the structures, functions, and characteristics of narratives and their contestation within and across societies. Though narratives can have lasting impact on individual or collective identities, research on their role has only just begun to flourish in the fields of European Studies and European Union (EU) studies. The articles in this special issue go beyond most existing work in three ways. First, they broaden out the study of narratives by closely examining the actors and networks in politics, society, and culture which create, foster, and disseminate narratives. Second, they do not treat isolated country cases. Instead, they address major narratives of at least a partly transnational nature – narratives developed and advanced by actors, ranging from EU institutions to political parties and social groups. These are themselves transnationally constituted or at least draw on transnational connections and learning processes. Third, to reconstruct these transnational actors and narratives, the authors transgress disciplinary boundaries, drawing on contemporary history, sociology, political science, and cultural studies.

Like most academic literature, we define narratives as a series of events or developments told, more or less cohesively, along a storyline or plot (Kaiser, 2015, p. 365), like the rags to riches story of Ireland's Celtic Tiger that Wolf Schünemann mentions in his article. The concept's roots in literary studies go back to the late 1950s, and several decades earlier in Russian language studies (Czarniawska, 2004, pp. 1–2). However, it gained wider academic currency after the so-called linguistic turn of the 1970s and

1980s (Maza, 1996, pp. 1493–1495; Shenhav, 2005, pp. 76–78), especially through concepts of 'grand', 'master' and 'meta' narratives originally developed by Hayden White (1973) and Jean-François Lyotard (1979). Many historians, sociologists, anthropologists, cultural studies scholars and others eagerly engaged with the linguistic turn. They assume that the motivations behind social (including political) interpretations and actions are as often swayed by cultural habits, as by attempts to maximize the individual or group interests that rational choice-informed literature emphasizes.

More recently, research in a growing number of academic disciplines has used the concept of narrative as a key to understanding discourse and its impact on politics, society, and culture, not least because it offers an indispensable antidote to 'the essentializing tendencies of "identity politics" around categories like race, sex, and gender' (Hammack & Pilecki, 2012, p. 77). Moreover, human beings have a 'natural tendency to think in narratives' (Shenhav, 2005, p. 76). This gives storytelling its unrivalled power to make ideas about 'cultural, socio-economic and political developments' seem significant, understandable, and plausible (Della Sala, 2010, p. 4; Kaiser, 2015, p. 2).

For this reason, psychologists have been increasingly captivated by narratives since the 1980s. Some rate them as our 'primary' way of linking 'the individual mind' to political and social realities and investing emotionally in them (Hammack & Pilecki, 2012, pp. 76–78). The coherent identities of individuals and social groups depend heavily on the sense of continuity that narratives provide (Hammack, 2008, pp. 10–11). Crucially, narratives do not just describe what happens. They construct how we perceive, remember and tell stories about what happens (Maza, 1996, p. 1495; Roberts, 2006, p. 710). The story we believe in influences how we react, engage, make demands and more generally, seek to shape our social and political environment. Parables and epics have therefore been mainstays of socialisation throughout human history, and they are formidable political weapons. Master narratives have, for example, played a key role in the social construction of nations and in the political integration of states since the nineteenth century. Nationalists have narrated, and continue to narrate, key events of their countries' histories as episodes in a struggle for national independence, security, power or glory (Anderson, 2000).

This article will first set out the special issue theme of narratives in European integration. It will then introduce the articles and their individual and collective contribution to understanding these stories of integration and the roles of actors and networks in telling them. The article will go on to explore theoretical, conceptual and methodological issues of researching actors and narratives, and how the authors deal with them, before ending with some concluding comments.

Narratives in European integration

This special issue focusses on narratives that are widely disseminated in European society and can therefore have significant political impact. Such narratives have been crucial in defining myths about the origins of the present-day EU as well as its spatial scope, political finality, and policy objectives. Such narratives of European integration seek to explain it as a 'process', to legitimise (or call into question) the EU, its institutions and policies, or to describe, critically evaluate and contextualize them for citizens.

The EU's socio-economic crisis and political turmoil since 2008, including the possibility of individual member states like the United Kingdom leaving the organisation, has challenged the existing narratives that helped sustain public support for European integration. It has therefore stimulated political and academic interest in European narratives and discourse more generally. Sarah Maza identifies such crises as points when 'meanings have become indeterminate', allowing social actors to 'attempt to impose fixed meanings on social experience' (1996, p. 1500). Initially, many Europeans gave passive support to European integration, because it brought material benefits such as increased trade and prosperity as well as peace for Western Europe (Della Sala, 2010, p. 3). Following early left-wing criticism of the EU as a driver of economic liberalisation at the expense of social security and stability from the 1970s onwards, the troubled ratification of the Maastricht Treaty in 1992–1993 accelerated the breakdown of this 'permissive' consensus (Hooghe & Marks, 2009), and initiated increasingly heated debate over what is called the EU's democratic deficit. As subsequent treaty changes up to the 2009 Lisbon Treaty hugely increased the EU's powers and ambitions, more politicians and citizens began to reject deeper integration outright or demand that it be matched by greater democratic legitimacy, accountability, and transparency in its institutions and policy-making processes.

Many embattled political leaders now see solid public identification with the EU, based on some kind of shared cultural identity and political allegiance to its institutions, as the only solution to the EU's legitimacy crisis. In the early years of the European Community, the European Commission in particular very much focussed on improving the lot of citizens through 'output' in the form of beneficial legislation that helped to break down national barriers and implement the four freedoms, including freedom of movement. Since then, it has somewhat modified this highly technocratic approach. The EU as a whole has for example made efforts to create some kind of European cultural identity and unity. Thus, in the 1980s the European Community introduced symbols like the European flag, anthem and day, in the hope that their use would foster some form of European constitutional patriotism and allegiance to EU institutions (Calligaro, 2013; Manners, 2011). The EU has redoubled these efforts at creating a more secure cultural basis for the European polity since the ratification crisis over the Maastricht Treaty – a crisis that dramatically highlighted that citizen support for European integration could no longer be taken for granted (Littoz-Monnet & McMahon, 2013, p. 225).

Why then has no previous collective publication foregrounded the crucial role of narratives in shaping European discourses and identity? By contrast, research in European Studies as a multi- and interdisciplinary field has, since the late 1990s, recognised and analysed other, related ideational factors such as identity (Risse, 2010), memory (Leggewie & Lang, 2011; Macdonald, 2013), myths (Della Sala, 2010), norms (Manners, 2002), and culture (Shore, 2000) to some extent. Recent changes in political language may help explain why research on narratives is only just beginning to flourish in European Studies. Though political actors have always told stories as part of the art of persuasion, they and the general public have only recently begun consciously and openly to discuss narratives as powerful political tools and ask what new narrative, or narratives, could buoy up public support for European integration. Thus, the 'New Narrative for Europe' project, which ran during 2013–2014 and is examined in Wolfram Kaiser's article in this special issue, marks the European Commission's first important foray into exploiting the notion and concept of narrative.

Narratives are one of many ideas about the importance and use of political discourse that have filtered into common and political currency from academia. Academic approaches to the relationship between politics and discourse may therefore explain the late uptake of the concept of narratives. Political scientists who study the EU initially concentrated on those products of discourse, such as identity, memory, myths, and norms, which have the most immediate impact on political outcomes. Frank Schimmelfennig (2001) and Helene Sjursen (2002), for example, attributed the EU's decision to enlarge eastward after the end of the Cold War to it having become rhetorically entrapped in its own normative discourse.

This emphasis on political impact is also central to discussion by scholars of the EU of the concept of myth (Della Sala, 2010, p. 2), which is closely related to that of narrative. They focus heavily on how myth 'distorts', in order to give 'intention a natural justification' (Stråth, 2005, p. 260), and some discursive elements that they discuss as myths have no apparent story structure at all (Hansen & Williams, 1999, p. 240). By contrast, the political role and impact of narratives, like those of metaphors (Hülsse, 2006), rituals, symbols (Manners, 2011) or tropes, is often less immediately visible. However, narratives are essential building blocks and motors for politically important products of discourse, giving them their emotional force and direction (Kølvraa, 2016, p. 170). After all, stories are a key way of defining and reinforcing people's identities, or whom they fundamentally understand themselves to be, and therefore which moral codes and actions they consider appropriate (Somers, 1994).

Analysing actors and narratives

The contributors to this special issue are exceptionally well placed to establish narratives as a key concept in European Studies and to analyse their role in European politics, society, and culture. They all have some disciplinary connections with political science. Adina Maricut, for example, works in the political science sub-field of public policy analysis, which is devoted to understanding institutional behaviour and policy processes. Wolf Schünemann is a scholar of comparative politics, hence his interest in exploring similarities and differences between national referendum debates and their transnational character. However, their research topics and interest in cultural dimensions of European integration take all authors beyond narrowly political-institutional concerns. Some work at the interface of political science with religious studies (Jim Guth) or draw on transnational history within the context of interdisciplinary European Studies (Wolfram Kaiser, Richard McMahon, Brent Nelsen). Nikola Petrović and Schünemann engage thoroughly with sociological concepts and insights. Ljiljana Radonić's interdisciplinary profile and track-record even includes elements of philosophy and theatre studies. As a result, their articles highlight and explore how political actors interact with intellectuals, artists, and citizens (Kaiser), academics (McMahon, Petrović), museum directors and curators (Radonić) and religious leaders (Nelsen and Guth) in attempts to produce narratives of European integration. Most articles analyse narratives in explicitly political speeches, manifestos, press reports, institutional documents and website forum comments, but McMahon, Petrović and Nelsen and Guth also examine academic and religious texts.

The articles cluster around two approaches to the present-day impact of political narratives in European integration. First, Kaiser, Maricut and McMahon focus on the use of narratives to support political agendas, which in turn respond to the persisting crisis of the EU. Examining evolving positions of the European Commission, Parliament and Council of Ministers on the free movement of persons, Maricut concludes that institutions develop particular entrenched narratives to support their vision of, and preferences for, a policy field. Kaiser focuses on one key institution, the Commission, and how it attempted to mobilise the concept of narrative in order to address the EU's legitimacy crisis and lack of public engagement. McMahon in turn examines EU Studies as the intellectual infrastructure of European integration and therefore a crucial informal institution. He traces the changing narratives that academics produce about European integration.

The other four articles also consider narratives that are used to advocate political positions on European integration. However they expand their focus to broad cleavages in the identity and culture of Europeans which shape and are shaped by narratives of integration. Schünemann looks at campaign narratives in three EU treaty referenda in order to examine a fundamental political issue for the EU, the emerging division between pro-Europeans, who have supported further deepening, and Eurosceptics. The other three articles address much older divisions. As Schünemann points out, a crucial factor structuring pro and anti-European positions is the traditional right-left divide in politics. Nikola Petrović traces the emergence of new pro-integration narratives among centre-left parties and public intellectuals in the 1990s. Many EU citizens traditionally either identify themselves with the left or the right in politics or are associated with them through family histories or social networks. This is even truer of the religious cleavage that Nelsen and Guth investigate, between Catholicism and Protestantism. By looking at the fundamentalist fringe of Protestantism, they argue that its cultural influence informs some forms of ingrained Eurosceptic narratives. Both narratives contrast with the dominant post-war pro-integration narrative of Christian Democracy – a narrative characterized by its predominantly Catholic origins, the belief in some kind of Christian cultural unity and a strong commitment to broadly federalist forms of integration (Kaiser, 2007). Finally, Radonić addresses another crucial cleavage, between east and west. She contrasts narratives in newer post-communist EU member states with those prevailing in Western Europe.

Narratives of European integration

As this brief outline suggests, contributors address major transnational narratives of European integration. Among them are the oldest central legitimising story about European integration as a promoter of peace and prosperity (discussed in Kaiser's article) and more recent narratives of the EU as a force for good, promoting human rights and other liberal values around the world (Maricut, Petrović). Radonić considers whether condemnation of the Holocaust has become a core element of this liberal European identity. McMahon discusses and Schünemann and Maricut reference a different, progressive narrative of continuously deepening integration (Gilbert, 2008).

Contributors portray narratives as a field of contestation and complexity. Nelsen and Guth's religious fundamentalists, for example, oppose European integration, believing it will precipitate the apocalypse. Schünemann and McMahon discuss battles between Eurosceptic and pro-European narratives in referendum campaigns and political science articles, respectively. McMahon's EU scholars disagree about whether the democratic deficit is a genuine problem. Maricut meanwhile shows how the European Parliament and the Council of Ministers prioritise diametrically opposed principles of free movement and security, respectively. Petrović analyses such oppositions by using the theoretical concept of transvaluation of values, from Liah Greenfeld's work on nationalism (1992). This states that nations and other political groups partly define their values (or narratives) to mark their difference from rivals. Petrović thus claims that Europe's social model emerged partly from tensions with Ronald Reagan's neoliberal America. While recognising elements of transvaluation of values in the narratives of rival institutions, Maricut emphasises the role of instrumentalisation. This is also a key element for Kaiser, McMahon, and Radonić. Radonić suggests that some central and eastern European museums referenced the Holocaust instrumentally to promote their countries' EU accession, while others relativised condemnation of National Socialism by suggesting that Soviet crimes were equally bad.

Actors producing narratives

Much of discourse analysis in literary studies, where the technique emerged, and in memory studies, is exclusively concerned with discourses alone, with texts. By contrast, a key innovation of this special issue is, as Schünemann puts it, drawing on Foucault, to bring 'the actors back into focus'. Each paper therefore begins by introducing the roles, identities, interconnections, and practices of the actors, who devise, disseminate and receive narratives of European integration. They do so in complex patterns, usually in some kind of formal or informal institutional structures, whose specific practices shape the narratives.

Several actors normally partake in shaping and contesting narratives. Contributors highlight that political actors interact with diverse social and professional groups to produce narratives of European integration. Among these groups are intellectuals and artists in Kaiser's article, academics in McMahon's and Petrović's, museum organisers in Radonić's and religious leaders in Nelsen and Guth's. Petrović, though he insists on the importance of individual inputs into the contingent evolution of narratives, traces the emergence of common narratives among a whole class of centre-left politicians and public intellectuals. Maricut meanwhile argues, from a policy network perspective, that institutions can also act in practice as corporate narrating actors, developing consistent narratives. Contributors thus treat EU institutions, political parties or social groups as well as cultural institutions such as museums as narrating actors. The organisation of groups in formal institutions, networks, or communities is therefore crucial to the production of narratives. Social science literature on epistemic communities, political and policy networks and communities of practice has increasingly striven to understand these organisational and relational issues (Davis Cross, 2013, pp. 139–140).

The special issue examines very diverse approaches to linking actors together across borders. The coherence of transnational bonds runs from tight and formal, in European institutions (Kaiser, Maricut), to nebulous, as in the cultural background that links Radonić's museum directors and curators and Nelsen and Guth's Protestant fundamentalists. Between these extremes, there are elements of network connection among McMahon's EU scholars and, to an extent, Nelsen and Guth's Protestants. Schünemann's campaign groups are meanwhile brought together by specific events, in this case referenda, and ideology also links these campaign groups and Petrović's left-wingers.

A by-product of this transnational approach is a tendency to focus on political or cultural elites. Elites are more transnationally connected than other people (Favell, 2011) and, as at national level in nineteenth century Europe, play a key role in developing the narratives with the greatest impact on the politics of European integration. Kaiser, Maricut, Petrović, and Nelsen and Guth thus all analyse narratives produced by EU political leaders and key institutions. Petrović's emphasis on individual actors, and how their ideologies and attitudes towards European integration are transformed, leads him to focus on pro-EU politicians and public intellectuals with 'a powerful influence on the framing of debates in the EU'. Kaiser's actors include a group specifically selected by the European Commission as representing Europe's cultural elites, while McMahon's research methodology deliberately aims to identify the most prominent EU scholars. Even Schünemann and Nelsen and Guth, who focus to a greater extent on fringe narratives in EU referendum campaigns and Protestantism, respectively, identify the most prominent proponents of these narratives. The only major exception to this concentration on high profile elites is Kaiser's analysis of public comments on a Commission internet forum which engaged with the newly developed elite narrative text.

This focus in this special issue on elite narratives neatly complements other transnational approaches, which address discourse among the majority of the population. The latter often apply strongly quantitative approaches, as in the venerable tradition of analysing Eurobarometer results, and studies of what sociologists call the 'horizontal integration' of European populations (Favell, 2011). Qualitative ethnographies and discourse analyses of ordinary citizens' experiences of the EU have also emerged, especially from ethnographers and geographers (Armbruster, Rollo, & Meinhof, 2003).

This special issue is also innovative in extending its focus on narrating actors to their practices of producing, disseminating and receiving narratives within particular social contexts. McMahon and Schünemann's articles demonstrate how political science, International Relations and European Studies have recently drawn on sociology of knowledge to develop concepts and notions of actors and practices. However, the roots of the linguistic turn in textual analysis and the habits of intellectual history and political theory have delayed a shift towards analysing actors and their practices. Although constructivism and sociological institutionalism have shown some interest in practices for example (e.g. Adler & Pouliot, 2011; Lewis, 1998), their main focus remains the study of texts and ideas. The disciplines of sociology and anthropology concern themselves especially with social and political practices. However, for European Studies, with the notable exception of French scholarship, they have only recently emerged 'from the wilderness' (Favell & Guiraudon, 2011, p. 1).

Contributors demonstrate that practices of narration impact on the narratives themselves. Kaiser's article, for example, describes how narratives emerged from interchange between the Commission's instincts for tightly controlled message management and the anarchic individualism of a committee of intellectuals and artists that it set up. Radonić's analysis of museum displays naturally places greater emphasis on the practices of narration than an analysis of written text or speech would. She describes for example how east-central European commemorative museums borrowed the aesthetics of Holocaust memorialisation to legitimise politically instrumental messages that in some cases relativized the Holocaust.

Theories, concepts, and methods

Informed by their diverse disciplinary and cross-disciplinary affiliations, contributors adopt key theoretical approaches for understanding narratives, discourse, and identity within the context of European integration. Radonić's memory studies examine, for example, how the past is officially and privately constructed and commemorated. It stresses the competition for interpretative authority between different social and political groups within states, but also the attempts to re-narrate the past as shared European history. Developed in France in the 1980s, the Historical Memory School has looked especially at the way that states and their institutions commemorate their past, including in the monuments and museums that Radonić studies. Maricut meanwhile draws on post-positivist approaches from the rich theoretical body of policy narratives literature. Schünemann uses the Sociology of Knowledge Approach to Discourse, which builds on Foucauldian discourse analysis, but is more interested in those who produce discourse.

A key theoretical tension concerns the degree to which the contributors treat the narratives of each individual narrating actor as autonomous or as part of a common cultural discourse. The articles in this special issue all focus on broader cultural narratives, which circulate within a community, told and retold, as long as they sound plausible to storytellers and listeners (Della Sala, 2010, p. 4; Eder, 2006, p. 257; Kaiser, 2015, p. 2; Maza, 1996, p. 1495). For della Sala, this process is crucial for providing political legitimacy (2010, p. 5). For Klaus Eder, it constructs the boundaries of communities (2006, p. 258), and for Ian Manners, collective memories (2010, p. 82). In this volume, Maricut describes policy narratives as designed to achieve 'institutionally constructed' roles. Individual narrators put 'their organization's hat on'.

Contributors nevertheless recognise that cultural narratives are established through multiple unique individual story-telling. Several articles therefore recognise both diversity and coherence among and within different narratives. McMahon, for example, contrasts the robust narrative of continuous progressive integration towards supranational government with a diversity of accounts of the EU's democratic deficit. Kaiser describes public comments on the 'New Narratives' project as 'a kaleidoscope of opinions'.

Petrović's paper explicitly problematizes this distinction between individual and aggregated narratives, especially where it concerns time. Echoing constructivist and post-modernist critiques, he objects to Thomas Risse (2010) tracing British representations of Europe to 'medieval English history', for creating a 'misleading', 'reified view of the social world'. He instead emphasises the 'need for a more flexible and change-sensitive approach' to studying political narratives, which can 'grasp changes in personal ideologies which can ultimately have a major influence'. Other contributors (Maricut, McMahon) by contrast track the rise and fall of multiple narratives over several decades, without strongly problematizing their internal change. Schünemann's snapshot of narratives at a particular time, the emphasis on contingency in Kaiser's account and Nelsen and Guth's intellectual history of the evolution of narratives over time are more compatible with Petrović's argument.

Until the late 1990s, research on ideational dimensions of European integration such as Ronald Inglehart's analyses of opinion poll results (e.g. 1970) generally used positivist, quantitative methods. By contrast, this special issue much more strongly reflects subsequent work, which has been influenced by the linguistic and cultural 'turns'. The articles therefore generally use various forms of comparative qualitative discourse analysis to identify narrative threads from disparate written or spoken texts. These texts include academic works (McMahon, Petrović), religious texts (Nelsen-Guth), political speeches and manifestos (Nelsen-Guth, Petrović, Schünemann), press reports (Maricut), institutional documents (Kaiser, Maricut), and website forum comments (Kaiser). Radonić also treats the aesthetic organisation of museums as texts, alongside more typical textual sources such as museums guides. Kaiser supplements discourse analysis with the other qualitative research techniques of semi-structured interviews and non-participant observation at planning meetings for the Commission's 'New Narrative' project.

Some articles also develop more or less elaborate analytical strategies to identify narrative patterns. McMahon represents normative expressions as the building blocks of narratives in academic works. He codes and quantitatively analyses their degrees of normativity and positive or negative tones. Schünemann systematically arranges organisations that campaigned in referenda on the Constitutional Treaty and the Lisbon Treaty along left-right and yes-no axes. Kaiser, Maricut, Nelsen and Guth and, to an extent, McMahon employ the historical narrative approach, tracing how contingent sequences of development shape the production of narratives.

Turning to the contributors' analyses of actors, Kaiser and Maricut study leading figures of formal transnational organisations and their statements. Where contributors research transnational connections of different sorts, other methodological approaches are required. A comparative approach, for example, identifies transnational narratives and themes by comparing examples across Europe of museums (Radonić), referenda (Schünemann) or political parties (Petrović, Nelsen and Guth). Nelsen and Guth, McMahon and Petrović use a third approach, tracing network connections. These can be formal, like the European Parliament group which links left wing parties; culturally validated, like the EU studies canon of most cited works; or historical, like the linkages which have disseminated millenarian protestant ideologies. Radonić's suggestion that museums create 'Europeanisation of memory' by borrowing 'internationally' established aesthetics of Holocaust memorialization also implies a network, through which particular cultural elements are diffused.

Conclusion

Narratives, or stories, are vitally important to European integration, shaping important policies and helping to define the major identities that affect integration. Researchers in European Studies, broadly conceived, are only just coming to appreciate this importance, as they turn from studying discourse and its actual or potential impact on politics, to exploring the mechanisms of actors producing and disseminating narratives, their transfer across borders and their contestation in the EU and other polities.

This special issue marks an important step in fostering this new research agenda. It adds two new elements to academic consideration of narratives. First, unlike much previous work, it emphasises the narrating actors, how they are organised and their practices. Second, it highlights a key organisational factor for narratives of European integration. Many of these are formulated by transnational communities and networks of narrating actors or by international institutions that themselves narrate. It remains to be seen how much impact the resulting narratives can have on European and EU politics. Perhaps they provide the EU as a polity with a cultural basis and increase its political stability. Alternatively, the heavy contestation over narratives could actually contribute to undermining the EU's apparently shallow legitimacy and even provoke its downfall and disintegration.

Disclosure statement

No potential conflict of interest was reported by the authors.

Funding

This work was supported by the Marie Curie Intra-European Fellowship (IEF) [FP7-PEOPLE-2013-625508].

References

Adler, E., & Pouliot, V. (2011). *International practices*. Cambridge: Cambridge University Press.
Anderson, B. (2000 [1983]). *Imagined communities: Reflections on the origins and spread of nationalism*. London: Verso.
Armbruster, H., Rollo, C., & Meinhof, U. H. (2003). Imagining Europe: Everyday narratives in European border communities. *Journal of Ethnic and Migration Studies, 29*(5), 885–899.

Calligaro, O. (2013). *Negotiating Europe: EU promotion of Europeanness since the 1950s*. Basingstoke: Palgrave Macmillan.

Czarniawska, B. (2004). *Narratives in social science research*. London: Sage.

Davis Cross, M. K. (2013). Rethinking epistemic communities twenty years later. *Review of International Studies, 39*(1), 137–160.

Della Sala, V. (2010). Political myth, mythology and the European Union. *Journal of Common Market Studies, 48*(1), 1–19.

Eder, K. (2006). Europe's borders: The narrative construction of the boundaries of Europe. *European Journal of Social Theory, 9*(2), 255–271.

Favell, A. (2011). *Eurostars and Eurocities: Free movement and mobility in an integrating Europe*. New York: Wiley.

Favell, A., & Guiraudon, V. (2011). Sociology of the European Union: An introduction. In A. Favell & V. Guiraudon (Eds.), *Sociology of the European Union* (pp. 1–24). Basingstoke: Palgrave Macmillan.

Gilbert, M. (2008). Narrating the process: Questioning the progressive story of European integration. *Journal of Common Market Studies, 46*(3), 641–662.

Greenfeld, L. (1992). *Five roads to modernity*. Cambridge, MA: Harvard University.

Hammack, P. L. (2008). Narrative and the cultural psychology of identity. *Personality and Social Psychology Review, 12*(3), 222–247.

Hammack, P. L., & Pilecki, A. (2012). Narrative as a root metaphor for political psychology. *Political Psychology, 33*(1), 75–103.

Hansen, L., & Williams, M. C. (1999). The myths of Europe: Legitimacy, community and the 'crisis' of the EU. *Journal of Common Market Studies, 37*(2), 233–249.

Hooghe, L., & Marks, G. (2009). A postfunctionalist theory of European integration: From permissive consensus to constraining dissensus. *British Journal of Political Science, 39*(1), 1–23.

Hülsse, R. (2006). Imagine the EU: The metaphorical construction of a supra-nationalist identity. *Journal of International Relations and Development, 9*(4), 396–421.

Inglehart, R. (1970). Cognitive mobilization and European identity. *Comparative Politics, 3*(1), 45–70.

Kaiser, W. (2007). *Christian democracy and the origins of European Union*. Cambridge: Cambridge University Press.

Kaiser, W. (2015). Clash of cultures: Two milieus in the European Union's 'A New Narrative for Europe' project. *Journal of Contemporary European Studies, 23*(3), 364–377.

Kølvraa, C. (2016). European fantasies: On the EU's political myths and the affective potential of utopian imaginaries for European identity. *Journal of Common Market Studies, 54*(1), 169–184.

Leggewie, C., & Lang, A. (2011). *Der Kampf um die europäische Erinnerung: ein Schlachtfeld wird besichtigt*. Munich: C.H. Beck.

Lewis, J. (1998). Is the 'hard bargaining' image of the Council misleading? The committee of permanent representatives and the local elections directive. *Journal of Common Market Studies, 36*(4), 479–504.

Littoz-Monnet, A., & McMahon, R. (2013). Cultures of defining culture: EU cultural policy in the context of the study of culture. In R. McMahon (Ed.), *Post-identity? Culture and European integration* (pp. 212–234). London: Routledge.

Lyotard, J. F. (1979). *La condition postmoderne: Rapport sur le savoir*. Paris: Les éditions de Minuit.

Macdonald, S. (2013). *Memorylands: Heritage and identity in Europe today*. Abingdon: Routledge.

Manners, I. (2002). Normative power Europe: A contradiction in terms? *Journal of Common Market Studies, 40*(2), 235–258.

Manners, I. (2010). Global Europa: Mythology of the European Union in world politics. *Journal of Common Market Studies, 48*(1), 67–87.

Manners, I. (2011). Symbolism in European integration. *Comparative European Politics, 9*(3), 243–268.

Maza, S. (1996). Stories in history: Cultural narratives in recent works in European history. *The American Historical Review, 101*(5), 1493–1515.

Risse, T. (2010). *A community of Europeans? Transnational identities and public spheres*. Ithaca, NY: Cornell University Press.

Roberts, G. (2006). History, theory and the narrative turn in IR. *Review of International Studies, 32*(4), 703–714.

Schimmelfennig, F. (2001). The community trap: Liberal norms, rhetorical action, and the Eastern enlargement of the European Union. *International Organization*, *55*(1), 47–80.

Shenhav, S. R. (2005). Thin and thick narrative analysis: On the question of defining and analyzing political narratives. *Narrative Inquiry*, *15*(1), 75–99.

Shore, C. (2000). *Building Europe: The cultural politics of European integration*. London: Routledge.

Sjursen, H. (2002). Why expand? The question of legitimacy and justification in the EU's enlargement policy. *Journal of Common Market Studies*, *40*(3), 491–513.

Somers, M. R. (1994). The narrative constitution of identity: A relational and network approach. *Theory and Society*, *23*(5), 605–649.

Stråth, B. (2005). Methodological and substantive remarks on myth, memory and history in the construction of a European community. *German Law Journal*, *6*(2), 255–272.

White, H. (1973). *Metahistory: The historical imagination in nineteenth-century Europe*. Baltimore: Johns Hopkins University Press.

Different narratives, one area without internal frontiers: why EU institutions cannot agree on the refugee crisis

Adina Maricut

ABSTRACT

This article contextualizes contemporary institutional responses of the European Union (EU) to the refugee crisis within the historical setting in which EU migration and asylum policies emerged – namely during the implementation of the border-free Schengen Area (1984–1995). Using the analytical framework of 'policy narratives', it argues that EU institutions have used the creation of the 'area without internal frontiers' to build coherent narratives about the nature and scope of EU action and of their own role in it. Such narratives became locked into the institutional discourse and influenced the subsequent evolution of EU politics on the topic.

The European Union's (EU) handling of the 2015 refugee crisis has constituted an amalgam of institutional approaches and reactions. Throwing into question what EU leaders repeatedly represent as 'one of Europe's basic principles' (German Chancellor Angela Merkel, cited in Karnitschnig, 2015) – free movement of people within the Schengen Area[1] – the crisis revealed underlying conflicts between different member states on one side, and between the national and the supranational levels on the other. The main EU institutions had diverging priorities on the matter. The Council of the EU ('the Council') reflected national concerns about security and administrative capacity to host refugees, but governments disagreed on possible solutions (Lehne, 2016). The European Commission ('the Commission') focused on safeguarding the borderless Schengen regime and ensuring burden-sharing regarding asylum-seekers (European Commission, 2016b). Finally, the European Parliament ('the Parliament') emphasized the necessity for a human rights approach in the treatment of refugees (European Parliament, 2015). While such policy differences can easily be taken for granted as part of the usual plurality in the EU decision-making process, they also represent institutional positions on asylum and migration which have been entrenched for three decades. This article examines their emergence in the particular historical context of the 1980s and 1990s, which has powerfully influenced contemporary responses of EU institutions to the refugee crisis.

Using the analytical framework of 'policy narratives', the article focuses on 'processes of argumentation' (Fischer & Forester, 1993, p. 2) present in institutional discourses, which identify a specific policy problem and provide corresponding solutions (Boswell, Geddes, & Scholten, 2011, pp. 4–5). This article argues that the Council, the Commission, and the Parliament[2] have used the creation of the free movement area in order to build coherent narratives about the nature and scope of EU action in migration and asylum, as well as of their own role in it. To demonstrate how they did this, the article focuses on the period 1984–1995, during which the abolition of internal border controls was implemented. This empirical analysis takes into account that the abolition of internal border controls was an objective pursued both within the European Community (EC) framework and outside of it through the intergovernmental Schengen system – inaugurated by the Schengen Agreement (1985) and its implementing Convention (1990), which officially entered into force in 1995 (van de Rijt, 1997).

It is posited that by relating their institutional mandates and tasks to the very purpose of the Schengen Area, the three actors inside the institutional triangle developed coherent narratives. The main themes of these narratives then became 'locked' into their institutional discourse (Pierson, 1996). Accordingly, the Council presented the area without internal frontiers as something in need of protection from security threats, both internal (cross-border crime) and external (terrorism and illegal immigration). The Commission advocated a balance between security and fundamental rights in a Schengen Area that, crucially, was to provide 'the EU right most cherished by Europeans' (European Commission, 2014). Finally, in order to distinguish its position, the Parliament established a reputation as the 'watchdog of fundamental rights and democratic scrutiny' (Carrera, Hernanz, & Parkin, 2013, pp. 1–2) in a Schengen space designed to ensure 'an area of freedom' for all citizens, regardless of their nationality. The findings are based on discourse analysis of official documents from the three institutions, secondary literature, and newspaper coverage of institutional preferences in the field.

This exercise is valuable for at least three reasons. First, the purpose is to demonstrate that current institutional positions on refugee inflows are a direct repercussion of the genesis of migration and asylum policy at the EU level, as side effects of the abolition of internal border controls, rather than as policy fields in their own right. While the institutions might have updated their narratives throughout the years, the main leitmotifs remained intact: 'security' for the Council, 'fundamental rights' for the Parliament, and 'freedom of movement' for the Commission. Second, the goal is to show that it is very difficult to speak of 'heroes' and 'villains' when it comes to EU institutional behaviour in the fields of migration and asylum, because in many respects each institution sees itself as the 'hero' of its own story. This interpretation is contrary to more typical portrayals of institutions as 'the good' (the Parliament), 'the bad' (the Council), and 'the ugly' (the Commission) – in line with a 1966 Sergio Leone movie – offered by liberal-oriented commentators (Acosta, 2009). The point is that glorifying or, alternatively, vilifying the activity of an institution ultimately depends on one's personal stance in the narrative presented. Third, the paper is an empirical contribution to the broader academic debate on actor-produced narratives about Europe and European integration, emphasizing the value of studying the origin of such narratives for the evolution of given policy fields at the EU level.

To illustrate the argument, the article starts by introducing the concept of narratives in policy-making, grounded in the rapidly expanding public policy literature on the topic. Having highlighted the importance of framing in the policy process, the focus moves to exploring the abolition of internal border controls. This is the 'opening scene' of EU institutional narratives in policy areas associated with free movement. The purpose is to show how different institutional actors related to the area without internal frontiers either as a problem that required fixing (the Council), a potential accomplishment of the European integration project that needed to be carefully implemented (the Commission), or as an opportunity to enforce fundamental freedoms that had to be seized (the Parliament). The article concludes by reflecting on the implications of the creation of the Schengen Area for contemporary institutional narratives in the areas of migration and asylum.

Understanding actor-produced narratives in policy-making

Over the past two decades, the concept of 'policy narratives' has increasingly gained currency in the academic public policy literature.[3] Its origins can be found in post-positivist approaches (Fischer, 2003; Fischer & Forester, 1993; Roe, 1994; Stone, 2011), but also became applied over time in positivist research[4] (Jones & McBeth, 2010). Divided along ontological and epistemological lines, these two strands have developed in parallel, constructing a rich theoretical body of literature (for an analysis on the relationship between the two strands, see Jones & Radaelli, 2015). More importantly, there is no right way of employing 'policy narratives' in empirical research. What matters are the objectives of the researcher and the extent to which narratives are appropriately and consistently used as a means to reach those ends. Bearing in mind that the purpose of this article is to disentangle the construction of institutional narratives (about roles and scope of EU action in a given policy field) in relation to a historical event (the abolition of internal border controls), I have chosen to draw principally on post-positivist or interpretive approaches. I briefly outline these below.

Accordingly, the most common understanding of policy narratives refers to 'stories participants are disposed to tell about policy situations' (Fischer & Forester, 1993, p. 11). Nonetheless, this is merely one level of analysis – the others being interpretation by an academic author ('narrative of narrative') and reconstruction by a reader ('narrative of narrative of narrative') (Riessman, 2008). Throughout this paper, the focus remains on the first level, that is, policy narratives as 'organized forms of discourse' put forward by actors involved in the policy process who 'share a social construct' and actively 'try to impose their views of reality on others'. Most crucially, narratives are problem-setting, meaning that they identify policy problems [often metaphorically] and causally link them to proposed solutions, which is why they are sometimes associated with ideas of framing or packaging. In this respect, narratives serve a functional purpose. They 'fix the assumptions for decision-making under conditions of high ambiguity' (Roe, 1994, p. 37) by providing arguments in support of one course of action or another (Boswell et al., 2011, p. 4). In other words, when confronted with complex social phenomena, political actors use narratives to process and convey information as well as to guide their behaviour, thus rendering that complexity intelligible (Jones & McBeth, 2010, p. 330).

From the perspective of the 'storytellers' themselves, policy narratives aim at the 'construction of meanings relevant to the achievement of goals and purposes' (Fischer, 2003, p. 166). Indeed, narratives can be instrumental tools for advancing one's objectives, regardless of whether they are introduced consciously or not. When it comes to policymakers, such objectives are most often 'institutionally constructed' (DiMaggio & Powell, 1991, p. 28), meaning that individuals make sense of the roles attributed to them inside institutions and act accordingly. Putting their organization's hat on (Laffan, 2004, p. 85), officials construct narratives which they perceive to be in their institution's best interest.

In this context, narratives can be read as stories about policy situations, told by actors with their own agenda about 'what has to be done and what the expected consequences will be' (Fischer, 2003, p. 161). Nevertheless, within the EU institutional framework, the way in which narratives are built is far from straightforward, especially when it comes to an intricate objective such as the abolition of internal border controls, championed by the Schengen Agreement and discussed below.

Before moving forward, a few methodological considerations are in order. Since this paper deliberately treats institutional positions as homogenous (for the purposes of empirical illustration), it overlooks some of the intra-institutional diversity that existed during the period investigated. To focus on official institutional positions, the article uses official policy documents as its main source of data (together with newspaper coverage and secondary literature). The degree to which document authors have internalized political decisions to pursue any one specific institutional narrative depends partly on whether they are political or technocratic officials. However, the nature of their employment does not undermine the identification of dominant institutional narratives regarding free movement of people in connection to immigrant and refugee inflows. I found that these were rooted in the ways in which different institutions originally framed the abolition of internal controls. The following sections present the historical context and the ensuing construction of institutional narratives.

Origins of narratives: abolishing internal frontiers (1984–1995)

The origins of institutional narratives in the EU areas of migration and asylum are closely linked to the historical circumstances surrounding the emergence of these policy fields. In 1986, EC member states signed the organization's first major treaty revision in two decades, the Single European Act (SEA), and established a concrete deadline for the completion of the 1992 internal market programme. The implementation of this objective, set out in a Commission White Paper (European Commission, 1985) and endorsed by the European Council (European Council, 1985), would come to dominate Community affairs until the mid-1990s, marking the transition towards the EU. But while the SEA promised to deliver the 'four freedoms' entailed in the single market (of goods, capital, persons, and services), the abolition of internal border controls was a particularly contentious issue. Though specifically requested by heads of states and governments during a summit meeting in Fontainebleau (European Council, 1984), the British government vetoed the pursuit of the measure through a Community instrument. It opposed any form of elimination of frontier checks inside the EC on the grounds of their indispensability for identifying third country nationals trying to enter the country illegally (Whitaker, 1992, p. 201).

Under the circumstances, France and Germany sought to provide a political alternative by pursuing a gradual relaxation of border controls at their common frontiers through a bilateral agreement signed in Saarbrücken, Germany, in 1984 (Schutte, 1991, p. 549). The arrangement was joined a year later by the Benelux countries, at a meeting in the small Luxembourg village of Schengen, and became known as the Schengen Agreement. Nowadays considered a landmark of European integration, the establishment of the Schengen Area set in motion a series of subsequent measures designed to compensate for the abolition of internal frontiers inside the EC. They included immigration and asylum and constituted the core of the EU's so-called third or Justice and Home Affairs

(JHA) pillar, established by the 1993 Maastricht Treaty (De Lobkowicz, 2002, p. 17). For this reason, the Schengen Agreement is often understood in EU studies as an example of functional spill-over pressures theorized by neo-functionalism. More specifically, neo-functionalists consider that the abolition of internal border controls raised significant security concerns among the member states, who only agreed to relinquish frontier checks if compensatory measures were put into place in the fields of JHA (Niemann, 2012, p. 217). In contrast, authors who disagree with the neo-functionalist hypothesis point to the absence [or minor role] of supranational institutions from the original intergovernmental arrangement (Ette, Parkes, & Bendel, 2011, p. 17), as well as to the centrality of government officials in the initial years of EU migration and asylum policy (Guiraudon, 2003, p. 264). In other words, the abolition of internal border controls might have created spill-over pressures, but the initial compensatory measures accompanying the Schengen Agreement were 'the result of a negotiated compromise among key European governments who, acting rationally according to their self-interest and political leverage, were trying to address common problems characterizing the border control domain in the region' (Zaiotti, 2011, p. 7).

In fact, governments' perception of common border problems during the period played a crucial role in the consolidation of the Schengen Agreement. In the early 1990s, Western Europe experienced a refugee crisis, albeit of smaller proportions than during 2015–2016. On the one hand, the end of the Cold War and German reunification created a feeling of insecurity in home affairs ministries owing to fears of large-scale immigration and organized crime from the east (Geddes, 2007, p. 453). On the other hand, the Yugoslav wars of the 1990s resulted in subsequent refugee waves, which governments wanted to limit (van Selm-Thorburn, 1998, p. 3). The Schengen signatories in particular received the highest number of asylum applications; consequently, their concerns about security, stability, and administrative capacity to host refugees became translated in the newly created third pillar (Lavenex, 2001, p. 858). However, since not all countries were affected equally by refugee inflows, [German] calls for solidarity and burden-sharing went unanswered (Léonard, 2007, p. 26) – a situation mirrored during the 2015–2016 crisis.

Indeed, as public policy scholars know too well, crises offer decision-makers the opportunity to frame their narratives in the context of emergency and the necessity to ensure the security of the public (Stone, 2011, p. 152). According to the Copenhagen School in International Relations, Western Europe witnessed in the early 1990s a shift in the public discourse on migration and asylum; specifically, policy-makers and think tanks in the field of security started to frame refugee inflows as a security rather than a humanitarian question (Huysmans, 2006, p. 16). In countries with large immigrant populations such as France, Belgium, and Germany, framing immigrants and asylum-seekers as a security problem was linked to negative perceptions of national citizens about foreigners, as revealed in public opinion studies (Lahav, 2003, p. 82). In other words, the adoption and implementation of the Schengen Agreement occurred in a political context marked by the desire to abolish internal border controls for economic reasons and the priority to control who crossed the external borders for security reasons. It was under these circumstances that institutional narratives in the fields of migration and asylum were developed and consolidated at the EU level. Indeed, all the main institutional actors at the Community level held a firm position on the objective of abolishing internal border controls. Not all of these were expressed it in a systematic manner, however. The Council did not have an official say in areas associated with free movement until the introduction of the third pillar; moreover, its formal legislative competences over the border-free regime entered into force only after the incorporation of the Schengen acquis into the EU legal framework with the Amsterdam Treaty (1999). But while the JHA Council was formally established in March 1994 (Monar, 1994, p. 80), decision-making by officials from justice and especially home affairs ministries existed well before that date. There is general consensus that home affairs representatives came to dominate the Schengen governance arrangement as well as other working parties created in the area (e.g. the Ad-Hoc Group on Immigration), thus 'ousting' officials from foreign affairs ministries who were originally in charge of negotiating the Schengen Agreement (Guiraudon, 2003, p. 267). In turn, the Commission and the Parliament also developed particular narratives from the start, although they had no competences regarding the practical abolition of internal border controls. Unsurprisingly, the two supranational institutions created specific structures to deal with JHA after the entry into force of the Maastricht Treaty, which created the legal basis for such a move.

The Council: guardian of national security

In light of the Schengen Agreement and the 1992 deadline for the completion of the internal market, the work of relevant ministries across member states intensified exponentially. Under the Schengen Secretariat, several working parties were established,[5] while the 1988 European Council in Rhodes demanded the additional creation of a Coordinators' Group on the Free Movement of Persons, tasked with conducting the necessary preparations for the abolition of internal borders (Niemeier, 1995, pp. 322–325). With home affairs officials dominating these groups, the priorities focused from the beginning on how, in the absence of internal frontiers, to provide national citizens with the same level of internal security as before (De Lobkowicz, 2002, p. 17). Indeed, for people who work in law enforcement and border control, national frontiers delimit the space within which they are supposed to ensure public order (Anderson et al., 1995). Unlike heads of state or government, who viewed the completion of the single market as a politically desirable economic goal for the EC, national representatives from home affairs ministries were mainly concerned with how to prevent the free movements from creating safe havens for criminals. The free movement of people in particular was expected to foster cross-border crime, allowing perpetrators to move from one country to another in order to avoid arrest and prosecution (Bache, George, & Bulmer, 2011, p. 469). Moreover, as explained in the previous section, the management of refugee inflows coming from the East and the Western Balkans was considered particularly problematic for security professionals (Geddes, 2007, p. 453). Under the circumstances, the main objective of cooperation accompanying the Schengen Agreement was to ensure that:

> measures are adopted in order to avoid the elimination of controls at borders between Member States being a source of abuse, facilitating crime, terrorism or drug trafficking, or increasing illegal immigration. (Group of Coordinators 'Free Movement of People,' 1993)

In addition, an Ad-Hoc Group bringing together ministers responsible for immigration and asylum, and their close advisors, was created in 1986 following a proposal from the British government, based on a SEA annex specifying the preservation of member states' competences in dealing with third country nationals (SEA, General Declaration Art 13–19). The

Group worked on the development of Eurodac, a database envisaged to prevent asylum-shopping in different member states (Ad Hoc Group Immigration, 1992a), as well as on issues related to the expulsion of illegal immigrants, deportees, or failed asylum-seekers (Ad Hoc Group Immigration, 1992b). This implied that policy interventions were to be geared toward providing mechanisms of protection. It was in this context that security became the overarching theme in the narrative of Council groups.

Over time, the security narrative of the Council consolidated. In the first years of post-Maastricht activity, the agenda was full of measures designed to protect the newly established single market through the enforcement of external borders, closer police cooperation fostered by the newly created Europol organization, or judicial cooperation in criminal matters (De Lobkowicz, 2002; Niemeier, 1995). In a similar vein, immigration and asylum, the other major areas of compensatory measures to the abolition of border controls, became framed in negative terms as problems related to 'asylum-shopping' and 'immigration risks' – which the Council considered it necessary to tackle (Guiraudon, 2003, p. 264). The 2001 terrorist attacks in the United States followed by the 2004 Madrid and 2005 London attacks marked a watershed in the priorities of the Council, which shifted its security concerns towards the external threat posed by terrorism (Argomaniz, 2009). Associated policy areas such as immigration and asylum also came to be framed as 'security threats' during this period (Huysmans, 2006). Against this background, it is hardly surprising that one of the main reactions of the JHA Council to the 2015 refugee crisis was to allow the temporary reintroduction of some internal border controls in defence of national security and state capacities.

The European Commission – creating European citizens

Under the powerful presidency of Jacques Delors (1985–1995), the European Commission was very proactive in advocating the removal of physical barriers inside the Community, articulating its vision in the White Paper on *Completing the Internal Market* (European Commission, 1985, Art 47–56). A staunch supporter of the area without frontiers, the Commission initially sought to achieve the gradual elimination of frontier checks through a Community instrument, the Border Controls Directive that it initiated in 1985. Its proposal became deadlocked in the Council due to opposition led by the British government, however (Whitaker, 1992, p. 201). This experience made the Commission acutely aware of the futility of putting forward legislation that would never pass in the Council (European Commission, 1988b, p. 3). In addition, the signing of the intergovernmental Schengen Agreement outside the EC framework made it clear 'which way the wind was blowing' (Peers, 2011, p. 139). In this context, the choice for the supranational institution was between being completely excluded from on-going discussions or of participating in some capacity, even as an observer (Zaiotti, 2011, p. 77). Martin Bangemann, Vice-President of the Commission at the time, described his institution's approach as 'pragmatic rather than doctrinaire', opting 'for making progress rather than fighting time-consuming battles for competence' (European Parliament, 1991a).

Therefore, the Commission focused on branding the abolition of internal border controls as part of the advent of what it called the 'People's Europe' or 'Citizens' Europe' (Shore & Black, 1994, p. 275). The move is not surprising, bearing in mind the growing criticisms in the 1990s of the EC's democratic deficit at the time and the difficulties in defending an unelected Brussels-based bureaucracy (Habermas, 1999, p. 49). While the political and economic circumstances of the 1980s had allowed the revival of European integration, Commission President Jacques Delors and fellow leading officials understood very well that their institution required an effective legitimating strategy in order to buttress its position in the EC's institutional system (Schrag Sternberg, 2013, p. 76). Their solution was to bring 'Europe closer to its citizens' through a narrative that described an emerging European identity. This was directly linked – but not limited – to the achievement of free movement of persons (Shore, 1993, p. 787). For example, in its 'Europe 1992' campaign on an 'area without frontiers', the Commission envisaged a symbiosis between the elimination of borders and the emergence of European citizens:

> The removal of physical, technical, and fiscal barriers is bound to improve the Community's image in the eyes of its citizens. (…) The broadening of horizons strengthens the sense of a common identity, the feeling of belonging to the same Community. (European Commission, 1988a, p. 2)

Thus, the abolition of internal border controls provided what soon became one of the Commission's major *raisons d'être* in the EU political system – protecting free movement of persons as a tangible achievement of European integration. Nevertheless, this institutional goal had to be carefully balanced against the need to respect member states' sovereignty in the process, as they rejected Commission authority over 'high politics' issues related to internal security (De Lobkowicz, 2002).

The partial communitarization of the third pillar after the Amsterdam Treaty meant that the Commission slowly moved 'from the sidelines to the centre stage' in policy areas associated with free movement (Ucarer, 2001). Often described as 'hovering between vision and Realpolitik' in the fields of migration and asylum (Papagianni, 2006, p. 234), the Commission has constantly attempted to place itself midway between the two poles of security and fundamental rights, siding on some issues with the Council (e.g. fighting illegal migration) and on others with the Parliament (e.g. rights for asylum-seekers) (Kaunert, 2009, p. 160).

Following the entry into force of the 2009 Lisbon Treaty and the empowerment of the Commission in the area of freedom, security, and justice more broadly (Ucarer, 2013), the Commission consolidated its position and became more vocal on issues related to free movement. This was obvious in the way in which the Commission used a 2011 mandate from the European Council to introduce legislation allowing the temporary reintroduction of border controls in the Schengen Area but shifting responsibility for such a decision from the Council to itself (Bocquillon & Dobbels, 2014, p. 33). As former Home Affairs Commissioner Cecilia Malmström put it, only the Commission is able to ensure that 'Schengen exists to defend freedom of movement' (Vandystadt, 2012). This institutional positioning is mirrored in the way in which the Commission has handled the 2015 refugee crisis, with the Commission president making a solemn promise that 'Schengen will not be abolished under my Commission' (Juncker, 2015, p. 52).

The European Parliament – the defender of fundamental rights

For its part, the European Parliament welcomed the Schengen Agreement's implementation of the free movement of persons, which it had advocated for years. However, it strongly criticized the use of intergovernmental means to achieve it, 'outside the democratic control of the Parliament' (European Parliament, 1991a). Calling for the lawful adoption of Community instruments to regulate the abolition of internal frontiers and the ensuing consequences, the Parliament was enraged by the Commission's collaboration with member states in the development of the Schengen system, perceived as 'capitulation' to national governments (Monar, 1994, p. 76). On the one hand, the Parliament opposed François Mitterrand's idea of 'a Europe of different speeds or variable geometry' (Mitterrand, 1984), which materialized with Schengen because its membership did not coincide with that of the EC as a whole. On the other hand, the Parliament deplored the lack of parliamentary or judicial control over the Schengen governance arrangements (European Parliament, 1990).

Nevertheless, there was not much the Parliament could do to prevent the evolution of the intergovernmental Schengen regime. In a radical move, it challenged the Commission before the European Court of Justice for failure to uphold the SEA regarding the free movement of persons (Case C-445/93). However, the case was dismissed when the Commission put forth three proposals for directives to this effect in 1995, which were again blocked in the Council (Zaiotti, 2011, p. 122).

In the face of this fait accompli, members of the European Parliament (MEPs) decided to change strategy and profit from the Parliament's internal reorganization, triggered by the Maastricht Treaty, in order to strengthen their institutional position (Shackleton, 2012, p. 129). Accordingly, on 16 January 1992, a new standing committee with 30 members and substitutes was established: the Committee on Civil Liberties and Internal Affairs (LIBE) (Esders, 1995, p. 260). The Parliament's Committee on Legal Affairs and Citizens Rights (JURY) was not thrilled about the new structure, which they saw as 'stripping away some of its powers' (European Parliament, 1991b). However, it was decided that a different committee was necessary in order to mirror the creation of the new Council formation (the JHA Council). It would address issues 'directly or indirectly linked to abolition of internal frontiers in the Community by 1993' (Turner, 1992).

The mandate of the committee was clear from the start, covering first and foremost matters relating to 'human rights problems in the Community, [and second] civil liberties in the Communities' (European Parliament, 1992). In itself, the Parliament's focus on human rights was not a novelty – as the External Affairs Committee held a debate every year on the state of human rights *outside* the Community. In contrast, the explicit agenda of LIBE to protect fundamental rights *inside* the newly founded EU was both unprecedented and regarded as a provocation to member states, who considered themselves to have an outstanding human rights record (De Capitani, 2010, pp. 125–126).

This nuance between outside and inside has to be understood in the context of the Maastricht Treaty, which gave no legislative competence to the Parliament in the third pillar but only provided that the institution was to be 'informed' of on-going discussions and its opinions 'duly taken into consideration' (Art K.6). Under the circumstances, the Parliament sought alternative avenues to have its voice heard. For example, it chose the title 'Civil Liberties' for its committee as opposed to the Council's plain 'JHA'. In a move consistent with the Parliament's tendency to exploit existing powers (Corbett, 1998, p. 92), the LIBE Committee based its fundamental rights mandate on a different Maastricht Treaty provision (Art K.2[1]), which clearly specified that policy areas accompanying the free movement of persons were to comply with the 1950 European Convention for the

Protection of Human Rights and Fundamental Freedoms. In the first years of LIBE activity, MEPs focused on the annual political debates in JHA, which attracted a lot of media attention and became increasingly lively, often antagonizing the Council (De Capitani, 2010, p. 125).

Consequently, the abolition of internal border controls had important consequences for the Parliament in terms of both its internal organization and taking a substantive policy stance. My interpretation is that MEPs needed a different strategy to gain a legitimate say in the border-free regime particularly because the European Council and the Commission had already framed the area without frontiers for the benefit of the European people, the usual constituency of the Parliament (Wessels, 1999, p. 209). Excluded from decision-making in the intergovernmental Schengen club, the Parliament found an alternative way to get involved in the third pillar, as the defender of European values (European Parliament, 2008). In the end, it was exactly the Parliament's exclusion from decision-making in the third pillar that forced it to seek a different narrative to legitimize its relevance. The Parliament found its mission in the third pillar as the human rights advocate. This was a position that they have kept, albeit with variation, throughout the evolution of migration and asylum policy at EU level (European Parliament, n.d.). For example, the Parliament has fought under the consultation procedure to protect the human rights of asylum-seekers coming to the EU in terms of both reception conditions and admittance criteria (Ripoll Servent & Trauner, 2014). While the consistency of such narratives has diminished to a certain extent since the Lisbon Treaty and the empowerment of the Parliament in other JHA domains like criminal justice (Carrera et al., 2013), the supranational institution still remains devoted to its original mission, as confirmed by its activity during the refugee crisis.

Conclusion

Watching the refugee crisis unfold in 2015, numerous commentators have argued that the Schengen system is failing and EU institutions are incapable of finding a coordinated response (*The Economist*, 2015). This article has provided some much needed historical context for understanding the fragmentation of institutional positions on the matter, shown to have originated in the ways in which different institutions 'narrated' the establishment of free movement of people in the first place. Indeed, institutional actors used the abolition of internal border controls as the setting for their narratives, framing the emergence of the Schengen Area as a policy problem (the Council), a potential accomplishment of European citizenship (the Commission), and an opportunity to strengthen Europe's commitment to fundamental rights (the Parliament). Specifically, from the perspective of member states in the Council, the abolition of internal borders was a clear threat to the security of the Community, which had to be protected through a coherent agenda of 'flanking measures'. For the Commission, implementing the free movement of people was an ambition comparable to the single market and hence had to be implemented at all costs, even if that implied having less influence for itself within an intergovernmental governance arrangement. Finally, while the Parliament initially viewed Schengen as an affront to the Community method of decision-making, it soon found its vocation, in the context of the 'area without frontiers', as the chief advocate of fundamental rights.

Over time, what started as isolated narratives about a policy episode developed into coherent institutional narratives about EU policy action more broadly, influencing the way in which fields like migration and asylum evolved at the EU level. In many respects, this is a fine example of the sector-to-sector integration expected in neo-functionalist theorizing (Schmitter, 2004). The objective of establishing the single market included (1) the implementation of free movement in people, which entailed (2) the abolition of internal frontiers, which in turn required (3) compensatory measures for a range of domains, including migration and asylum. And since the Council dominated decision-making in these areas up to the Lisbon Treaty (Nilsson & Siegl, 2010), security has long been the main priority – while the other institutions tried to counter-balance it. Clearly, the narratives that crystallized around the abolition of internal frontiers were reactions to ongoing developments, through which each institution sought to legitimize its own actions.

The institutional responses to the refugee crisis of 2015–2016 did not diverge from this pattern. In fact, what we witnessed was an upgrading of the security narrative of the Council, as some member states invoked a provision of the Schengen Borders Code in order to frame the refugee inflows as 'serious threats to public policy or internal security' (Art 25) and thus justify the [temporary] reintroduction of border controls (Ghimis, 2015). For example, during the period November 2015 to February 2016, four Schengen member states – Austria, Germany, Norway, and Norway – notified the Commission of 'the temporary reintroduction of border control at internal borders' on account of a 'continuous big influx of persons seeking international protection' (European Commission, 2016a). As of October 2016, these four countries, together with Sweden, still maintain temporary internal border controls (European Commission, 2016b). Under the circumstances, it is entirely possible that the same driving policy goal that accompanied the creation of Schengen, namely the necessity to ensure the same level of security in the absence of internal borders, will be the central theme of the institutional narrative justifying its dissolution, that is the necessity to maintain the same level of security in the face of a refugee inflow, when the absence of internal borders becomes unsustainable.

One caveat needs to be considered in relation to the security narrative of the Council. In a similar way to the refugee crisis of the 1990s, the events of 2015–2016 sowed dissension among member states regarding possible solutions. Generalized disagreement characterized not only Council structures but also the heads of state or government meeting in the European Council – the self-appointed crisis manager of the EU in recent years (Maricut, 2016, p. 545). Specifically, two groups took shape during the period: on the hand member states which followed Germany's lead in attempting to reach a deal with Turkey on the relocation of refugees, and on the other hand the Visegrad countries which opposed intra-EU relocation as a matter of principle and advocated instead for strong border controls, even through the erection of fences as exemplified by Hungary (Lehne, 2016). On top of this, a coalition of 10 countries led by Austria, including both EU and non-EU states, initiated in February 2016 a so-called 'closing down of the Balkan route'; the measure was designed to stop migrant flows but effectively stranded refugees in Greece (Smale, 2016). In the end, these measures were implemented simultaneously and are still ongoing, while the relocation scheme was largely unsuccessful considering that only 5651 persons were relocated as of September 2016 (European Commission, 2016b). On the whole, the 2015–2016 refugee crisis produced a split in the Council's narrative about the security of the Schengen Area.

The reasons for the split between member states go back to the discussion regarding perceptions of the crisis in the public sphere of different countries. In Germany, commentators attribute the Chancellor's initial openness towards refugees to an emotional reaction to the powerful imagery coming every day from the news in the late summer of 2015: the picture of the three-year-old Alan Kurdi found drowned on the shores of Turkey, the truck in Austria abandoned with 71 dead refugees, or the thousands of people stranded in Budapest's international train station (Spiegel Online, 2016). It is difficult to establish why perceptions of crises change over time; for example, why was there no similar outcry in the case of the Lampedusa shipwreck a few years before? (Kirby, 2016). The symbolism of Alan Kurdi's photo in particular is considered to have altered the course of the refugee crisis for several European leaders, not just Chancellor Angela Merkel; however, a year after his death the discursive shift in the narrative about refugees seems to have been temporary (Kingsley, 2016). At the most recent meeting of the JHA Council in October 2016, the Slovak Minister of Interior and current president of the Council declared that the institution 'does not yet fully agree with the European Parliament' on the matter of systemic checks at the border because for them 'security comes first' (Justice and Home Affairs Council, 2016).

In contrast, the Commission remained faithful to the leitmotif of its original institutional narrative in the area, namely ensuring free movement of people. It even consolidated its position by forcefully arguing that this right of EU citizens enshrined in the treaties is non-negotiable, regardless of the pressures put on it (cited in Palmeri, 2015). In a similar vein, the Parliament continued to defend its fundamental rights narrative, seeking to explain that Europe is not at fault for the current refugee crisis but that it is necessary to respond in line with European values that dictate a humanitarian approach to people who have fled war zones (Schulz, 2015). In other words, actor-produced narratives can constantly be updated on the basis of current events, but they maintain the guiding principles which informed their inception.

Keeping this in mind, the present article has sought to put into perspective the whole discussion about 'heroes' and 'villains' when it comes to institutional behaviour in the EU areas of migration and asylum. Even if one wanted to use normative categories for identifying 'the good, the bad, and the ugly' in the activities of the Council, the Commission, and the Parliament (Acosta, 2009), the institutions themselves can always present their decisions not only as legitimate but also as completely necessary. For example, the JHA Council, bringing together representatives of law enforcement and border authorities, will always be able to portray 'security' as the most important 'fundamental right'. In the end, this is a classic case of Miles's law 'where you stand depends on where you sit' (Miles, 1978); or, to put it differently, 'the story you tell depends on your institutional affiliation'.

Notes

1. The Schengen Area became operational in 1995 and expanded over time to 26 European countries, including non-member states Norway, Iceland, Switzerland, and Liechtenstein, but currently excluding EU member states United Kingdom, Ireland, Cyprus, Bulgaria, Romania, and Croatia (European Commission, n.d.).
2. The analysis excludes the European Council, which only became institutionalized in the Single European Act in 1987 and has no role in day-to-day decision-making in the field (Nilsson & Siegl, 2010, pp. 69–72).

3. See also the political science literature on discursive institutionalism, which explores the role of ideas in the official discourse of institutions (Schmidt, 2008). As its name suggests, the narrative approach seeks to disentangle the storyline aspect within an institutional discourse and does not just focus on the driving ideational forces behind it.
4. The main difference between the two is methodological. Post-positivists, who prefer to call themselves interpretivists, focus on narratives as 'meaning-making', inductively looking at how human beings make sense of the world and their own experiences in specific contexts by means of language. Positivists are interested in narratives as discourses that can be objectively measured based on unambiguous concept operationalization in a way that is both generalizable and falsifiable (Schwartz-Shea & Yanow, 2012, Chapter 3).
5. The working parties tackled specific topics: police and security, free movement of persons, transport, and checks on goods (Schutte, 1991, p. 549).

Disclosure statement

No potential conflict of interest was reported by the author.

Funding

This work was supported by the Central European University through its standard doctoral scholarship program.

References

Acosta, D. (2009). The good, the bad and the ugly in EU migration law: Is the European Parliament becoming bad and ugly? (The adoption of directive 2008/15: The returns directive). *European Journal of Migration and Law*, *11*(1), 19–39.

Ad Hoc Group Immigration. (1992a). *EURODAC: Progress report to ministers by the ad hoc group on immigration*, 16 November 1992 (No. SN 4683/92 WGI 1271).

Ad Hoc Group Immigration. (1992b). *Recommendation regarding practices followed by Member States on expulsion*, 16 November 1992 (No. SN 4678/92 WGI 1266).

Anderson, M., Boer, M. D., Cullen, P., Gilmore, W., Raab, C., & Walker, N. (1995). *Policing the European Union: Theory, law and practice*. Oxford: Clarendon Press.

Argomaniz, J. (2009). Post-9/11 institutionalization of European Union counter-terrorism: Emergence, acceleration and inertia. *European Security*, *18*(2), 151–172.

Bache, I., George, S., & Bulmer, S. (2011). *Politics in the European Union* (3rd ed.). Oxford: Oxford University Press.

Bocquillon, P., & Dobbels, M. (2014). An elephant on the 13th floor of the Berlaymont? European Council and commission relations in legislative agenda setting. *Journal of European Public Policy*, *21*(1), 20–38.

Boswell, C., Geddes, A., & Scholten, P. (2011). The role of narratives in migration policy-making: A research framework. *The British Journal of Politics & International Relations*, *13*(1), 1–11. doi:10.1111/j.1467-856X.2010.00435.x

Carrera, S., Hernanz, N., & Parkin, J. (2013). The 'Lisbonization' of the European Parliament: Assessing progress, shortcomings and challenges for democratic accountability in the area of freedom, security and justice. *CEPS Paper on Liberty and Security in Europe*, (58). Retrieved from: https://www.ceps.eu/system/files/LSE%20No%2058%20Lisbonisation%20of%20EP.pdf

Corbett, R. (1998). *The European Parliament's role in closer EU integration*. Basingstoke: Palgrave Macmillan.

De Capitani, E. (2010). The evolving role of the European Parliament in the AFSJ. In J. Monar (Ed.), *The institutional dimension of the European Union's area of freedom, security, and justice* (pp. 113–144). Brussels: Peter Lang.

De Lobkowicz, W. (2002). *L'Europe et la sécurité intérieure. Une élaboration par étapes [Europe and internal security. An elaboration in stages]*. Paris: La Documentation Française.

DiMaggio, P., & Powell, W. W. (1991). Introduction. In W. W. Powell & P. DiMaggio (Eds.), *The new institutionalism in organizational analysis* (pp. 1–38). Chicago: University of Chicago Press.

Esders, E. (1995). The European Parliament's Committee on Civil Liberties and Internal Affairs – the committee responsible for justice and home affairs. In R. Bieber & J. Monar (Eds.), *Justice and home affairs in the European Union: The development of the third pillar* (pp. 259–275). Brussels: European Interuniversity Press.

Ette, A., Parkes, R., & Bendel, P. (2011). The diversity of European justice and home affairs cooperation: A model-testing exercise on its development and outcomes. In P. Bendel, A. Ette, R. Parkes, & M. Haase (Eds.), *The Europeanization of control: Venues and outcomes of EU justice and home affairs cooperation* (pp. 9–38). Münster: LIT Verlag.

European Commission. (1985, June 14). *Completing the internal market*. White Paper from the Commission to the European Council. COM (85) 310 final. Retrieved from http://aei.pitt.edu/1113/1/internal_market_wp_COM_85_310.pdf

European Commission. (1988a, July 7). *A people's Europe*. Communication from the Commission to the European Parliament. COM (88) 331 final. Retrieved from http://aei.pitt.edu/3831/1/3831.pdf

European Commission. (1988b, December 7). *Communication of the Commission to the Council on the abolition of controls of persons at intra-Community borders*. COM (88) 640 final. Retrieved from http://aei.pitt.edu/3807/1/3807.pdf

European Commission. (2014, January 15). *Press release – European Commission upholds free movement of people* (MEMO/14/9). Retrieved from http://europa.eu/rapid/press-release_MEMO-14-9_en.htm

European Commission. (2016a, January 4). *Full list of member states' notifications of the temporary reintroduction of border control at internal borders pursuant to article 23 et seq. of the schengen borders code*. Retrieved January 6, 2016, from http://ec.europa.eu/dgs/home-affairs/what-we-do/policies/borders-and-visas/schengen/reintroduction-border-control/docs/ms_notifications_-_reintroduction_of_border_control_en.pdf

European Commission. (2016b, September 28). *Press release – Delivering on migration and border management: Commission reports on progress made under the European Agenda on Migration* (IP/16/3183). Retrieved from http://europa.eu/rapid/press-release_IP-16-3183_en.htm

European Commission. (n.d.). *Directorate-general migration and home affairs: Schengen, borders & visas – Schengen Area*. Retrieved September 21, 2015, from http://ec.europa.eu/dgs/home-affairs/what-we-do/policies/borders-and-visas/schengen/index_en.htm

European Council. (1984). *Conclusions of the European Council*. Fontainebleau, 25–26 June 1984. Retrieved from http://aei.pitt.edu/1448/1/Fountainebleau__june_1994.pdf

European Council. (1985). *Conclusions of the European Council*. Milan, 28–29 June 1985. Retrieved from http://aei.pitt.edu/1421/1/Milan_June_1995.pdf

European Parliament. (1990, December 14). *Oral question (0-0388/90) by Mrs Roth, Mrs Tazdait, Mr Taradash, Mrs Aglietta and Mr Melandri, on behalf of the Green Group to the Council*. European Parliament Session Documents, 83-1852/90/rev. Retrieved from http://aei.pitt.edu/48230/1/A9487.pdf

European Parliament. (1991a, October 14). *Resolution on the free movement of persons and security in the European Community* (OJ C 267/197). Luxembourg: European Parliament Historical Archives.

European Parliament. (1991b, December 11). *Minutes of the committee in legal affairs and citizens' rights* (PE/VII/PV/20). Luxembourg: European Parliament Historical Archives.

European Parliament. (1992, January 16). *Decision on the number and membership of parliamentary committees* (B3-0036/92). Luxembourg: European Parliament Historical Archives.

European Parliament. (2008). *The European Parliament as a champion of European values.* Brussels: Office for Official Publications of the European Communities.

European Parliament. (2015, September 10). *European Parliament resolution of 10 September 2015 on migration and refugees in Europe.* 2015/2833(RSP). Retrieved from http://www.europarl.europa.eu/sides/getDoc.do?pubRef=-//EP//TEXT+MOTION+B8-2015-0837+0+DOC+XML+V0//EN

European Parliament. (n.d.). *Civil liberties, justice and home affairs – welcome words.* Retrieved March 10, 2015, from http://www.europarl.europa.eu/committees/en/libe/home.html

Fischer, F. (2003). *Reframing public policy: Discursive politics and deliberative practices.* Oxford: Oxford University Press.

Fischer, F., & Forester, J. (1993). Editors' introduction. In F. Fischer & J. Forester (Eds.), *The argumentative turn in policy analysis and planning* (pp. 1–17). London: UCL Press.

Geddes, A. (2007). The politics of EU domestic order. In K. E. Jørgensen, M. A. Pollack, & B. Rosamond (Eds.), *Handbook of European Union politics* (pp. 449–462). London, CA: Sage.

Ghimis, A. (2015, September 22). The refugee crisis: Schengen's slippery slope. *European Policy Centre.* Retrieved from http://www.epc.eu/pub_details?cat_id=4&pub_id=5963

Group of Coordinators 'Free Movement of People'. (1993). *Work program of the Belgian presidency* (No. CIRC 3653/93). Retrieved from http://www.statewatch.org/semdoc/assets/files/keytexts/ktch1.pdf

Guiraudon, V. (2003). The constitution of a European immigration policy domain: A political sociology approach. *Journal of European Public Policy, 10*(2), 263–282.

Habermas, J. (1999). The European nation-state and the pressures of globalization. *New Left Review, I* (235), 46–59.

Huysmans, J. (2006). *The politics of insecurity: Fear, migration, and asylum in the EU.* London: Routledge.

Jones, M. D., & McBeth, M. K. (2010). A narrative policy framework: Clear enough to be wrong? *Policy Studies Journal, 38*(2), 329–353. doi:10.1111/j.1541-0072.2010.00364.x

Jones, M. D., & Radaelli, C. M. (2015). The narrative policy framework: Child or monster? *Critical Policy Studies, 9*(3), 339–355. doi:10.1080/19460171.2015.1053959

Juncker, J.-C. (2015, September 9). State of the Union by Jean-Claude Juncker, President of the European Commission. *European Commission.* Retrieved from http://ec.europa.eu/priorities/soteu/docs/state_of_the_union_2015_en.pdf

Justice and Home Affairs Council. (2016). Highlights of the Justice and Home Affairs (Home Affairs) on 13 October 2016 in Luxembourg. Retrieved June 2, 2015, from http://www.consilium.europa.eu/en/meetings/jha/2016/10/13-14/

Karnitschnig, M. (2015, August 31). Merkel warns Schengen could be at risk. *POLITICO.* Retrieved from http://www.politico.eu/article/merkel-warns-schengen-at-risk-germany-refugees-migration-quotas-travel/

Kaunert, C. (2009). Liberty versus security? EU asylum policy and the European Commission. *Journal of Contemporary European Research, 5*(2), 148–170.

Kingsley, P. (2016, September 2). The death of Alan Kurdi: One year on, compassion towards refugees fades. *The Guardian.* Retrieved from https://www.theguardian.com/world/2016/sep/01/alan-kurdi-death-one-year-on-compassion-towards-refugees-fades

Kirby, E. J. (2016, October 7). Compassion fatigue and the optician of Lampedusa. *BBC News.* Retrieved from http://www.bbc.com/news/world-europe-37485824

Laffan, B. (2004). The European Union and its institutions as 'identity builders'. In R. K. Herrmann, T. Risse-Kappen, & M. B. Brewer (Eds.), *Transnational identities: Becoming European in the EU* (pp. 75–96). Lanham, MD: Rowman & Littlefield.

Lahav, G. (2003). *Immigration and politics in the new Europe: Reinventing borders.* Cambridge: Cambridge University Press.

Lavenex, S. (2001). The Europeanization of refugee policies: Normative challenges and institutional legacies. *JCMS: Journal of Common Market Studies, 39*(5), 851–874.

Lehne, S. (2016, February 4). How the refugee crisis will reshape the EU. *Carnegie Europe*. Retrieved from http://carnegieeurope.eu/2016/02/04/how-refugee-crisis-will-reshape-eu/itj7

Léonard, S. (2007). *The 'securitization' of asylum and migration in the European Union: Beyond the Copenhagen school's framework*. In Paper presented at the SGIR Sixth Pan-European International Relations Conference, 12–15 September 2007, Turin. Retrieved from http://www.jcer.net/index.php/jcer/article/view/239

Maricut, A. (2016). With and without supranationalisation: The post-Lisbon roles of the European Council and the Council in justice and home affairs governance. *Journal of European Integration, 38*(5), 541–555.

Miles, R. E. (1978). The origin and meaning of miles' law. *Public Administration Review, 38*(5), 399–403. doi:10.2307/975497

Mitterrand, F. (1984). *Speech by François Mitterrand to the European Parliament (24 May 1984)*. Retrieved from http://www.cvce.eu/content/publication/2001/10/19/cdd42d22-fe8e-41bb-bfb7-9b655113ebcf/publishable_en.pdf

Monar, J. (1994). The evolving role of the Union institutions in the framework of the third pillar. In J. Monar & R. Morgan (Eds.), *The third pillar of the European Union: Co-operation in the fields of justice and home affairs* (pp. 69–83). Brussels: European Interuniversity Press.

Niemann, A. (2012). The dynamics of EU migration Policy: From Maastricht to Lisbon. In J. Richardson (Ed.), *Constructing a policy-making state? Policy dynamics in the EU* (pp. 209–232). Oxford: Oxford University Press.

Niemeier, M. (1995). The K.4 committee and its position in the decision-making process. In R. Bieber & J. Monar (Eds.), *Justice and home affairs in the European Union: The development of the third pillar* (pp. 321–331). Brussels: European Interuniversity Press.

Nilsson, H. G., & Siegl, J. (2010). The Council in the area of freedom, security and justice. In J. Monar (Ed.), *The institutional dimension of the European Union's area of freedom, security, and justice* (pp. 53–82). Brussels: Peter Lang.

Palmeri, T. (2015, August 24). Europe stands by Schengen. *Politico Europe*. Retrieved from http://www.politico.eu/article/europe-stands-by-schengen-free-movement-thalys-attack-border-control/

Papagianni, G. (2006). *Institutional and policy dynamics of EU migration law*. Leiden: Martinus Nijhoff.

Peers, S. (2011). *EU justice and home affairs law* (3rd ed.). Oxford: Oxford University Press.

Pierson, P. (1996). The path to European integration: A historical institutionalist analysis. *Comparative Political Studies, 29*(2), 123–163. doi:10.1177/0010414096029002001

Riessman, C. K. (2008). *Narrative methods for the human sciences*. Los Angeles, CA: Sage.

van de Rijt, W. (1997). Schengen et les pays nordiques: Aperçu de la situation actuelle [Schengen and the Nordic countries: Overview of current situation]. In M. den Boer (Ed.), *Schengen, judicial cooperation and policy coordination* (pp. 29–37). Maastricht: European Institute of Public Administration.

Ripoll Servent, A., & Trauner, F. (2014). Do supranational EU institutions make a difference? EU asylum law before and after 'communitarization'. *Journal of European Public Policy, 21*(8), 1142–1162.

Roe, E. (1994). *Narrative policy analysis: Theory and practice*. Durham, NC: Duke University Press.

Schmidt, V. A. (2008). Discursive institutionalism: The explanatory power of ideas and discourse. *Annual Review of Political Science, 11*(1), 303–326.

Schmitter, P. C. (2004). Neo-neofunctionalism. In A. Wiener & T. Diez (Eds.), *European integration theory* (1st ed., pp. 46–74). Oxford: Oxford University Press.

Schrag Sternberg, C. (2013). *The struggle for EU legitimacy: Public contestation, 1950–2005*. Basingstoke: Palgrave Macmillan.

Schulz, M. (2015, September 11). Don't blame Europe for the refugee crisis. *The Washington Post*. Retrieved from https://www.washingtonpost.com/opinions/dont-blame-europe-for-the-refugee-crisis/2015/09/11/e253c15a-573d-11e5-b8c9-944725fcd3b9_story.html

Schutte, J. J. (1991). Schengen: Its meaning for the free movement of persons in Europe. *Common Market Law Review, 28*(3), 549–570.

Schwartz-Shea, P., & Yanow, D. (2012). *Interpretive research design: Concepts and processes*. New York, NY: Routledge.

van Selm-Thorburn, J. (1998). *Refugee protection in Europe: lessons of the Yugoslav crisis*. The Hague: Martinus Nijhoff Publishers.

Shackleton, M. (2012). The European Parliament. In J. Peterson & M. Shackleton (Eds.), *The institutions of the European Union* (3rd ed., pp. 124–246). New York, NY: Oxford University Press.

Shooting Schengen. (2015, September 19). *The Economist*. Retrieved from http://www.economist.com/news/leaders/21665021-only-eu-wide-agreement-asylum-can-save-passport-free-travel-europe-shooting-schengen

Shore, C. (1993). Inventing the 'people's Europe': Critical approaches to European community 'cultural policy'. *Man, 28*(4), 779–800.

Shore, C., & Black, A. (1994). Citizens' Europe and the construction of European identity. In V. A. Goddard, J. R. Llobera, & C. Shore (Eds.), *The anthropology of Europe: Identity and boundaries in conflict* (pp. 275–298). Oxford: Berg.

Smale, A. (2016, February 24). With E.U. paralyzed, 10 nations try to stem migrant flow. *The New York Times*. Retrieved from http://www.nytimes.com/2016/02/25/world/europe/refugees-migrants-austria-greece.html

Spiegel Online. (2016, August 24). Two weeks in September: The makings of Merkel's decision to accept refugees. *Spiegel Online International*. Retrieved from http://www.spiegel.de/international/germany/a-look-back-at-the-refugee-crisis-one-year-later-a-1107986.html

Stone, D. A. (2011). *Policy paradox: The art of political decision making* (3rd ed.). New York, NY: W.W. Norton & Company.

Turner, A. (1992, January 21). *Letter to Martin Bangemann, Vice-President of the Commission of the European Commission on the occasion of the establishment of the LIBE Committee*. Luxembourg: European Parliament Historical Archives.

Ucarer, E. M. (2001). From the sidelines to center stage: Sidekick no more? The European Commission in justice and home affairs. *European Integration Online Papers (EIoP), 5*(5). Retrieved from http://eiop.or.at/eiop/pdf/2001-005.pdf

Ucarer, E. M. (2013). The area of freedom, security, and justice. In M. Cini & N. Perez-Solorzano Borragan (Eds.), *European Union politics* (4th ed., pp. 281–295). New York, NY: Oxford University Press.

Vandystadt, N. (2012, May 14). Home affairs council: Schengen – ministers uncomfortable with Franco-German letter. *Europolitics*.

Wessels, B. (1999). Whom to represent? Role orientations of legislators in Europe. In H. Schmitt, & J. Thomassen (Eds.), *Political representation and legitimacy in the European Union* (pp. 209–234). Oxford: Oxford University Press.

Whitaker, E. (1992). The Schengen agreement and its portent for the freedom of personal movement in Europe. *Georgetown Immigration Law Journal, 6*, 191–222.

Zaiotti, R. (2011). *Cultures of border control: Schengen and the evolution of European frontiers*. Chicago, IL: University of Chicago Press.

The Promethean role of Europe: changing narratives of the political and scholarly left

Nikola Petrović

ABSTRACT

The gradual abandoning of the 'socialism in one country' doctrine during the post-war period and the intensive transformation of European social democracy in the 1990s pushed social democratic politicians and intellectuals into the front line of advocates of a unified and powerful Europe. They contributed to the inclusion of social democratic and environmentalist values in the EU's official narrative. The success of European integration and George W. Bush's presidency created the narrative of the Promethean role of Europe. Scholars with a social democratic or environmentalist background created this narrative and it was also shaped by authors' national contexts.

Visions of Europe as the continent that is already leading the world towards a better future emerged at the beginning of the twenty-first century during a period of tense relations between the EU and the US. The transatlantic drift and the significant deepening and enlargement of European integration (the introduction of the Euro, the Constitutional Convention, the Eastern enlargement) contributed to the reinterpretation of the EU's role in the world and to an intensified search for a distinct European identity (Petrović, 2016). These geopolitical and institutional changes created the exalted narrative of the Promethean role of Europe. Just as the legendary Prometheus brought fire to humanity, this narrative claimed Europe and the EU delivered to the rest of the world a path beyond the nation-state, plus also ecological consciousness, pacificism and social cohesion. This article argues that this narrative was also a result of the changing global and European ideological landscape.

The middle of the 1990s was a period of significant change in the thought and practice of the European left. Successive election wins by European social democratic parties or centre-left coalitions created temporary centre-left domination in the EU at the end of the 1990s. Poul Nyrup Rasmussen became Prime Minister of Denmark in 1993 and immediately succeeded in getting the Maastricht Treaty approved through a second referendum, Wim Kok became Dutch Prime Minister in 1994, Ingvar Carlsson returned to the position of Swedish Prime Minister in 1994, leading the country in the European Union in 1995, Paavo Lipponen became Finish Prime Minister in 1995, Romano Prodi led the centre-left coalition to triumph in Italy in 1996, and in 1997 French socialist Prime Minister Lionel Jospin started his cohabitation with Jacques Chirac. However, the most significant social democratic electoral gains were in Britain and Germany. Tony Blair became Prime Minister in 1997 and Gerhard Schröder became Chancellor in 1998 in Germany's first Red-Green coalition. At the end of the 1990s, social democratic parties participated in governments in twelve of the EU-15 states. Moreover, for the first time they simultaneously controlled national governments in the biggest EU countries – Germany, France, the United Kingdom and Italy (Ladrech, 2000; Paterson & Sloam, 2006). However, by 2006, only the UK had a centre-left prime minister. Therefore, this was not the long-term structural hegemony of social democrats, as was the 'hegemony by default' (Kaiser, 2007, p. 263) of Christian democracy in Western Europe after 1945. Nevertheless, social democratic domination and the rise of the greens had an important transnational dimension. Transnationalisation was evident in the enhanced cooperation of ideological families at the European level and it influenced European integration and narratives about it at the beginning of the twenty-first century.

The transformation of European social democrats and their rising support for European integration has been researched in various ways. Most notable are analyses of the organizational and ideological Europeanisation of social democratic parties and their influence on EU politics (Ladrech, 2000) and of the convergences and divergences among European social democrats (Pollack, 2000). Crucially, Thomas Risse (2010) argued that the transformation of social democrats in Germany and France contributed to the growing compatibility of Germanness and Frenchness with Europeanness, as it created a centre-right and centre-left pro-European integration consensus. However, the transformation of British Labour also had an impact on the growing compatibility of Englishness with Europeanness, as the electoral success of New Labour temporarily silenced the hard left in the Labour Party and even contributed to the construction of the narrative of the Promethean role of Europe at the beginning of the 2000s. Risse traced the incompatibility of English nation-state identity with European identity to medieval English history. It is argued here that using the concept of nation-state identity that traces its foundation so far back in history could be misleading because it creates a reified view of the social world, which in reality is highly contingent (Brubaker & Cooper, 2000; Malešević, 2006). The concept of European identity is also used to reify a process of European integration that in reality is contingent (Petrović, 2016). Various group ideologies compete in a common public sphere with their visions of a nation-state or a 'region-state', as Vivien Schmidt defines the EU (2016). At a particular moment one vision can prevail and construct the identity of the organization through the creation of specific narratives such as that of Europe's Promethean role (on nation-states as organizations see Malešević, 2013). When researching the creation and influence of national or European identity, there is a need for a more flexible and change-sensitive approach that is able to grasp changes in group and personal ideologies which can ultimately have a major influence.

The present article argues that the long-term process of ideological repositioning of the European left across Europe influenced a new emerging narrative that emphasized the positive role of the EU in global affairs. The gradual abandoning of the 'socialism in one country' doctrine during the post-war period and the intensive transformation of European social democracy in the 1990s pushed social democratic politicians and intellectuals into the front line of advocates of a unified and powerful Europe. They saw the EU as the level where the main goals of their ideologies could be achieved. The first part of the article compares earlier forebears with creators of the narrative of the Promethean role of Europe. The second part explains how the changing morphology of social democracy and green ideology turned them into major contributors to the emerging Promethean narrative. The third part shows how social democrats and greens, while working together at the EU level, contributed to the inclusion of social democratic and environmentalist values in the EU's official narrative and how was this interpreted by scholars. The last part analyses how national debates in which centre-left actors participated, were transposed onto the European-level Promethean role of Europe narrative.

Forebears and creators of the narrative of the Promethean role of Europe

The narrative of the Promethean role of Europe has earlier forebears, but they were not so self-confident, comprehensive and coherent, and did not initiate a string of similar narratives, as was the case with the narrative of European exceptionalism at the beginning of the 2000s. Earlier accounts of the European role in the world praised the retreat of the nation-state in Europe (Haas, 1961) and Europe as a potential first world civilian power (Duchêne, 1972), but did not argue that Europe could be the moral leader for the rest of the world. Two books written during the relaunch of European integration in the mid-1980s by two prominent pro-Europeans with a Proudhonist background had a more ideological content and more optimistic outlook for the European role in the world. Veteran European federalist Hendrik Brugmans, in his book *Europe: A leap in the dark*, compared the capabilities of Europe, the USSR, the US, Islam and China and concluded that Europe could become a future global role model (1985). This was accompanied by Brugmans' proclamation of the failure of the American dream (1985, p. 31).[1] However, the outcome of the relaunch was still uncertain and Brugmans asked himself if this internal change – that is, the marriage of unity and diversity – could be achieved. Brugmans gave a recipe for the European economic model resembling that promoted by the modern catch-all social democracy: 'Solidarity between the investor and the trade unionist, not forgetting the ecologist' (1985, p. 78).

Jacques Delors, the then president of the European Commission, wrote the other book, *Our Europe* (1992). This elaborated his vision of a social Europe and regulated capitalism (Hooghe & Marks, 1997). His vision encompassed elements such as the unique European model of society, a combination of cooperation and competition, an emphasis on solidarity and collective bargaining and successful management of European diversity, but also responsibility towards less developed nations and Eastern European countries and a warning of the resurgence of American conservatism. In both of these books, the future motto of the EU is mentioned, as Brugmans quoted Proudhon's prediction of 'a world of federalism, "union in diversity"' (1985, p. 12) and Delors called for 'a Europe united in diversity' (1992, p. 158). Both books were written during Ronald Reagan's presidency, which was marked by neoliberal and neoconservative policies and his insistence on American exceptionalism. Although Brugmans and Delors helped establish the vision of Europe as a future moral leader and linked that vision to socialist values, the post-Maastricht disenchantment, and especially the Yugoslav wars, made this vision seem unrealistic.

There is a need to differentiate between those earlier narratives of Europe as a potential normative power, which had the function of mobilising pro-European forces for further integration, and which can be characterised as prophetism. Biebuyck and Rumford use the term 'Euro-prophets' (2012) when writing about some of the authors that are considered here as the creators of the emerging narrative at the beginning of the 2000s. However, in order to make a clear distinction to the prophetism of the mid-1980s, the term the Promethean role of Europe is used for the depiction of this new narrative. This term emphasizes the emerging perception of the already existent power of Europe as a role model promoting positive values and ideologies such as social democracy and environmentalism, which were considered to be absent in American policies, to the whole world.

In order to explore an emerging narrative of the Promethean role of Europe, the article analyses a limited number of key pro-EU politicians and scholars, who promoted social democratic or environmentalist values and had a powerful influence on the framing of debates in the EU at the beginning of the 2000s. These include the most powerful politicians in the EU institutions – such as the social democratic presidents of the European Commission or European Commissioners and of leading social democratic and green politicians in the three biggest EU member states (Germany, France and the United Kingdom), who were at that time intensifying their interactions. As in Liah Greenfeld's analysis of the emergence of nationalism (1992), they are treated as the creators and carriers of this narrative, taking into account the situational constraints they faced. Scholars and politicians formed national and transnational intellectual networks, out of which the narrative emerged. Ideological discourse analysis of books, articles, speeches and interviews by these scholars and politicians was performed (van Dijk, 1998). These written and spoken acts were analysed through time, with a special emphasis on the context in which actors produced them. In order to connect the development of a personal ideology to a broader historical context, the concept of epiphany – that is, of a key turning-point moment that shapes an individual's life – is used (Denzin, 2014). It is argued that globally and nationally important events serving as the causes of epiphanies have the power to transform personal ideologies.

Differentiation between pragmatic and ideological entrepreneurship was analysed. Drawing on the differences between those politicians who are more responsive to changes in the social and political environment and those who put more emphasis on ideas (Rousseau, 2006), analysis centres on when politicians adapt their discourse to the changes in European integration to remain relevant and when their ideological backgrounds push them towards promotion of European integration.

Numerous scholars contributed to the construction of European identity, driven by the same political changes as politicians, and by their ideological orientations on the scholarly left. Scholars that are analysed here have previously publicly espoused adherence to social democratic or green political ideologies. Special emphasis is given to the scholar-politician nexus, which is the result of an often symbiotic relationship between these two sorts of actors. Scholars, especially public intellectuals, often want to see their ideas materialise and politicians need intellectual legitimization of their policies and positions. There may also be some sort of indirect dialogue between these two types of actors and a reinforcement of an emerging narrative. This reinforcement of a narrative was analysed in the case of Ian Manners, one of the most influential EU studies scholar, and the then President of the European Commission José Manuel Durão Barroso. Barroso positively acknowledged Manners' concept of 'Normative Power Europe' in an interview, and Manners then used the quotation from this Barroso's statement in another scholarly paper in order to reinforce his concept and prove that the EU is a normative power (Adler-Nissen & Kropp, 2015).

The Promethean narrative is the result of the profound ideological, institutional and geopolitical changes at the end of the twentieth century and the beginning of the twenty-first century. Ideological changes are mostly analysed in the following section and institutional and geopolitical in the third section. However, all of these types of causes cannot be easily discerned from each other as they are interconnected, so they sometimes occur in both of these sections and they are all used to explain national narratives in the last section.

Transformation of the European left and European integration

New geopolitical, economic and social circumstances in the post-Maastricht EU brought the need for a theoretical repositioning of European social democracy. British and German centre-left intellectuals and politicians for the most part performed this repositioning as witnessed in the 'Third Way' and 'Die Neue Mitte' varieties of European social democratic ideology. One of the key tenets of the new European social democracy was a growing enthusiasm for European integration (Hooghe, Marks, & Wilson, 2002). Anthony Giddens, the key theorist of the Third Way, incorporated the EU in his ideology in the following way:

> The European Union began as part of the bipolar system, but should be understood today as a response to globalization. What matters is not so much that it defines an entity, 'Europe', as that it is developing social, political, political and economic institutions that stretch above the nation-state and reach down to the individual. ... even in its current form it offers a model capable of wider application, and could play a direct role in providing it. (1998, pp. 141–142)

Giddens and his German colleague, sociologist Ulrich Beck, both proponents of the social theory of reflexive modernisation, were also both staunch EU supporters, but their emphases on key European problems differed according to national contexts. Visions of European integration by social democratic politicians also differed according to national and party contexts, ranging from Schröder's call for a 'European government' (Radikale Schritte, 2001), through Jospin's more cautious 'federation of nation-states' (2001) to Blair's announcement of 'EU – a superpower, but not a superstate' (2000). Despite these differences, it was significant that the EU became an inevitable element of the politics of all social democratic leaders. Both as a political actor and as an organizational model for other regions, it represented for them the framework through which world peace and global social justice could be pursued. This enthusiasm for European integration was even more pronounced in the narratives of green politicians such as the German Foreign Minister Joschka Fischer and Daniel Cohn-Bendit, the co-president of European Greens. Green parties were becoming more influential on a European scale at the end of the 1990s, with German and French Green parties participating for the first time in national governments. In his speech at Humboldt University, Fischer called for the establishment of a European federation and thus inspired a debate on the deepening of political integration (2000). Many of the actors from this social democratic and green wave at the end of the 1990s played crucial roles in EU politics: they strongly influenced EU politics and deepened European integration. In cooperation with like-minded intellectuals, they also created a new European narrative that advocated promoting European integration and specific positive European values to the rest of the world.

Apart from globalization and Europeanisation, which pushed the European centre-left towards promoting Europe, ideational factors also played an important role. Non-communist leftism has been a recurring feature of fervent federalism and Europeanism since Spinelli's Ventotene Manifesto. In a clearly revolutionary spirit, Spinelli, after he denounced Stalinism, wrote about the moment of new action and 'the moment for new men: the moment for a free and united Europe' (Spinelli & Rossi, 1944). After the Second World War and at the advent of the Cold War, other socialist actors such as the Socialist Movement for the United States of Europe also prioritised the achievement of European unification over their socialist ideological goal.

The differing communist left and non-communist left perspectives on European integration can be most clearly discerned from the end of the 1960s debate between Jean Jacques Servan-Schreiber and Ernst Mandel. Servan-Schreiber, a publicist and future president of the French centre-left Radical Party, called for European federalism and the pooling of European economies as an answer to the American challenge – that is, the danger of the US economy dominating the European one (1967). Belgian Trotskyist Mandel accused Servan-Schreiber of being a technocratic ideologist. He sent this call to the European socialists: 'Forward, against American and European monopolists, to the United Socialist States of Europe!' (Mandel, 1970, p. 154). However, the most positive stance of more radical and communist leftists towards European integration can be described as 'reluctant Europeanism' (Almeida, 2012, p. 69). Politicians belonging to the European United Left/Nordic Green Left and scholars primarily occupied with class issues (van Apeldoorn, 2002) remain concerned about what they see as the imperialistic and neoliberal foundations of the EU. They also see the centre-left as betrayers of the socialist cause, because they abandoned Keynesian policies and therefore are responsible for growing inequality.

Nevertheless, ideologies have a number of core concepts and one of the core concepts of the socialist ideology is that of 'history as the arena of (ultimately) beneficial change' (Freeden, 1996, p. 426). Modern social democrats – and especially the Third Way Labour – put the core concept of equality of outcomes to the side, but at the same time they got involved in the deepening of European integration or even European federalism as the radical construction of the future. European integration was for them the beneficial change that provided the historical opportunity in which social equality could be achieved and global justice pursued. Michael Freeden, a leading expert in the study of political ideologies, elaborated this characteristic of socialist ideology:

> Socialism entails a massive leap of faith and imagination, an emotional as well as an intellectual effort to claim that what has never been, or what belongs to a conjectural history, is nevertheless normal and proper to human beings and their societies. (1996, p. 418)

Therefore, social democratic politicians and scholars could engage in the construction of an optimistic narrative, as they preserved the core concept of belief in progressive change.

On the other hand, there was a lack of exalted Christian democratic narratives on Europe's role in the world. As Kaiser argues, transnational Christian democracy has crucially shaped the EU and it still does, but already since the beginnings of European integration for 'the Christian democratic elites, creating an integrated core Europe did not promise the dawn of a new millennium' (2007, p. 172). Enabled by their ideological fervour and by their belief in constant progress, leftists have been offering bold visions of Europe since

Spinelli's revolutionary calls. Another concept that became one of the core concepts of European social democracy was supranationalism (Hooghe & Marks, 1997). This was a modification to the internationalism of the old social democracy (Giddens, 1998). As the differences between the economic policies of the centre-left and centre-right decreased, there was a greater need for the centre-left to differentiate itself from the nationalism and conservatism of the right. Rising emphasis on the promotion of the rights for ethnic and sexual minorities played that role. Supranationalism of the new social democrats also became an important addition to this increasingly important cleavage.

Cohn-Bendit and Fischer were far from single-issue green ideologists and they also belonged to the non-communist left. At the end of 1960s, they were searching for the New Left alternative to 'obsolete communism' (Cohn-Bendit & Cohn-Bendit, 2000). Green ideology served as a kind of sanctuary for these two 1968 radicals after the demise of the New Left movement in the 1970s. Elisabeth Bomberg also traces links between the green ideology and radical federalists and critics of the nation-state such as Denis de Rougemont (1998). These links make some strands of green ideology more responsive to the idea of European federalism. Larger green European parties, except those with hard left leanings such as the Irish and Swedish parties, turned towards pro-European positions during the 1990s (Hooghe et al., 2002, p. 984).

Rising supranationalism of the European left enabled its actors to search for their identity on a European level and create new pro-European narratives, but also to cooperate with like-minded politicians.

Transnational framing of the EU's role in the world

Transnationalisation was an important factor in the process of the transformation of the European centre-left, as it created an opportunity to discuss different national versions of their ideologies and to influence EU policies. Besides the electoral gains on the national level, the 1990s brought integration to the European centre-left on the European level. Already at the beginning of the 1990s the Confederation of Socialist Parties of the European Community (CSPEC) recognised the need for more intensive European cooperation in a changing world. They concluded that the democratic 'control of the future remains possible, provided that those elements of sovereignty which can no longer be exercised in a purely national framework are pooled' (CSPEC, 1990, p. 1). The Party of European Socialists (PES) was founded as the successor to the CSPEC in 1992, thus acknowledging the new reality of deeper European integration. PES's activism contributed significantly to the inclusion of the Employment Chapter in the Amsterdam Treaty in 1997 (Ladrech, 2000). In accordance with the Third Way ideology, the Treaty also mentioned technological and globalization challenges to high level of employment and emphasized the need for a 'skilled, trained and adaptable workforce and labour markets responsive to economic change' (Treaty of Amsterdam, 1997). The Amsterdam Treaty had an even more significant inclusion, the Social Protocol, which was a direct result of Labour's victory in Britain. A new centre-left government ended 'both British exceptionalism and differentiated integration with respect to social policy' (Dinan, 2010, p. 425). The Amsterdam Treaty was also a victory for the European greens as it emphasized sustainable development. This was the result of the influence of the 'green' Nordic countries whose political clout was strengthened by the 1995 entrance of Sweden and Finland in the EU (Moravcsik & Nicolaïdis, 1999), but it also represented an attempt to search for a common goal and a new identity in the post-Maastricht EU (Baker, 2007).

Like the other main party families (liberals and Christian democrats) socialists 'gradually converged on moderately pro-Integration positions' between 1976 and 1994, (Hix, 1999, p. 37). In 1994, European green parties also 'agreed to a joint manifesto that stressed reform "from within" rather than the anti-EU stance of some earlier campaigns' (Bomberg, 1998, p. 95). Cohn-Bendit was a perfect symbol of the transnationalisation of the European left, entering the European Parliament (EP) on the German list in 1994 and the French Green list in 1999.

The impact of the transformation of the European centre-left was also felt through the creation of various transnational think tanks that promoted a federal Europe and whose members were leading left-wing politicians and scholars. In 1996, Delors founded the social democratic think tank 'Notre Europe', whose prominent members are contributors to the Promethean role of Europe narrative such as Pascal Lamy and Maria João Rodrigues. In 2010, an initiative for a federal Europe, the 'Spinelli Group', was founded in the EP with prominent outside supporters such as Fischer, Beck and Delors. Members of the European Parliament such as Cohn-Bendit and Guy Verhofstadt, who recently co-authored the *Manifesto for a postnational revolution in Europe* (2012), and German social democrat and former radical leftist Jo Leinen have occupied key places in the 'Spinelli Group'.

The Lisbon Strategy of 2000, a continuation of the 1997 Luxembourg process, also had a transnational social democratic imprint. It combined the Third Way's reformism and its orientation towards competitiveness, with social cohesion and sustainability, which would soon be reinterpreted as innate European values. Blair initiated the reformist tone of the Lisbon Strategy, Rasmussen's concept of flexicurity was reflected in it and the main author of the Strategy was a Portuguese social democrat, Rodrigues, a former Minister of Labour. Rodrigues explained the background of the Strategy and its emphasis on distinct European values, arguing that Europe was losing ground to the United States, but this did not mean Europe had to copy the US (2003). This was a clear example of the transvaluation of values, in this case American values, a process that Greenfeld identifies in the creation of various nationalisms (1992, p. 16). She argues that nationalists often define 'national' values in opposition to those of their geopolitical rivals.

These distinct European values were the result of the changing relations between the US and the EU in a post-Cold War environment that was marked by growing independence of European states from America. This new constellation can be discerned from the statements of leading European politicians. Blair called for the shaping of a responsive European Union: 'a civilised continent united in defeating brutality and violence; a continent joined in its belief in social justice' (2000). Jospin stated that 'Europe is called upon to point globalization in the direction of law and justice' (2001). Prodi, as the president of the European Commission, said: 'We are an emerging power, dare I say "a potential power"' (2001).

US-EU relations grew particularly acrimonious at the beginning of the twenty-first century as the US President George W. Bush pursued unilateral actions such as the invasion of Iraq and the non-ratification of the Kyoto protocol. Especially symbolic was the 2001 Gothenburg European Council, where the EU outlined strategies for the sustainable development and combating climate change. At the same time, the newly elected Bush, who also came to Gothenburg for an EU-US summit, was met with public demonstrations. Subsequently, numerous centre-left and pro-EU scholars took the calls of Blair, Jospin and Prodi even further, arguing that Europe has already became a superpower, albeit a different kind from the US. Numerous intellectuals and social scientists, inspired by the success of European integration at the beginning of the twenty-first century, were engaged in the promotion of the new global role for Europe.

Manners inaugurated the new narrative with his normative power Europe concept. He was inspired by EU–US differences, which he embodied in the Texan Governor George W. Bush receiving protests from the EU against the death penalty (2002, p. 248). Manners' concept was also aimed at the construction of European identity (Diez, 2005). However, it was more important that prominent and more explicitly ideological public intellectuals were constructing the new narrative. This indicated the increasing importance of the EU. For instance, Jürgen Habermas and Jeremy Rifkin were not primarily EU experts, but they wrote highly influential texts on European integration as the first step towards Kantian perpetual peace and towards the establishment of the global society. This narrative of the Promethean role of Europe declared Europe to be the only society that is already capable of comprehending and solving global inequalities and ecological crisis.

Prophetism was prevalent in the quoted statements of centre-left European leaders before the Iraq war. But authors such as Habermas (Habermas & Derrida, 2003), Rifkin (2004), T. R. Reid (2004), Mark Leonard (2005), John McCormick (2007, 2010) and Steven Hill (2010), whether in the lead-up to the Iraq War, during it or in its aftermath, created a new narrative proclaiming that Europe is a sort of Prometheus already serving as a global role model.

The narrative consisted primarily of comparisons between European and American values, which deemed European values to be superior. These comparisons were kindled by attacks by neoconservative politicians such as Donald Rumsfeld and scholars such as Robert Kagan (2003) on what they perceived as out-of-touch European values. On the other hand, authors of the narrative emphasized the deep ideological roots of European superiority. Habermas writes about the links between the European workers' movement and the Christian socialist tradition (Habermas & Derrida, 2003, p. 296) and McCormick saw social democracy as being rooted in European society and European values (2010, p. 118). Environmentalism was also often invoked as an ideology close to Europeans and reflected in EU policies (McCormick, 2010; Rifkin, 2004). Ideological backgrounds of these authors and their dissatisfaction with US policies drove them to create a new narrative that was meant to become the cornerstone of European identity.

The national roots of the Promethean role of Europe narrative

Geopolitical and institutional changes, as well as transnational debates, created the Promethean role of Europe narrative, but it was also shaped by specific national contexts, which were also influenced by these same changes. Some of the national debates from the 1990s and 2000s were transposed to a transnational narrative of the Promethean role of Europe. However, all of these national emphases included the same mechanism of leftist actors ideologically repositioning themselves in a rapidly changing world.

France

To begin with, France, for most of the history of European integration the most powerful member state, produced numerous narratives on the future of Europe. Earlier visions were still preoccupied with geopolitical considerations, whether it was de Gaulle's vision of Europe as a superpower led by France, which contained a strong notion of French grandeur, or Duchêne's civilian power Europe. On the French left, Servan-Schreiber timidly pointed out that some welfare indicators such as the access to medical care are better in Europe than in the US, but on the other hand he argued that the US was superior in access to education (1967). Servan-Schreiber predicted that only a non-dogmatic and reformed European left could modernise Europe so that it would then be able to compete with the US. He singled out François Mitterrand as the representative of this reformed European left (1967, p. 237). And it was precisely Mitterrand who, as the French president, abandoned Keynesian policies and pushed the French left towards fully embracing European integration.[2]

The U-turn of the French socialists and the ideas of French political elites had a strong influence on the relaunch of European integration during the 1980s (Parsons, 2003; Schmidt, 1996), but also on the new visions of social Europe. After Mitterrand and Delors performed their U-turn in 1983, they became the most vociferous promotors of social Europe. However, there is a need to deal with the background of these ideas on a personal level, which can be traced in individual actors' reactions to major historical events, their ideological profiles and their socialisation in European affairs. Mitterrand is regarded as an inconsistent politician with various controversies following him through his political career. Yet there was a level of ideological entrepreneurship in his position on European integration, as Mitterrand's 'consistently pro-European attitude provided one source of cohesion throughout his career' (Cole, 1994, p. 118). Tiersky argues that Mitterrand's experience of two World Wars 'convinced him that some structure beyond the nation-state was necessary' (2003, p. 163). In 1948, Mitterrand participated in the Congress of Europe in The Hague. As a long-time opponent of de Gaulle, Mitterrand also opposed his European policies.

Delors did not have the same sort of prominent pro-European history as Mitterrand, but he had a specific ideological background that prepared him for becoming the most prominent president of the European Commission. In 1959, inspired by Proudhon's ideas, he founded a left federalist club, which opposed de Gaulle's European policies and perceived European integration as a 'need to build a regional bloc capable of independence vis-à-vis the USA' (Drake, 2000, p. 34). In addition, he had a brief period of socialisation in European affairs, as in 1979 he became a member of the European Parliament. His father had been wounded in the First World War and he lost his best friend at Auschwitz. Delors' influence in constructing the European narrative was far reaching, as in the 1980s he popularised the term 'European social model', which was meant to be an alternative to the American form of capitalism (Jepsen & Serrano Pascual, 2006), and introduced the concept of social cohesion into EU politics (Hooghe, 1996). These concepts remained prominent in the EU's official discourse and were used by scholars at the beginning of the 2000s when they described the exceptional social solidarity of Europe.

Lamy also participated in the U-turn as an advisor to Delors and, as the European Commissioner for Trade and as the General Director of the World Trade Organization, promoted an ideology of harnessed globalization: a European opposition to the American ad hoc version of globalization (Abdelal & Meunier, 2010). He proposed this term in 1999 and in 2006 described unharnessed globalization as 'an export of American values without going through any negotiation phase. Harnessed globalization is much more consensual' (quoted in Abdelal & Meunier, 2010, pp. 353–354). This strongly resonated with Jospin's previously quoted call for Europe to become the frontrunner of a just globalization. Jospin was also forced to push the debate on the consequences of globalization on the European level, although he was never an enthusiastic supporter of European integration and opposed the liberalisation of French socialists.

Germany

Unification changed Germany's role in Europe, making it the most populous EU member state by a large margin and subsequently giving it much stronger influence on EU politics. It also ended an important constraint to German elites' complete immersion in European integration. Even Willy Brandt, a committed European, had to devote most of his foreign policy efforts in the Ostpolitik. Unification's influence was apparent in the change of focus that Habermas described in his case. In a recent interview, Habermas acknowledged that his interest in Europe 'gained momentum with the German unification, which was a key moment for my country' (Habermas & Meyvis, 2013). Habermas became the first world-renowned intellectual to engage in the construction of the Promethean role of Europe, while claiming that the EU 'already offers itself as a form of "governance beyond the nation-state", which could set a precedent in the post-national constellation' (Habermas & Derrida, 2003, p. 294).

Apart from a national context, Habermas was driven by his theoretical and ideological project of reconstructing left thought (1976). Although he had a Marxist background, Habermas was never overly interested in the issues of class and class relations. In 2005, he responded to accusations that he made a liberal turn in the 1980s: 'I was a "left-liberal, left of Social Democracy" in the '60s also. But my interest in political economy, in which I had never felt at home, declined' (quoted in Specter, 2010, p. 209). At the end of the 1990s, Habermas became primarily concerned with the question of the postnational constellation and the EU (1998). Habermas belongs to the '58ers generation of German intellectuals, who witnessed the collapse of the Third Reich and tried to overcome the German Nazi past, while opening Germany to the West (Specter, 2010). These experiences could partly explain Habermas's embrace of the postnational EU. This plays well with Risse's argument that Germany's historical experiences pushed German elites, in this case intellectual elites, to welcome European integration (2010). However, various experiences and ideological backgrounds among German elites led them to perceive European integration in different ways and even oppose it. For example, the German New Left or the '68ers were also confronting the German Nazi past, but their revolutionary denouncement of a Western-type democracy put them at odds with some of the '58ers. This was exemplified by Habermas' conflicts with radical students at the end of 1960s.

However, individual actors are not completely constrained by belonging to a group ideology: their personal ideas and experiences allow them to overcome their group ideology and this can become relevant if they occupy an important political position. This was the case with Fischer, who became associated with European federalism after he abandoned his previous core concepts, such as pacifism. Habermas and Fischer also exemplify a scholar-politician nexus and Habermas got engaged in the construction of new narratives on Europe during the rise of Europeanism in the German Red-Green coalition. During the mid-1980s, they ran seminars together in Frankfurt and both abandoned radical left positions. This culminated with their unexpected support of the NATO intervention during the War in Kosovo (Müller, 2004). In Habermas's 2003 essay on European identity, Fischer is the only political actor mentioned as an example of a genuine European politician (Habermas & Derrida, 2003, p. 292). Fischer's Europeanism can be explained by the confrontation of the '68ers with the German Nazi past and his personal ideological transformation, during which he gradually abandoned the '68ers radicalism. Anti-nationalism was a prominent element in the German Green Party, whose members included both Fischer and Cohn-Bendit. Moreover, Fischer used the notion of Auschwitz as the justification for his decision to abandon the use of violent tactics after the anti-Semitic behaviour of German hijackers during the Entebbe plane hijack in 1976, but also for his support of the NATO intervention in Kosovo and Serbia. Fischer's anti-nationalistic ideological entrepreneurship continued as he initiated a debate on European federalism after the period of post-Maastricht disenchantment and thus gave a push to the deepening of European integration. In the Humboldt University speech, he used powerful arguments such as the need to overcome the Westphalian system, the shortcomings of Monnet method and the constitutional treaty as 'a deliberate political act to re-establish Europe' (2000) in order to put federalism back in the debate.

With the Red-Green coalition calling for a federal Europe and the long tradition of German Christian Democrats' federalism, Germany indeed looked like having reconciled 'Germanness' and 'Europeanness' at the beginning of the twenty-first century. However, the contingency of the creation of national identities and their instability should always be kept in mind, as in von Beyme's analysis of the shifting German national identities and even of East and West Germany not having a unified national consciousness (1999). The recent rise of the Alternative für Deutschland shows that there are formidable political forces which could easily make 'Germanness' less compatible with 'Europeanness'.

The United Kingdom

Eurosceptic forces traditionally play an important role in British politics and can now claim victory in the EU referendum. However, there was a considerable move towards pro-European attitudes at the end of the 1990s in the Labour Party. In addition, it should not be forgotten that in the 1930s and 1940s, quite a number of leftist British federalists were not constrained by Englishness in creating bold visions of a federal Europe. For example, Barbara Wootton argued in 1941 that socialism in Europe could be achieved only when the nation-state was superseded and European federation accomplished. However, the Labour government's decision to boycott the 1948 Hague Congress of Europe, a seminal event for planning the institutions of post-war European integration, was just the first of numerous events that alienated the British left from European integration and caused a lack of socialisation in European affairs. On the other hand, German Social Democrats also considered the option of boycotting the Council of Europe, but eventually opted for participation. Their participation in early European institutions 'during the late 1950s and early 1960s certainly prompted the SPD to adopt a more positive stance towards European integration' (Lodge, 1976, p. 33).

Nevertheless, there were important events in the post-war period that caused epiphanies and created convinced pro-European Labourites. For instance, one pro-European witness claims that Harold Wilson's failure to modernise British industry led him to swing to Europe. Roger Liddle concluded that 'nation state social democracy seemed incapable of either securing fairness and prosperity in Britain or exercising moral leadership in the world' (2014, p. xii). Furthermore, Margaret Thatcher's Euroscepticism gave an incentive to Labour not to support policies that their main rival promoted. This was evident in Neil Kinnock's embrace of European integration during his time as the leader of the Labour Party and as the Leader of the Opposition during Thatcher's reign. With this move, Kinnock also wanted to neutralise the rise of the most pro-European British political force: the SDP-Liberal alliance (Gowland, Turner, & Wright, 2009).

Another scholar-politician nexus that was important for the creation of the Promethean role of Europe narrative was a constituent part of New Labour's turn towards the EU. Giddens is often considered the chief advisor to Blair, but their versions of the Third Way differed. Giddens' Third Way has been interpreted as 'posttraditionalist' and Blair's as 'social moralist' (Driver & Martell, 2000). However, both of them accepted the new realities of globalization and especially of a globalized economy. This drove them to see Britain as a natural part of the EU. Blair was, arguably, more interested in another topic that did not belong to the core of the Third Way ideology. It was the doctrine of humanitarian intervention and an interest in foreign policy, which marked his term in office. He put the British Armed Forces on the world stage again and was interested in strengthening European Security and Defence Policy. However, he did not aim for his opening to Europe to undermine the NATO alliance and the UK's relationship with the US. Despite this search for balanced relations with both his American and European allies, Blair went down in history as an ally of Bush during the Iraq War.

However, Blair's alliance with Bush was one of the reasons why some centre-left British intellectuals, while distancing themselves from this alliance, contributed to the Promethean role of Europe narrative. Mark Leonard, as a young member of the Demos think tank, was part of Blair's project of rebranding the Labour Party. In 2005, he published a book called *Why Europe will run the 21st century*, where he criticised Bush's aggressive politics and praised the European approach that was able to transform non-democratic regimes. He saw Europe as the epitome of the Third Way, a 'synthesis of the energy and freedom that come from liberalism with the stability and welfare that come from social democracy' (Leonard, 2005, p. 7). Europe also became a beacon for the rest of the world: 'In every corner of the world countries are drawing inspiration from the European model and nurturing their own neighbourhood clubs' (Leonard, 2005, p. 7). He, like Brugmans, compared Europe to China and the US, but contrary to Brugmans, concluded that already 'the new global order is being shaped in the one place where most Americans would least expect to find it: in "Old Europe"' (Leonard, 2005, p. xi). Leonard, like Blair, was critical of the idea of European federalism. However, he was heavily involved in the promotion of Europe as a transformative power. Also in those years, McCormick was concerned with the EU as a new sort of power (2007) and they were both, in a way, transposing the debates on the UK's global influence onto the European level.

The intellectual networks that created this narrative were not just transnational, but also transcontinental. McCormick, the author of the most comprehensive analysis of European identity (2010), is a British citizen who lives in the US and is influenced by both public spheres. American scholars, journalists and political analysts, disappointed by their homeland's global impact, significantly contributed to the creation of the narrative with strong expressions such as the 'European dream' (Rifkin, 2004) and the 'European way' (Hill, 2010). In the discourse of American scholars, there was also a significant leap from Euro-prophetism to the Promethean role of Europe narrative. In 1992, American economist Lester Thurow compared Japan, the US and Europe and concluded that future 'historians will record that the twenty-first century belonged to the House of Europe!' (1992, p. 256). After three years of George W. Bush's presidency, American authors were already offering the EU and Europe as a role model for the US. They argued either that Americans were not aware that the European model of society was already surpassing them (Reid, 2004) or that the EU was already a global role model (Rifkin, 2004).

Prior to getting involved in the construction of European identity, both McCormick and Rifkin were environmental activists and experts. They both saw the EU as the leader in the protection of the environment and Europe as a breeding ground of environmental values. Rifkin was involved in influencing EU policies, as he claimed that he served as an advisor to Romano Prodi, 'the president of the European Commission and, in that capacity, provided the strategic memorandum that led to the adoption and implementation of the EU hydrogen plan' (2004, p. 413). In another example of a scholar-politician nexus contributing to an emerging narrative, Rifkin then used Prodi's call for a turn towards renewable energy as proof of the EU's commitment to sustainable development. American authors were also writing in the aftermath of the transformation of the American left. This transformation was the result of the success of the New Democrats during Bill Clinton's presidency, marked by, among other things, their growing internationalism and by Clinton's vice president Al Gore's intense focus on environmentalism. It was also indicative that, at least in the US, the Promethean narrative survived Blair's alliance with Bush, the election of Barack Obama and a string of electoral defeats of European social democrats.

The different twentieth century historical experiences and political paths of the nation-states analysed here had diverse impacts on the emergence of a new narrative. When compared to the German and French experiences, the British experiences of the Second World War had a far lower capacity to create major epiphanies for future pro-European ideological entrepreneurs. In France and especially in Germany, there was a considerable impetus for intellectuals and politicians on the left to search for anti-nationalistic solutions. When confronting its national past, the British left was more preoccupied with British imperial history and this often created strong anti-imperialist narratives within the Labour Party. Moreover, both Eurosceptics and pro-Europeans within the Labour Party used anti-imperialist rhetoric to support their policies. Pro-Europeans, such as Roy Jenkins, had argued since the 1960s that the Labour Eurosceptics' preoccupation with the Commonwealth rather than European integration was also playing into the hands of British imperialism (Cotton, 2010). However, as the pro-European faction's power declined especially after Jenkins left the Labour to form the SDP in 1981, their version of anti-imperialist Europeanism also lost its relevance. Kinnock's pragmatic Europeanism was left to struggle with the anti-imperialism of the hard left. Their anti-imperialism is an ideology that conflates the critique of capitalism with the critique of the imperial past and present of Western states. The strength of such views within the Labour Party is not just a result of British imperial history, but also of the British political system. French and German anti-imperialism have their parliamentary representatives in radical left parties, while in the UK the radical left is still strongly represented and quite influential in the Labour party.

Risse argued that Europe was Britain's 'other', whereas Germany's or Spain's 'other' was their troubled pasts. This enabled Germany and Spain to replace traditional national identities with Europeanness (2010). However, every European nation-state has a troubled past that can be used in an attempt to promote or oppose European integration, as the complex case of the British Europeanism and Euroscepticism demonstrates. The British two-party system, which does not incentivise rebels to form new parties, and the legacy of Thatcher (Fontana & Parsons, 2015) are more important factors when analysing the strength and outlook of British Euroscepticism, than is Englishness. As the recent Brexit debates and the result of the EU referendum suggest there are at least two visions of the UK. The sovereignist vision prevailed, but the internationalist vision remains present and their confrontations still shape English and British identity. Every nation-state is a potentially divided society and in every EU member state there is at least one fifth of the population that thinks their country could better face the future outside of the EU (European Commission, 2016). However, not every member state has a formidable Eurosceptic political forces that can stir up social divisions and take their country out of the EU. The content of national identities is the result of constant negotiations between various political and intellectual elites; ditto for European identity. The outcome of these negotiations depends on the balance of political power and the relevance of certain actors and their legacies.

Conclusion

The Promethean role of Europe narrative came out of different national and professional contexts. However, all of the actors who created it were influenced by profound geopolitical, institutional and ideological changes.

Europeanism has been a factor uniting all socialist parties since the 1990s, unlike Atlanticism, which does not have such consensual support (Sassoon, 2000). It is an ideological loophole that enables European social democrats to criticise the role of the US in global affairs. A major event creating this resentment and causing important epiphanies was the Vietnam War. American war crimes in Vietnam changed the perception of the US, especially among the European left, and transformed numerous personal ideologies. It influenced both the creation of the New Left, which rejected many elements of Western civilization, and the shaping of those disquieted by both American policies and the radical left's solutions. Both those on the centre-left trying to find a European balance between American deviations and radical leftism (Servan-Schreiber, Brugmans, Habermas) and former radical leftists (Fischer, Cohn-Bendit, Rifkin) found a new ideological goal in advocating the European cause.

The development of the Promethean narrative demonstrates the contingency of its emergence. The specific period in which a particular centre-left government was in power and precisely how it was transformed were crucial for its contribution to the narrative. Failures in pursuing Keynesian policies constituted another major force that transformed European social democrats and pushed them towards the promotion of European solutions. French socialists finally obtained power and abandoned 'socialism in one country' during a make-or-break moment for European integration, which allowed them to project their values at the European level. Their German and British colleagues were governing their countries during the institutional stagnation of European integration and the vagaries of the post-1973 economy.

When social democrats came back to power in the 1990s, they had already jettisoned Keynesianism and found themselves in a deeply integrated EU. Together with greens, a new political force, they succeeded in implementing their values in the official narrative of the EU and, as a result, their identification with the EU grew stronger. Confrontation with geopolitical and ideological challenges from the US during the presidency of George W. Bush intensified this identification and created the narrative of the Promethean role of Europe. The narrative then reinforced social democratic and green connections to the constructed European identity, as the authors wrote about social democracy and the green ideology as ideologies that defined Europe. German debates on postnationalism, the French search for social cohesion or British debates on the UK's global influence were also, through individual contributions of the centre-left authors, imprinted on the emerging narrative.

Since then, European social democratic parties have experienced an electoral crisis and the green parties an electoral stagnation, which indicated that voters did not find that the Promethean narrative corresponded with the reality. The surge of new radical left parties, especially in Southern Europe, and the re-emergence of the anti-imperial Labour through the success of Jeremy Corbyn, present new challenges for the fervent Europeanism of the centre-left. The 2015 split in SYRIZA and the electoral failure of its more radical Popular Unity breakaway faction indicate that European integration is constraining the ruling radical left, as already happened with the Greek socialists in the 1980s. Corbyn also altered his former Eurosceptic stance when he became the Labour leader, although he remained a reluctant European, refusing to stand together with David Cameron in order to prevent the Brexit. The outcome of this new clash of leftist ideas with the reality of the EU as a coercive organization remains to be seen. A new, leftist, pro-European narrative might emerge, hinted at by SYRIZA's U-turn and stimulated by the election of Donald Trump as the new American president. A new narrative is emerging through an intellectual movement led by former Greek finance minister Yanis Varoufakis. Its manifesto resembles the prophetism of the 1980s. Though lamenting the EU's failure to become 'the Beacon on the Hill', the manifesto says the EU has a chance of becoming one through its democratization (DiEM25, 2016). However, if voters will not support these and similar political forces it will be of little avail to the construction of European identity.

Notes

1. It was a clear change from Brugmans' pro-American views during the intense Cold War, which he then shared with early socialist supporters of European integration such as Altiero Spinelli or Paul-Henri Spaak.
2. Mitterrand's presidency and his promise of creating social Europe even succeeded in attracting the attention of Olof Palme. However, his Swedish social democrats have not seriously considered the EC membership during their Cold War neutrality (see in Johansson & von Sydow, 2010).

Acknowledgement

I would like to thank Richard McMahon, Wolfram Kaiser, Vjeran Katunarić and Bart Kerremans for their help and support.

Disclosure statement

No potential conflict of interest was reported by the author.

Funding

This work was supported by the European Social Fund.

References

Abdelal, R., & Meunier, S. (2010). Managed globalization: Doctrine, practice and promise. *Journal of European Public Policy*, *17*(3), 350–367.

Adler-Nissen, R., & Kropp, K. (2015). A sociology of knowledge approach to European integration: Four analytical principles. *Journal of European Integration*, *37*(2), 155–173.

Almeida, D. (2012). *The impact of European integration on political parties: Beyond the permissive consensus*. Abingdon: Routledge.

van Apeldoorn, B. (2002). *Transnational capitalism and the struggle over European integration*. London: Routledge.

Baker, S. (2007). Sustainable development as symbolic commitment: Declaratory politics and the seductive appeal of ecological modernisation in the European Union. *Environmental Politics*, *16* (2), 297–317.

Beyme, K. V. (1999). Shifting national identities: The case of German history. *National Identities*, *1*(1), 39–52.

Biebuyck, W., & Rumford, C. (2012). Many Europes: Rethinking multiplicity. *European Journal of Social Theory*, *15*(1), 3–20.

Blair, T. (2000, October 7). Warsaw speech. 'A superpower, but not a superstate'. *Guardian*. Retrieved from http://www.guardian.co.uk/politics/2000/oct/07/uk.tonyblair

Bomberg, E. E. (1998). *Green parties and politics in the European Union*. London: Routledge.

Brubaker, R., & Cooper, F. (2000). Beyond 'identity'. *Theory and Society*, *29*(1), 1–47.

Brugmans, H. (1985). *Europe: A leap in the dark*. Stoke-on-Trent: Trentham Books.

Cohn-Bendit, D., & Cohn-Bendit, G. (1968/2000). *Obsolete communism: The left-wing alternative*. San Francisco-Edinburgh: AK Press and Cohn-Bendit.

Cohn-Bendit, D., & Verhofstadt, G. (2012). *For Europe! Manifesto for a postnational revolution in Europe*. CreateSpace Independent Publishing Platform.

Cole, A. (1994). *François Mitterrand: A study in political leadership*. London: Routledge.

Cotton, C. M. M. (2010). Labour, European integration and the post-imperial mind, 1960-75. In B. Frank, C. Horner, & D. Stewart (Eds.), *The British labour movement and imperialism* (pp. 149–172). Newcastle: Cambridge Scholars.

CSPEC. (1990). *Confederation of socialist parties of the European community*. Party leaders' declaration on the intergovernmental conferences. Madrid, December 10.

Delors, J. (/1988/ 1992). *Our Europe* (B. Pearce, Trans.). London: Verso.

Denzin, N. K. (2014). *Interpretive autoethnography*. Thousand Oaks, CA: Sage.

DiEM25. (2016). A manifesto for democratising Europe. Retrieved from https://diem25.org/wp-content/uploads/2016/02/diem25_english_long.pdf

Diez, T. (2005). Constructing the self and changing others: Reconsidering 'normative power Europe'. *Millennium-Journal of International Studies, 33*(3), 613–636.

van Dijk, T. A. (1998). *Ideology: A multidisciplinary approach*. London: Sage.

Dinan, D. (2010). *Ever closer union. An introduction to European integration*. Basingstoke: Palgrave Macmillan.

Drake, H. (2000). *Jacques Delors: Perspectives on a European leader*. London: Routledge.

Driver, S., & Martell, L. (2000). Left, right and the Third Way. *Policy & Politics, 28*(2), 147–161.

Duchêne, F. (1972). Europe's role in world peace. In R. Mayne (Ed.), *Europe tomorrow: Sixteen Europeans look ahead* (pp. 32–47). London: Fontana.

European Commission. (2016). *Standard Eurobarmeter 85. Spring 2016*. Brussels: European Commission.

Fischer, J. (2000). *Vom Staatenverbund zur Föderation – Gedanken über die Finalität der europäischen Integration. Rede am 12*. Mai in der Humboldt-Universität in Berlin. Retrieved from http://www.cvce.eu/viewer/-/content/4cd02fa7-d9d0-4cd2-91c9-2746a3297773/de

Fontana, C., & Parsons, C. (2015). 'One woman's prejudice': Did Margaret Thatcher cause Britain's anti-Europeanism? *Journal of Common Market Studies, 53*(1), 89–105.

Freeden, M. (1996). *Ideologies and political theory: A conceptual approach*. Oxford: Oxford University Press.

Giddens, A. (1998). *The Third Way: The renewal of social democracy*. Cambridge: Polity Press.

Gowland, D., Turner, A., & Wright, A. (2009). *Britain and European integration since 1945: On the sidelines*. Abingdon: Routledge.

Greenfeld, L. (1992). *Nationalism: Five roads to modernity*. Cambridge, MA: Harvard University Press.

Haas, E. B. (1961). International integration: The European and the universal process. *International Organization, 15*(3), 366–392.

Habermas, J. (1976). *Zur Rekonstruktion des historischen Materialismus*. Frankfurt am Main: Suhrkamp.

Habermas, J. (1998). *Die postnationale Konstellation: Politische Essays*. Frankfurt am Main: Suhrkamp.

Habermas, J., & Derrida, J. (2003). February 15, or what binds Europeans together: A plea for a common foreign policy, beginning in the core of Europe. *Constellations, 10*(3), 291–297.

Habermas, J., & Meyvis, L. (2013, May 24). *Europe is no longer an elite project*. Retrieved from http://www.kuleuven.be/english/news/interview-with-jurgen-habermas-europe-is-no-longer-an-elite-project

Hill, S. (2010). *Europe's promise: Why the European way is the best hope in an insecure age*. Berkeley, CA: University of California Press.

Hix, S. (1999). Dimensions and alignments in European Union politics: Cognitive constraints and partisan responses. *European Journal of Political Research, 35*(1), 69–106.

Hooghe, L. (1996). *Cohesion policy and European integration: Building multi-level governance*. New York, NY: Oxford University Press.

Hooghe, L., & Marks, G. (1997). The making of a polity: The struggle over European integration. *European Integration Online Papers, 1*(4).

Hooghe, L., Marks, G., & Wilson, C. J. (2002). Does left/right structure party positions on European integration? *Comparative Political Studies, 35*(8), 965–989.

Jepsen, M., & Serrano Pascual, A. (2006). The concept of the ESM and supranational legitimacy-building. In M. Jepsen & A. Serrano Pascual (Eds.), *Unwrapping the European social model* (pp. 25–47). Bristol: The Policy Press.

Johansson, K. M., & von Sydow, G. (2010). Swedish social democracy and European integration. In D. G. Dimitrakopoulos (Ed.), *Social democracy and European integration: The politics of preference formation* (pp. 157–188). Abingdon: Routledge.

Jospin, L. (2001, May 28). Excerpts from Jospin's European vision speech. *BBC News*. Retrieved from http://news.bbc.co.uk/2/hi/world/monitoring/media_reports/1355981.stm

Kagan, R. (2003). *Of paradise and power: America and Europe in the new world order*. New York, NY: Random House.

Kaiser, W. (2007). *Christian democracy and the origins of European Union*. Cambridge: Cambridge University Press.

Ladrech, R. (2000). *Social democracy and the challenge of European Union*. Boulder, CO: Lynne Reinner.

Leonard, M. (2005). *Why Europe will run the 21st century*. New York, NY: Public Affairs.

Liddle, R. (2014). *The Europe dilemma: Britain and the drama of EU integration*. London: IB Tauris.

Lodge, J. (1976). *The European policy of the SPD*. London: Sage.

Malešević, S. (2006). *Identity as ideology. Understanding ethnicity and nationalism*. Basingstoke: Palgrave Macmillan.

Malešević, S. (2013). *Nation-states and nationalisms: Organization, ideology and solidarity*. Cambridge: Polity.

Mandel, E. (/1968/ 1970). *Europe vs. America. Contradictions of imperialism*. New York, NY: Monthly Review Press.

Manners, I. (2002). Normative power Europe: A contradiction in terms? *Journal of Common Market Studies, 40*(2), 235–258.

McCormick, J. (2007). *The European superpower*. Basingstoke: Palgrave Macmillan.

McCormick, J. (2010). *Europeanism*. Oxford: Oxford University Press.

Moravcsik, A., & Nicolaïdis, K. (1999). Explaining the treaty of Amsterdam: Interests, influence, institutions. *Journal of Common Market Studies, 37*(1), 59–85.

Müller, J.-W. (2004). Is Euro-patriotism possible? *Dissent, 51*(2), 13–17.

Parsons, C. (2003). *A certain idea of Europe*. Ithaca, NY: Cornell University Press.

Paterson, W., & Sloam, J. (2006). Is the left alright? The SPD and the renewal of European social democracy. *German Politics, 15*(3), 233–248.

Petrović, N. (2016). EU ideology. *Innovation: The European Journal of Social Science Research, 29*(1), 56–76.

Pollack, M. A. (2000). Blairism in Brussels: The 'Third Way' in Europe since Amsterdam. In M. Green Cowles & M. Smith (Eds.), *The state of the European Union: Risks, reform, resistance, and revival* (pp. 266–291). Oxford: Oxford University Press.

Prodi, R. (2001, May 29). *For a strong Europe, with a grand design and the means of action*. Paris: Speech at the Institut d'Etudes Politiques. Retrieved from http://europa.eu/rapid/press-release_SPEECH-01-244_en.htm

Radikale Schritte. (2001, April 30). *Spiegel*. Retrieved from http://www.spiegel.de/spiegel/print/d-19075581.html

Reid, T. R. (2004). *The United States of Europe. The new superpower and the end of American supremacy*. New York, NY: Penguin Books.

Rifkin, J. (2004). *The European dream: How Europe's vision of the future is quietly eclipsing the American dream*. New York, NY: Penguin Books.

Risse, T. (2010). *A community of Europeans? Transnational identities and public spheres*. Ithaca, NY: Cornell University Press.

Rodrigues, M. J. (2003). *European policies for a knowledge economy*. London: Edward Elgar.

Rousseau, D. L. (2006). *Identifying threats and threatening identities: The social construction of realism and liberalism*. Stanford, CA: Stanford University Press.

Sassoon, D. (2000). Socialism in the twentieth century: An historical reflection. *Journal of Political Ideologies, 5*(1), 17–34.

Schmidt, V. A. (1996). *From state to market? The transformation of French business and government*. Cambridge: Cambridge University Press.

Schmidt, V. A. (2016). Conceptualizing Europe as a 'region-state'. In A. Petros Spanakos & F. Panizza (Eds.), *Conceptualising comparative politics* (pp. 17–46). Abingdon: Routledge.

Servan-Schreiber, J.-J. (1967). *Le défi américain*. Paris: Denoël.

Specter, M. G. (2010). *Habermas: An intellectual biography*. Cambridge: Cambridge University Press.

Spinelli, A., & Rossi, E. (1944). *The Ventotene manifesto*. Retrieved from http://www.altierospinelli.org/manifesto/en/pdf/manifesto1944en.pdf

Thurow, L. C. (1992). *Head to head: The coming economic battle among Japan, Europe, and America*. New York, NY: Morrow.

Tiersky, R. (2003). *François Mitterrand: A very French president*. Oxford: Rowman & Littlefield.

Treaty of Amsterdam. (1997). Retrieved from http://www.europarl.europa.eu/topics/treaty/pdf/amst-en.pdf

Almost the same stories: narrative patterns in EU treaty referendums

Wolf J. Schünemann*

ABSTRACT

The article analyses narratives that favoured or opposed European integration in three referendum debates held during the constitutional process of the 2000s: in France and the Netherlands in 2005 (Constitutional Treaty) as well as the first vote in Ireland on the Lisbon Treaty in 2008. In all debates examined, speakers used similar narratives of European integration. While most narrative patterns have transnational character, however, they are also remarkably country-specific. They depend on the specific cultural context and the social positions of the speakers articulating them.

When political actors campaign for a Yes or No vote in a European treaty referendum, their argumentation reflects and displays recurrent narratives of Europe, European integration and the nation state. However, referendum research normally shows not much interest on narratives. It mostly concentrates on the vote as the politically decisive moment in the course of a referendum, to which it applies the tools of opinion research and political sociology (Franklin, Marsh, & Wlezien, 1994; Hobolt, 2009). Thereby most studies reflect an artificial separation between the result of a referendum and the voters' motivation, which are most intensely studied relying on exit polls, on the one hand and the debate that led to it and provided individual voters with the evaluative capacity and knowledge to make their choice on the other. This knowledge most basically includes the knowledge on European integration that appears and processes deeply embedded in stories told and re-told by everybody engaged in a debate. Studying discourses allows for a much deeper analysis and arguably better understanding of referendums than the often rather superficial interpretations of exit polls. So for instance, the latter regularly show a tendency to over-estimate the second-order-quality of European Union (EU) referendums (Franklin et al., 1994b; Le Gall, 2005) because they see national motives clearer than the EU-related stories behind them (more detailed argument in Schünemann, 2014, 2016). Comparative discourse analysis helps to identify, analyse and compare narratives of European integration, to understand their origins and to grasp their transnational or country-specific qualities. Drawing on comparative discourse analysis, this article examines the EU treaty referendum debates in three countries: France, the Netherlands and Ireland during the European constitutional process between 2005 and 2008. While pointing out the

*Present address: Institute of Political Science, Heidelberg University, Germany.

similarities of narratives in the cases studied as an indicator for transnational discursive patterns, the paper also highlights the country-specific qualities of most narratives identified. In contrast to more optimistic outlooks regarding a transnationalisation of European public spheres (e.g. Koopmans & Erbe, 2004; Risse, 2010; Trenz, 2004), it argues that interdiscursive dissonances still indicate a clear national structuration of political meaning making in EU political debates.

This article uses a discourse analytical research design in a Foucauldian tradition. Discourse research comes with theoretical implications. The basic thought is that socio-historically contingent knowledge orders structure the ways of meaning-making that can be followed by actors in a given situation of social communication. While actors thus cannot be seen as masters of the discourse freely adapting their rhetorical action to their respective goals, they should not be reduced to materialisation machines of predetermined statements neither. They have a certain discursive leeway, and this is, where concepts of socialisation and interpretation in a sociology of knowledge tradition come into play. Thus, to assess the (trans-) national quality of discursive elements, it matters not only what is told, but also who tells it. Thus, this article's first step will be to identify and analyse the collective actors who engaged in the debate on the national level and attempted to persuade the public to vote Yes or No. The selection of relevant collective actors was based on explorative research on national media reporting of the referendum debate. The resulting lists of actors were checked and modified on the basis of 29 background interviews with active campaigners in the debates.

For discourse analysis meanwhile, representative samples of written or transcribed texts were compiled (F: 620, NL: 294, IRL: 528). Most of these texts were accessible on the websites of the respective actors or campaigns or via news archives. The data were examined in detail, drawing on a methodology based on the Sociology of Knowledge Approach to Discourse (SKAD), developed by the German sociologist Keller (2011, 2013). Beyond the mainstream of EU referendum research, a smaller number of studies have indeed examined debates in more or less systematic ways. However, most of the respective works showed a lack of systematic methodology. Other more systematic studies focussed only on a single case study (Aboura, 2005; Kleinnijenhuis, Takens, & van Atteveldt, 2005) and/or their interpretive analytics was concentrated on a very special aspect of economic and monetary integration for instance (Bélorgey, 2005; Jonung, 2004).

The first section briefly introduces SKAD, concentrating on its basic theoretical assumptions and on the role that narratives play in the analytic framework. The following section shortly sketches the sets of actors that campaigned in the three referendums. The narratives produced are then interpreted and compared. The article argues in conclusion that while the identified narrative patterns show traits of transnational diffusion of knowledge, there are important country-specific peculiarities in how the stories are told. Thus so-called interdiscursive dissonances between the debates in different countries remain and deliver an indicator for the still prevailing structural fragmentation of a European public sphere.

SKAD and the role of narratives

Story-telling as a social practice is embedded in a socio-cultural context and depends on the position of the speaker who tells the story and the knowledge resources available to him or her. SKAD as a research approach is particularly suited to empirical comparative research. It combines Foucauldian discourse analysis, as laid out most clearly in *Archeology of Knowledge* (Foucault, 1969/1981), with key assumptions of sociology of knowledge, primarily from *The Social Construction of Reality* (Berger & Luckmann, 1969). According to SKAD, discourse is understood as the material manifestation and circulation of knowledge of all kinds, which manifests itself in different forms of meaningful articulation (Keller, 2011). Regarding the referendum campaigns, key knowledge would concern European integration, the EU as a political institution, the nation state, relevant policies such as foreign, economic, social or environmental policies and finally, broader concepts such as constitution, sovereignty, neoliberalism, globalisation, etc. These knowledge elements often develop over time and appear and re-appear, embedded in stories that actors tell – or in the narratives to be analysed later on.

The statements identified through discourse analysis can be analysed for all sorts of interpretive schemes, one of which is the narrative. Narratives are special patterns of meaning making. Narrative structures can frequently be found in political communication. They are understood here as a combination of statements that are organised along a storyline or a plot, which effectively tell a story about something developing in a temporal dimension (Viehöver, 2006). The progressive narrative of European integration dissected by Gilbert (2008) is an example of such a transnational narrative and an important element in the Yes discourses in all the cases studied here. Other examples might have less transnational quality and are cultivated more by national discourse communities. The 'Celtic Tiger' narrative, for example, tells the story of the apparently miraculous economic transformation of Ireland, while an inverse story of decline, sketching the development of France from 'grande nation' to a nation 'which is falling down', is broadly shared by many speakers in the French debate (Baverez, 2003).

During the research process, natural data from the respective debates (campaign texts and material of all sorts) were interpretively analysed, coded and ascribed to arguments as overarching categories (e.g. the Sovereignty Argument or the Economic Argument). Within the resulting set of codings for each argument, I identified the recurrent narratives (e.g. narratives of economic development or narratives of national sovereignty in the EU, see below) for each country and compared the results between the cases.

Who tells? The actors behind the stories

Referendums in general are particularly telling examples of manifest interpretive conflicts in which many salient issues in the respective societies are transformed into publicly debated arguments. Moreover, such debates are very good cases to study as they widen the scope of speakers beyond the set of actors engaged and listened to in daily politics, to include political parties, associations, interest groups and ad hoc campaign organisations. Given this variety of actors engaged in the referendum debates, it is a challenging task to reduce complexity to a manageable degree for illustration. One common observation, which is in line with literature on Euroscepticism (Hooghe, Marks, & Wilson, 2002; Taggart, 1998) is that in the three debates examined, a mainstream bloc of the leading office-seeking parties, grouped around the centre of the left-right spectrum, supported the ratification of the treaties. They played central roles in the respective Yes camps of the debates. In each case, this bloc was opposed by the 'patchwork of protest' (Harmsen, 2005, p. 5) or 'the unusual coalition' (de Vreese & Semetko, 2004, p. 3) –

though quite 'usual' in the tradition of Euroscepticism in Western Europe (Taggart, 1998). This was composed by more or less diverse sets of actors from the left and right margins of the political spectrum. The following sections list the actors state by state. Divergences from the general pattern of EU political conflict will be highlighted.

France 2005: a chance for dissidents

In the French referendum in 2005, the supportive block included the conservative Union pour un movement populaire (UMP) of President Jacques Chirac, which was in government at the time, as well as the Parti Socialiste (PS) as the major opposition party. The centre-right Christian democratic Union pour la démocratie française (UDF) and Les Verts, the Green party on the Left, also campaigned in favour of the treaty. All these parties except for the UDF struggled with intra-party dissidents, however. For the Gaullist movement, which has a considerable discursive heritage of Euroscepticism, support for European integration was traditionally uncertain. This time, however, with an UMP President in power and having posed the referendum question to the people, only a small group of dissidents appeared on the scene. The split in the PS was much deeper. It had major implications for the party and for the whole referendum campaign. As the first party to put the Constitutional treaty to an internal referendum, the PS attracted most public attention from the beginning and fought turf battles in the spotlight of the media. Dissidents included the political heavyweights Henri Emmanuelli and the former Prime Minister Laurent Fabius.

Otherwise, the No camp included the communists and Trotskyites on the Left and the Neo-Gaullists and nationalists on the Right. On the extreme Left, the Parti Communiste Français (PCF) campaigned alongside two Trotskyite sister parties, the Ligue Communiste Révolutionnaire and Lutte Ouvrière. On the far Right, the Mouvement pour la France (MPF) led by Philippe de Villiers, campaigned alongside the Front National (FN) with its leader Jean-Marie Le Pen.

All political parties in both camps benefitted from transnational networks to a greater or lesser extent. The mainstream parties and the PCF, MPF and FN particularly profited from their representation in the European Parliament and support from the respective groups therein. While the political parties were clearly the most intensive campaigners in the French case, the major trade unions as well as the main employers' association also gave their members informal voting advice to support the treaty. Some smaller trade unions joined the No campaign however. Some of these participated in a quite visible cooperation network, which was temporarily institutionalised under the umbrella name of Non de Gauche (NdG). Allied to the NdG, but separate from it, the anti-globalisation Attac organisation played a crucial role. It conducted its own No campaign within a wide transnational network of globalisation critics.

Netherlands 2005: low intensity and reluctant leadership in the Yes camp

Compared to the other cases, the set of actors in the Dutch referendum debate is less complex. All mainstream parties campaigned for the Constitutional Treaty: Partij van de Arbeid (PvdA), the left-liberal D66, the liberal-conservative Volkspartij voor de Vrijheid en Democratie (VVD), and the Green Party (GL). The leading party of the government coalition at the time, the Christian Democratic Appeal (CDA), engaged only reluctantly and did not play a leadership role. This was mainly because of its concern over the use of a referendum as a mechanism to decide the question. All of the mainstream parties were well connected transnationally and had members in the European Parliament party groups who were often important speakers for the respective campaigns.

On the Left, the No camp was dominated by the Socialist Party (SP). Moreover, a new formation of ecologists on the Left, the Partij voor de Dieren (Party for Animals) used the referendum campaign to gain broader public attention for the first time ever. On the political Right, the two orthodox-Calvinist parties opposed the constitution. While the Christen Unie (CU) represented a more moderate conservative voice against ratification, the Staatkundig Gereformeerde Partij was more sectarian in its opposition (Slotboom & Verkuil, 2010, p. 144). On the extreme Right, the Lijst Pim Fortuyn (LPF) was still in existence three years after the death of its charismatic leader, but its campaign was not very visible. Fortuyn's position as *agent provocateur* in Dutch politics was more and more being taken over by Geert Wilders and his movement (Groep Wilders, GW) at that time.

It is peculiar to the Dutch referendum debate that all leading interest groups, including trade unions, business associations, and the churches, refused to engage in the debate and refrained from making any voting recommendations. An ad hoc organisation, the Stichting Beter Europa, was however created to campaign for a Yes vote. Within the No camp, the so-called Comité Grondwet Nee, an ad hoc organisation created by loosely connected activists with links to the transnational NGO Attac, campaigned intensely on the issue.

Ireland 2008: strong engagement of civil society

In the Irish case, the central supportive bloc was made up of the two opposing catch-all parties Fianna Fáil (FF), the leading party in the government coalition at that time, and Fine Gael (FG). While FF always had to deal with members who were critical of the EU, FG has traditionally shown a stronger commitment to an 'ever closer union' portraying itself as the 'Party of Europe' (Quinlivan & Schön-Quinlivan, 2004, p. 88). The smaller coalition partner, the Progressive Democrats (PDs), also supported ratification. Finally, the Labour Party (LP) joined the Yes camp despite internal conflicts over the European issue. Intra-party controversies of this kind caused the Irish Green Party to remain neutral.

The No camp only included one party represented in the parliament, the left-nationalist Sinn Féin (SF). Additionally, a number of splinter parties and movements on the extreme Left such as the SP, People Before Profit Alliance or Éirígi also campaigned against ratification. While the mainstream parties were members of European Parliament groups, SF, the SP and other actors in the No camp on the political left formed part of the transnational network Campaign against the European Constitution (CAEUC)/NotoLisbon.

Beyond the political parties, a broad range of other actors actively participated in the referendum debate. They included some of the leading business associations and trade unions.

Due to the importance of neutrality for Irish foreign policy and its role in the referendum campaign, some organisations from the traditionally strong peace movement, including the Peace and Neutrality Alliance (PANA), also campaigned against ratification. In addition, the People's Movement (PM), founded in 2004, conducted an intensive No campaign. Moreover, the well-known Irish Eurosceptic Anthony Coughlan and his National Platform EU Research & Information Centre provided the campaigners on the No side with critical expertise.

On the Right, Declan Ganley and his neo-conservative Libertas Institute featured prominently in the media and developed into a leading campaign organisation for the No camp. Although less present in the media, the campaign organisation Cóir successfully mobilised activists across the country. It had historical forerunners in the No-to-Nice-campaign at the start of the 2000s and was closely affiliated to the traditionally powerful pro-life movement in Ireland.

What is told? Narratives of European integration

In the referendum debates examined, both sides used a long list of arguments with transnational or country-specific qualities (see Schünemann, 2014). This article focuses on some central narratives, however, which appear and reappear in Yes and No discourses. These can be regarded as meta-narratives as they tell an overarching story of European integration, transcending the narrower scope of the treaty at hand.

Success stories, gratefulness and responsibility: historical narratives

For a long time, the historiography of the present-day EU was characterised by a Whiggish teleological approach (Kaiser, 2006, p. 193). Similarly, Europhiles of all sorts ranging from politicians to journalists and academics have shared and reproduced a progressive narrative (Gilbert, 2008). All actors in the pro-treaty camps in all three debates produced meta-narratives of this sort. They have in common that they completely transcend the content and quality of the treaty and frame the ratification as a collective decision of historical importance, or a collective performative act of the nation that determines the fate of the historical project of European integration in future: 'Let's not roll back forty-five years of history' (Ollier, 2005). The issue of ratification was set in the context of EU history, the European 'success story' (Veld, 2005) was marked by a sequence of milestones, which were the treaty reforms. In their speeches and pamphlets, the advocates of a Yes vote derived from the historical record almost a moral obligation for the nation or even the individual voter to support the treaty, almost regardless of what it actually contained. Thus, 'Europe merits YES' (UMP, 2005b) and 'Europe deserves Yes' (CDA, 2005) were the campaign slogans of two leading mainstream parties in the French and the Dutch campaigns.

Nevertheless, there are also remarkable differences in how success stories were told. In the French and Dutch cases, the underlying narrative was predominantly a continental European story of peace and stability – 'peace project Europe' (Halsema, 2005) – after centuries of conflict and war between European nation states (Poniatowski, 2005). In his intervention in the French Senate the French PS politician and former Prime Minister Pierre Mauroy, referring to the 'founding fathers' of the Communities, listed peace as the primary reason to vote Yes to the treaty: 'The first objective of those who engaged in the European construction after the Second World War was to create peace' (Mauroy, 2005). Also in the Dutch case, the narrative of the peace project prevailed. As D66 politician in 't Veld put it:

The truth is that Europe is an unknown success story. Sixty years ago, Europe rose from the ashes produced by hate, intolerance and violence and it succeeded in living the dream of a free and peaceful continent. (2005)

French historical narratives were special, however. They pointed to the historical responsibility of the French for the European project as their own invention, as a success story of their own ideas and values. According to some leading campaigners, it has been 'French ambition' (Delors, 2005) that has driven European integration since the creation of the first communities.

In contrast with the French and Dutch discourses, the continental European narrative of integration as a peace project was mostly absent from those of Irish Yes campaigners. Interestingly, the only exceptions are rare references to the Northern Irish question: 'Without the support and example of the EU it is difficult to imagine Northern Ireland at peace with itself, the Republic and the United Kingdom' (Costello, 2008).

Between catalyst and straightjacket: narratives of economic development

Often related to historical narratives, but analytically separable, are the narratives of economic development that appear in all debates. At least until the Euro crisis, it seemed an easy task and it was certainly a frequent practice to narrate European integration as an economic success story. While one could evaluate the achievements of the EU in specific policy fields very differently, many observers took for granted that regional integration had positive economic effects for member states and their societies. Thus, such stories were often used to make a case for why continued integration in general and the ratification of the treaty in particular would serve economic development.

Narratives of economic development frequently appeared in the Dutch case. There was hardly a treaty proponent who did not emphasise the export-orientation of the country as an 'open economy' (Nicolaï, 2005) being particularly dependent on economic exchange with its EU partners: 'Open borders, the Euro and the free competition on the European market constitute the lifeline of our economy' (Kroes, 2005). In the face of the challenges of globalisation, treaty proponents urged a sign of commitment to the integration project: 'We need a strong European economy in order to compete on the global level. We cannot do that by ourselves, therefore we simply need Europe' (PvdA, 2005). In this vein, it was tempting for proponents to transform narratives into scenarios of isolation and economic damage in the case of a No vote. Economics Minister Laurens Jan Brinkhorst for instance was criticised for his warning that in the case of a No vote 'the lights will go out in the Netherlands' (cited in Voerman & Van de Walle, 2009, p. 110).

In the Irish Yes discourse, narratives of economic development were quite similar to the Dutch case. Ireland was portrayed as a particularly open and globalised economy, 'the best gateway to Europe' (Burke, 2008), which was heavily dependent on foreign direct investment (FDI). European market integration was said to strengthen this position. A Yes to the treaty would preserve Ireland as an 'attractive location for FDI' (Whelan, 2008). However, the economic success story of European integration was told in a country-specific way, combining it with the (at least then) ubiquitous narrative of the so-called Celtic Tiger. The apparently miraculous transformation of Ireland from the 'poorest of the rich' (Economist, 1988) to 'Europe's shining light' (Economist, 1997) was still the prevalent narrative pattern in the Irish debate. Thus, in the Irish narratives, European integration and the EU were not so much seen as a success story in themselves, but as a catalyst and facilitator of the country's economic development: 'EU membership has been pivotal to Ireland's success story' (Kenny, 2008).

In contrast to the Dutch and Irish cases, in the French debate, references to Europe as an economic success story were rare. Some UMP politicians highlighted that exports to other EU states constituted two-thirds of France's total exports (Poncelet, 2005). Such references did not make a clear and strong narrative, however. Quite contrary to this, many treaty proponents conceded negative economic developments in France and partly attributed these to structural problems of the EU, with its economic and financial policy often seen as a 'corset' (ATTAC, 2005, p. 109). Against the background of such a counter-narrative, treaty provisions were depicted as a remedy at best: 'People are understandably troubled by the displacement of firms [...] The only way to move forward is via an avant-garde of states willing to proceed further (enhanced cooperation made easier by the treaty).' Most of all, the treaty would finally allow for the establishment of an 'economic government' (PS, 2005), a well-established vision in French EU discourses. Such a 'government for the Euro zone' could balance the allegedly one-sided activities of the European Central Bank (Hollande, 2005). Moreover, it could help to soften the Stability and Growth Pact (Fillon, Anciaux, & Bouvard, 2005). Finally, the treaty would provide for stronger fiscal coordination in order to prevent fiscal dumping (UMP, 2005a).

A question of modernisation: narratives of institutional development

As a third notion, narratives of institutional development in all debates make a case for modernisation of the EU's institutional structures. Having been developed for the original community of six and insufficiently modernised since then, the institutional structures were presented as unsuitable for coping with the realities of a community of 25 or 27 member states. Thus, the Dutch PvdA politician Timmermans argued:

> Since May last year, the European Union has 25 member states. However, the European government still works under an institutional model that was developed for six states. [...] If we do not make quick changes, it will end up in deadlock. (2005)

Institutional reform to prepare for Eastern enlargement had been especially unsatisfactory. Thus, UMP leader Nicolas Sarkozy emphasised 'that the institutions of the Europe of six, or even fifteen, are not suitable for a Europe of 25' (Sarkozy, 2005). Finally, a similar story was told in the Irish debate, although with a different starting point:

> When Ireland joined the EEC in 1973 there were nine members. Now that the Union has expanded to 27 member states, common sense dictates that a larger organisation needs to revise its rules to advance the common good. Streamlining the decision-making process of the EU institutions will make them more effective, efficient and flexible. (Perry, 2008)

Beyond this modernisation-as-consolidation argument, a more abstract narrative of institutional development appeared in the cases examined, closely connected to the progressive meta-narrative of European integration. It depicted every new treaty as a necessary next step on the road of integration: 'Now it is time for the next step, with the Lisbon Treaty', as FG MEP Mitchell (2008) put it. Thus, the statements of treaty proponents are not concerned with the potentially controversial reform of the EU, but its timely development. The reform is not a matter of politics, but of modernisation (White, 2008). As in the case of the bicycle metaphor first introduced by the first Commission President Walter Hallstein, proponents of such narratives suggested that any form of stagnation in the EU's institutional development would constitute an existential risk for integration as such. PD politician and former EP President Pat Cox explained in the Irish campaign, for instance: 'Timely and appropriate reform is the lifeblood of all successful organisations' (2008). Against this background, for UMP politician Alain Lamassoure, the treaty would bring the necessary institutional reforms for preserving the union and its governability in the twenty-first century: 'This new century requires a new Europe' (Lamassoure, 2005). Similarly, in the Irish debate the treaty was defended as '[a] Reform Treaty for a 21st century Europe' (Ahern, 2008).

French narratives of institutional development were special in that they explicitly opened up the vision of a political union. This vision and the notion of 'political union' is a traditional element of French EU discourse. It implies a commitment to European integration according to a French or continental model (see the famous press conference of de Gaulle, 1967; Moreau Defarges, 2006). Nowadays, it serves as an opposed term to what is intensely criticised as the neo- or ultraliberal agenda of EU integration. The basic idea is that instead of orienting merely towards market ideology, the EU should increase its efforts in positive integration following political objectives. By reforming the EU, the treaty would make the EU more political in the described sense: 'With the constitution, Europe will most of all be more political in character' (Sarkozy, 2005). The treaty ratification would finally create the political Europe desired for so long: 'The treaty is the first text which creates a political Europe' (Verts, 2005).

Provinces of a European super state: narratives of national sovereignty in the EU

Moving on to the core narratives on the No side, it makes sense to start with the overarching anti-federalist narrative of the dangerous European super state. It is prominent in the discourses of almost all No campaigners. They told the story of the EU successively undermining national autonomy and transforming member states into mere provinces of a new federal state. Unsurprisingly, the far Right expounded this narrative most dramatically. 'No to the European super state' (LPF, 2005) was one of the central slogans of Pim Fortuyn's LPF party in the Dutch debate, for example. In the French debate, the leader of the FN, Le Pen, derived the supposed state quality of the new union directly from its constitutional symbolism: 'A constitution is a founding act of a State [...] A European constitution is therefore a founding act of a European super state' (2005a). From the perspective of the critics, federalisation had always been the hidden agenda behind European integration. As leading politicians of the CU asserted, 'European integration has a history of creeping federalisation' (Rouvoet & van Middelkoop, 2005). In contrast, the nation state was depicted by UMP dissident Labaune (2005) for instance as being finally reduced to the status of 'a province of Europe governed by Brussels'. The Dutch right-wing populist Wilders claimed:

> The European constitution abrogates the principle of primacy of national democracy and political independence of member states. Both, in a judicial and a political sense, the Netherlands will become the province of a European super state. (2005a)

Even the Dutch SP leader warned that the Netherlands would degenerate into a powerless province (Marijnissen, 2005). The term province, of course, has special connotations in the Dutch historical context of the Republic of the Seven United Netherlands. Wilders, for instance, used this intertextual reference when naming the central document of his campaign 'independence declaration' (Wilders, 2005b).

The varied meanings of the terms province or union become very clear in the Irish case in the context of a more vivid post-colonial trauma. Speakers often dramatised the fear of a European super state by warning against a new empire oppressing the young Irish nation. Thus, PANA speaker Roger Cole argued: 'Of course Ireland was part of a militarised, centralised, neo-liberal Superstate before, it was called the British Union and Empire' (2008). The term 'province' offered an opportunity for intertextual references in the Irish case, too. Thus, Cóir warned in a leaflet: 'We'll be a province once again' (2008), thereby referring to the famous Irish rebel song 'And Ireland, long a province, be A Nation once again!'

The business agenda behind EU integration: narratives of neo-liberal reform

Critical narratives of neo-liberal reform, enforced through European integration, were present in each of the three debates examined. Obviously, they drew on a storyline that is used more widely by the political Left throughout Europe. It alleges that European integration is essentially driven by big business and finance, with a hidden neo-liberal agenda. This narrative represents market ideology as the leading idea of integration, resulting in ruinous deregulation, the undermining of welfare states and threats to democracy.

In no other case were narratives of neo-liberal reform as central to the No discourse as in France. Practically all treaty opponents told the story of European integration as driven by 'the neoliberal ideology' (Hoang-Ngoc, 2005) and referred to the treaty as the 'neoliberal constitution' (Généreux, 2005). These notions activate a powerful meta-narrative, which is deeply embedded in French EU discourse and appeared frequently in the campaign material: 'For fifty years of European construction by politicians their aim has been to create a market covering the entire continent where capital and goods can move freely to facilitate the expansion of the largest businesses' (Laguiller, 2005). In an allegedly teleological sequence of neo-liberal reforms of the EU, the treaty was depicted as a culmination point. It would even constitutionalise this dangerous economic ideology and make it permanent for the future. This was one of the main reasons given by the left-republican splinter movement Mouvement Républicain et Citoyen to say 'No to neoliberalism forever' (MRC, 2005).

While especially central to the French debate, narratives of neo-liberal reform also frequently appeared in the Dutch and Irish cases, where their articulation was, however, more clearly limited to campaigners on the Left. For instance, the socialist politician Harry van Bommel clarified: 'In my opinion, with the more moderated Lisbon agenda, it just confirms what we knew for a long time anyway; the European Union is an economic union in the first place, predominantly oriented towards a liberal internal market' (Van Bommel, 2005). In a central document of CAEUC, it becomes obvious how the Lisbon Treaty was portrayed as one element in a long series of treaty reforms dedicated to a neo-liberal agenda: 'Neoliberalism is EU policy, and it is pushed further by this renamed constitution' (CAEUC, 2008). Many other campaigners in the Dutch and Irish debates criticised the 'ultraliberal character of the EU' (Kox, 2005) or the 'neo-liberal EU superstate' (Cole, 2008).

Despite all similarities, remarkable differences become obvious where the opponents list the ingredients of the alleged neo-liberal reforms. While the sanctification and con-stitutionalisation of free-market-ideology and warnings against social dumping or a 'race to the bottom' (CGN, 2005b; Généreux, 2005; Higgins, 2008) were common elements in all debates, other concerns were not. For instance, the problem of fiscal dumping played a central part in the French critique. However, it was completely absent from the Irish debate where economic success was pretty much attributed to low corporate tax rates, which attracted FDI. In contrast, the critique of enforced aus-terity through the Stability and Growth Pact was an important element, especially in the French debate where the 'stupid pact' (Lecourieux, 2005) featured prominently.[1] It also sometimes popped up in the Irish debate (Allen, 2008). It did not once appear in the Dutch case, however, as the Netherlands are traditionally attached to a stability dogma in financial policy, which, in turn, loomed large in other arguments of the debate.

Faceless Eurocrats in Brussels: narratives of the democratic deficit

Finally, the EU's democratic deficit has been a constantly and transnationally debated concern about European integration since at least the 1992–1993 Maastricht Treaty. The respective narratives appeared prominently in the three No discourses. While proponents admitted the deficit but depicted the reforms as a suitable remedy, opponents argued that they were insufficient or they criticised any further competence transfer to the EU as detri-mental to more authentic democracy at the national level.

In this context, particularly influential stories appeared, featuring the supranational institutions and especially the Commission as 'a non-elected Brussels Commission' (NP, 2008), 'Brussels bureaucrats and politicians' (Herben, 2005), 'a faceless bureaucracy' (Ó Snodaigh, 2008) and 'the tyranny of bureaucrats' (Le Pen, 2005b). Based in Brussels and far removed from the citizens and their needs, supranational institutions would gain even more powers through treaty reform. In the Dutch debate, Wilders was not alone in arguing: 'Europe is no longer a Europe of the people, but a Europe of bureaucrats from Brussels' (2005b). The French sovereignist MPF told the general story very similarly: 'Europe constructs itself without and against the citizens' (MPF, 2005). From this perspec-tive, the treaty was far from a remedy for the democratic deficit. The EU would not gain any democratic accountability. As the leftist Comité Grondwet Nee put it in the Dutch debate, 'It is even more problematic that fundamental causes of the democratic deficit have not been tackled. With this constitution, effective democratic control of European affairs remains a great dream for the moment' (CGN, 2005a).

What is more, the opponents actually talked about the treaty as aggravating the demo-cratic deficit: due to competence transfers to the EU level, it would further erode national democracies without building a sufficient alternative: 'Our national democracies are being killed without a true European democracy being created' (DLR, 2005). The narratives thus situated treaty provisions that prescribed the transfer of new competences from the national to the European level in a long line of disempowerment of national institutions, particularly democratically elected national parliaments. In this vein, Irish opponents depicted the Lisbon Treaty as a 'further erosion of our democratic rights' (Voteno, 2008).

Conclusion

This article has analysed a set of recurrent (meta-) narratives in three EU treaty referendum debates in France, the Netherlands and Ireland during the constitutional process of the 2000s. The empirical analysis used a discourse analytical research design based on the SKAD.

Narratives are a crucial structural element of meaning-making and constitute an interpretive scheme analysable in political discourses on European integration. In the literature on European identity and transnational public spheres, the development and promotion of transnational narratives (or *a* common narrative) by political elites are seen as very relevant for so-called Europeanisation (Risse, 2010, p. 62). Given such high expectations, this paper concentrated on the main meta-narratives of European integration that were observable on both sides of referendum debates during the constitutional process.

Comparing the debates in the three countries, many similarities stand out, indicating, to a certain extent, transnational diffusion of narrative patterns or the existence of European narratives. Treaty proponents in all debates told similar success stories of European integration and used almost the same teleological storyline to argue for the necessity of institutional reform. Among the opponents, the super state narrative has transnational quality. Similarly, the democratic deficit is repeatedly brought up by Eurosceptics across Europe as an argument against further EU integration. Finally, the traditional narrative of the political Left about big business and finance steering world politics according to their hidden neoliberal agenda was a strong argument against ratification in all cases. However, does this already indicate a transnationalisation or Europeanisation of discourses? The answer needs to be nuanced. For the pro camps in the three cases, narrative convergence is observable, but it seems highest for the progressive meta-narrative of institutional development, which builds the argumentative basis of a rather technocratic argument of pro-European elites. It is questionable, whether this narrative resonated very well in any of the debates examined. In contrast, stories of historical development as well as economic development and outlook showed more country-specific peculiarities.

For the no camps, divergence is obvious when it comes to the economic meta-narrative of the hidden neoliberal agenda. While all speakers in the French debate, thus regardless of institutional affiliation and political orientation, told the same story of a neoliberal EU, in the two other cases the narrative is only present in the statements from the political Left. Moreover, international comparison shows remarkable differences regarding the ingredients of the alleged neoliberal agenda. In contrast, on the No sides the narrative of the European super state as well as the story behind the so-called democratic deficit sounded similar and resonated well in all three debates.

All in all, it is remarkable that the campaign actors in different countries, although in some cases affiliated with the same parliamentary group in the EP, for example, mostly only tell *almost* the same stories, adding peculiar, country-specific elements or leaving aside others. The analysis has shown that the deeper the interpretive analysis goes, the more crucial differences (re-)emerge. They indicate culturally embedded knowledge elements that are not easy to translate or to transfer.

Discourse analytical comparison of narrative structures in national EU debates can reveal both the common stories or leading meta-narratives of integration and the different ways in which they are told. It helps to get a better understanding of the knowledge elements and evaluative capacity that is made available to voters during a referendum debate. Thus discourse research can make important contributions to referendum research, which so far concentrated mainly on votes and outcomes thus leaving aside the socio-culturally embedded communication processes that produced the results. While this study was not designed to examine any patterns of dissemination or track diffusion of trans-/national narratives, this would be a relevant follow-up question for further research in the field. On the higher level, this study can help to assess the chances of finding or creating European narratives or of building some form of European identity. For the special period of the constitutional process, however, it is fair to conclude that despite some narrative convergence, a Europeanisation of national EU discourses or the development of a common and – especially – a positive transnational narrative of European integration was not in sight. Given much less neo-federalist enthusiasm nowadays, it is fair to expect that country-specific elements will continue to guarantee a dissonant chorus in the near future.

Note

1. This very frequently appearing notion in the French debate actually refers to a quote by then President of the European Commission Romano Prodi, qui said in an interview with the newspaper Le Monde in October 2002: 'I know very well that the stability pact is stupid' (*Le Monde*, 18 October 2002).

Disclosure statement

No potential conflict of interest was reported by the author.

References

Aboura, S. (2005). French media bias and the vote on the European constitution. *European Journal of Political Economy, 21*(4), 1093–1098.

Ahern, D. (2008, March 11). Treaty will help to protect our hard won prosperity. *Irish Times*.

Allen, K. (2008). *Reasons to vote no to the Lisbon treaty*. EU Constitution Referendum. Retrieved from http://www.voteno.ie/resources/reasons-to-vote-no-to-the-lisbon-treaty.pdf

ATTAC. (2005). *Cette Constitution qui piège l'Europe*. Les petits libres: Vol. 57. Paris: Éd. Mille et une nuits.

Baverez, N. (2003). *La France qui tombe*. Paris: Perrin.

Bélorgey, G. (2005). La question économique dans le débat référendaire. *Revue politique et parlementaire, 2005*(1036), 96–108.

Berger, P. L., & Luckmann, T. (1969). *Die gesellschaftliche Konstruktion der Wirklichkeit. Eine Theorie der Wissenssoziologie*. Frankfurt am Main: Fischer.

Burke, C. (2008, June 3). *Vote 'Yes' for more jobs– Colm Burke MEP*. Retrieved from http://www.finegael.org/news/y/1010565/article

CAEUC. (2008). *Lisbon Treaty*. Vote No. Retrieved from http://www.campaign-against-eu-constitution.org/files/CAEUCpamphlet4Feb08.pdf

CDA. (2005, June 1). *Europa verdient ja!: Wat is de Europese grondwet?* Retrieved from http://nederland.archipol.ub.rug.nl/content/cda/20050530/www.cda.nl/domains/cda/pages/content0cdb.html?content=11010000004948_2_10000000001651&navid=10000000000724_11010000000079#samw

CGN. (2005a, February. 23). *Manifest tegen deze Europese Grondwet.* Retrieved from http://www.grondwetnee.org/grondwetnee2.php?category=4

CGN. (2005b, May 6). *5 redenen om tegen te stemmen.* Retrieved from http://www.grondwetnee.org/grondwetnee2.php?subaction=showfull&id=1115393004&archive=&start_from=&ucat=2&category=2

Cóir. (2008). *See how Lisbon will cost you. 4 things you should know.* Retrieved from http://www.coir-campaign.org/images/LeafletsPosters/leaflet_may08_final.pdf

Cole, R. (2008). *Partnership Europe or Imperial Europe.* Retrieved from http://www.pa-na.ie/idn/240408.html

Costello, J. (2008). *Defeat for Lisbon would rob workers north and south of major benefits.* Retrieved from http://www.labour.ie/press/listing/1211881008604603.html

Cox, P. (2008). *Voting YES will consolidate and enhance Ireland's European and global prospects into the future.* Retrieved from https://web.archive.org/web/20080517070521/http://yestolisbon.ie/index.php/component/content/article/49?ed=1

Delors, J. (2005, May 14). Interview de Jacques Delors. *Nord-Éclair.*

DLR. (2005). *L'Europe bureaucratique ou l'Europe des citoyens?* Retrieved from http://www.lachainedunon.com/

Europe's shining light. (1997, May 17). *The Economist.*

Fillon, F., Anciaux, J.-P., & Bouvard, M. (2005, March 31). Saisissez-vous du " Oui " pour bâtir une autre Europe ! *Le Figaro.*

Foucault, M. (1981). *Archäologie des Wissens. Suhrkamp-Taschenbuch Wissenschaft: Vol. 356.* Frankfurt am Main: Suhrkamp (Original work published 1969).

Franklin, M., Marsh, M., & Wlezien, C. (1994). Attitudes toward Europe and referendum votes: A response to Siune and Svensson. *Electoral Studies, 13*(2), 117–121.

de Gaulle, C. (1967, November). Pressekonferenz vom 27. *Europa-Archiv, 1967*(24), 553–561.

Généreux, J. (2005). *Au nom de l'Europe, c'est NON.* Retrieved from http://www.france.attac.org/a4910

Gilbert, M. (2008). Narrating the process: Questioning the progressive story of European integration. *JCMS: Journal of Common Market Studies, 46*(3), 641–662.

Halsema, F. (2005, May 27). *De Europese Grondwet verdient een progressieve voorstem.* Retrieved from http://europa.groenlinks.nl/nieuws/2006/09/19/de-europese-grondwet-verdient-een-progressieve-voorstem

Harmsen, R. (2005). *The Dutch referendum on the ratification of the European Constitutional Treaty.* EPERN Referendum Briefing Paper (No. 13).

Herben, M. (2005). Pleidooi voor een Europa van de menselijke maat. In B. J. Spruyt & E. B. Stichting (Eds.), *Samen Zwak. Pleidooien tegen de Europese Grondwet* (pp. 53–59). Amsterdam: Polpam.

Higgins, J. (2008). Why you should Vote No to Lisbon. *The Socialist*, p. 35.

Hoang-Ngoc, L. (2005, March 11). *L'idéologie néo-libérale du "gouvernement économique" européen.* Retrieved from http://www.nonsocialiste.fr/article/article-view/453/1/318/.

Hobolt, S. B. (2009). *Europe in question: Referendums on European integration.* Oxford [u.a.]: Oxford University Press.

Hollande, F. (2005, April 12). Mes 5 raisons de voter oui. *Tribunes Socialistes.*

Hooghe, L., Marks, G., & Wilson, C. J. (2002). Does left/right structure party positions on European integration? *Comparative Political Studies, 35,* 965–989.

Jonung, L. (2004). The political economy of monetary unification: The Swedish Euro Referendum of 2003. *Cato Journal, 24*(1–2), 123–149.

Kaiser, W. (2006). From state to society? The historiography of European integration. In M. Cini & A. K. Bourne (Eds.), *Palgrave advances. Palgrave advances in European Union studies* (pp. 190–208). Basingstoke: Palgrave Macmillan.

Keller, R. (2011). The sociology of knowledge approach to discourse (SKAD). *Human Studies, 34*(1), 43–65.

Keller, R. (2013). *Doing discourse research: An introduction for social scientists.* London: Sage.

Kenny, E. (2008, May 1). *Europe: Let's be at the heart of it - Kenny.* Retrieved from http://www.finegael.org/news/y/1009701/article/

Kleinnijenhuis, J., Takens, J., & van Atteveldt, W. H. (2005). Toen Europa de dagbladen ging vullen. In K. Aarts & Henk van der Kolk (Eds.), *Nederlanders en Europa: het referendum over de Europese grondwet* (pp. 123–144). Amsterdam: Bakker.

Koopmans, R., & Erbe, J. (2004). Towards a European public sphere? *Innovation: The European Journal of Social Science Research, 17*(2), 97–118.

Kox, T. (2005, April 15). *Frans nee heeft grote invloed op Nederlands euro-referendum.* Retrieved from http://www.sp.nl/nieuwsberichten/2681/050415-frans_nee_heeft_grote_invloed_op_nederlands_euro_referendum.html

Kroes, N. (2005, May 10). *Neelie Kroes, Europees Commissaris voor de Mededinging.* Retrieved from http://www.vvd.nl/index.aspx?FilterId=974&ChapterId=1147&ContentId=1790

Labaune, P. (2005). *Le combat de la France.* Retrieved from http://www.debout-la-republique.fr

Laguiller, A. (2005). Au référendum, c'est Non! *Lutte Ouvrière, 2005*(1921), 3.

Lamassoure, A. (2005, March 1). Ce siècle nouveau exige une Europe nouvelle. *Le Figaro.*

Le Gall, G. (2005). Le 29 mai entre mythe et réalités. *Revue politique et parlementaire 2005*(1036), 2–23.

Le Pen, J.-M. (2005a). *Intervention Parlement Européen, Strasbourg.* Retrieved from http://www.frontnational.com/doc_interventions_detail.php?id_inter=34

Le Pen, J.-M. (2005b). *Déclaration de M. Jean-Marie Le Pen, président du Front national, sur les raisons de voter "non" au référendum sur la Constitution européenne du 29 mai, Paris le 1er mai 2005.* Retrieved from http://www.frontnational.com/doc_interven-tions_details.php?id_inter=72

Lecourieux, A. (2005, April 11). *Quelques-uns des articles scélérats de la Constitution européenne.* Retrieved from http://www.france.attac.org/a4643

LPF. (2005). *Waarom 'NEE' tegen de Europese Grondwet.* Retrieved from http://nederland.archi-pol.ub.rug.nl/content/lpf/20050607/www.lijstpimfortuyn.nl/article4e8c.html?id=980

Lucardie, P. (2005). De campagne: David tegen Goliath? In K. Aarts & Henk van der Kolk (Eds.), *Nederlanders en Europa: het referendum over de Europese grondwet* (pp. 104–122). Amsterdam: Bakker.

Marijnissen, J. (2005, May 21). De ene Eurostaat komt er in een snel tempo aan. *Trouw.*

Mauroy, P. (2005). *Intervention de Pierre Mauroy: révision constitutionnelle (Sénat, 15 février 2005).* Retrieved from http://www.ouisocialiste.net/article.php3?id_article=358

Mitchell, G. (2008, March 25). Treaty will prepare EU for challenges of 21st century. *Irish Times.*

Moreau Defarges, P. (2006). *Ou va l'Europe?* Paris: Eyrolles.

MPF. (2005). *Constitution Europeenne.* Retrieved from http://www.mpf-villiers.com/mcgi/cgi.exe?exec=PRJ&TYP=2#

MRC. (2005). *Constitution européenne - C'est non!* Retrieved from http://www.mrc-france.org/tr23

Nicolaï, A. (2005). *Atzo Nicolaï: Een stem voor Europa is een stem voor jezelf!* Retrieved from http://www.vvd.nl/index.aspx?FilterId=974&ChapterId=1147&ContentId=1793

NP. (2008). **What the Lisbon Treaty would do … (Detailed Explanation).* Retrieved from http://www.nationalplatform.org/2008/05/03/23032008-what-the-lisbon-treaty-would-do

Ollier, P. (2005, March 30). Ne pas renier quarante-cinq ans d'histoire. Interview de Patrick Ollier. *Le Figaro.*

Ó Snodaigh, A. (2008, May 3). *Fine Gael must tell truth on Ireland's loss of VETO.* Retrieved from http://www.sinnfein.ie/contents/12485.

Perry, J. (2008, June 5). *Lisbon Treaty Referendum.* Retrieved from http://www.finegael.org/news/y/1010030/article

Poncelet, C. (2005, May 20). *Déclaration de M. Christian Poncelet, Président du Sénat, sur la campagne du référendum sur la Constitution européenne, à Epinal le 20 mai 2005.* Retrieved from http://discours.vie-publique.fr/notices/053001604.html

Poniatowski, A. (2005, February 9). Constitution européenne et la Turquie, parlons-en, justement. *Le Figaro.*

Poorest of the rich (Ireland Survey). (1988, January 16) *The Economist.*

PS. (2005). *Le vrai / Le faux sur le Traité constitutionnel*. Retrieved from http://www.ouisocialiste.net/IMG/rtf/Vrai-Faux_actu21-02.rtf

PvdA. (2005). *Factsheet Nederland Sterk en Sociaal in Europa*. Retrieved from http://www.pvda.nl/nieuws/nieuws/2005/04/Factsheet+Nederland+Sterk+en+Sociaal+in+Europa.html

PvdA, & Timmermans, F. (2005). *Europese grondwet verdient volmondig Ja*. Retrieved from http://www.pvda.nl/nieuws/nieuws/2005/02/Europese+grondwet+verdient+volmondig+--39-Ja--39-.html

Quinlivan, A., & Schön-Quinlivan, E. (2004). The 2004 European parliament election in the Republic of Ireland. *Irish Political Studies, 19*(2), 85–95.

Risse, T. (2010). *A community of Europeans?: Transnational identities and public spheres. Cornell paperbacks*. Ithaca, NY: Cornell University Press.

Rouvoet, A., & van Middelkoop, E. (2005). Een Grondwet met een verborgen agenda. In B. J. Spruyt & E. B. Stichting (Eds.), *Samen Zwak. Pleidooien tegen de Europese Grondwet* (pp. 81–88). Amsterdam: Polpam.

Sarkozy, N. (2005, April 14). Une nouvelle Europe plus politique, plus efficace, plus forte. *Le Figaro*.

Schünemann, W. J. (2014). *Subversive Souveräne: Vergleichende Diskursanalyse der gescheiterten Referenden im europäischen Verfassungsprozess. Theorie und Praxis der Diskursforschung*. Wiesbaden: Springer.

Schünemann, W. J. (2016). *In Vielfalt verneint. Referenden in und über Europa von Maastricht bis Brexit*. Wiesbaden: Springer.

Slotboom, R., & Verkuil, D. (2010). *De Nederlandse politiek in een notendop*. Amsterdam: Bert Bakker.

Taggart, P. (1998). A touchstone of dissent: Euroscepticism in contemporary Western European party systems. *European Journal of Political Research, 33*, 363–388.

Trenz, H.-J. (2004). Media coverage on European governance: Exploring the European public sphere in national quality newspapers. *European Journal of Communication, 19*(3), 291–319.

UMP. (2005a). *OUI pour donner une constitution à L'Europe*. Retrieved from http://www.u-m-p.org/site/dossiers/Europe/ActualiteEuropeAf-fiche.php?IdActualiteEurope=29

UMP. (2005b). *Le Journal gratuit du OUI !* Retrieved from http://www.u-m-p.org/site/InterviewAffiche.php?IdActualite=601

Van Bommel, H. (2005, April 16). Referendum na een Frans 'nee' afblazen schaadt vertrouwen in politiek. *Friesch Dagblad*.

Veld, Sophie in 't. (2005, May 21). *WAAROM IK VOOR DE EUROPESE GRONDWET STEM Sophie in 't Veld*. Retrieved from http://www.d66.nl/europa/nieuws/20050521/congrestoespraak_sophie_in_t_veld?ctx=vhopg90lkduz

Verts. (2005). *L'Europe avance à petits pas …* Retrieved from http://www.lesverts.fr/article.php3?id_article=2287.

Viehöver, W. (2006). Diskurse als Narrationen. In R. Keller, A. Hirseland, W. Schneider, & W. Viehöver (Eds.), *Handbuch sozialwissenschaftliche Diskursanalyse Bd. 1 Theorien und Methoden* (2nd ed., pp. 179–208). Wiesbaden: VS Verl. für Sozialwiss.

Voerman, G., & Van de Walle, N. (2009). *Met het oog op Europa: Affiches voor de Europese verkiezingen, 1979–2009*. Amsterdam: Boom.

Voteno. (2008). *Irish Leaders adopt increasing desperate tactics in effort to win Lisbon*. Retrieved from http://www.voteno.ie/html/press.htm#desperatetactics

de Vreese, C., & Semetko, H. A. (2004). *Political campaigning in referendums. Framing the referendum issue*. London [u.a.]: Routledge.

Whelan, J. (2008). *Lisbon vote critical for export industry*. Retrieved from http://www.irish-exporters.ie/LisbonVoteCritical.shtml

White, P. (2008, June 11). *Yes vote required to prevent Ireland's isolation and a loss of jobs*. Retrieved from http://www.irishtimes.com/newspaper/opinion/2008/0611/1213103047039.html

Wilders, G. (2005a). *EERSTE OPENBARE SPEECH GEERT WILDERS SINDS DE MOORD OP THEO VAN GOGH*. Retrieved from http://www.groep-wilders.nl/

Wilders, G. (2005b). *ONAFHANKELIJKHEIDSVERKLARING - een boodschap van hoop en optimisme*. Retrieved from http://www.geertwilders.nl/in-dex.php?option=com_content&task=view&id=120&Itemid=71

One narrative or several? Politics, cultural elites, and citizens in constructing a 'New Narrative for Europe'

Wolfram Kaiser

ABSTRACT

European Union (EU) institutions have cultivated narratives of European integration for a long time. For its 2013–2014 'A New Narrative for Europe' project, however, the European Commission for the first time explicitly used the 'narrative' label. Drawing on non-participant observation, semi-structured interviews and qualitative discourse analysis, this article contrasts the drafting process and the resulting declaration's narrative structure and content with its discussion by citizens in a web-based consultation. The analysis shows that participating citizens forcefully demanded a bottom-up debate and advocated pluralistic perspectives. In these circumstances, elite-driven attempts at strengthening European identity and EU legitimacy are likely to be ineffective.

When the European Commission invited comments on its 'A New Narrative for Europe' project and text on its website, one commentator called it a 'campaign of hypocrites'. This author demanded that the 'European commission has to uproot itself or be uprooted by the people of Europe, and start over. ... Talk is cheap, and yours, official Europe, is even cheaper.'[1] Even before the 'New Narrative' project, however, European Union (EU) institutions had developed and cultivated narratives of European integration for a long time. They craft and use them strategically, as in the case of the 'founding fathers' narrative about the role of leading politicians in the origins of European integration and their allegedly idealistic motives, for example.

Such processes of narrative construction are geared towards strengthening feelings of cultural commonality and social community within the EU to foster a trans- and supranational collective identity – processes that are broadly reminiscent of top-down strategies for national integration and state formation in the nineteenth century (Anderson, 1991; Hobsbawm & Ranger, 1983). At the very least, EU institutions hope that the construction of such narratives will help legitimize European integration and the EU and make it more popular among its citizens. Such attempts at narrative legitimation of European integration and the EU are not limited to public discourses in speeches. Thus, to give but one example, in 2007 the European Parliament initiated the House of European History project in Brussels, originally intended to enshrine a broadly federalist European integration narrative in a museum now to be opened in 2017 (Kaiser, 2016; Settele, 2015).

The pilot project 'A New Narrative for Europe', administered by the European Commission during 2013–2014, was the first EU-run project explicitly to use the 'narrative' label, however. It originated in a 2012 initiative of Morten Løkkegaard, a Member of the European Parliament (MEP) for the Danish right-liberal Venstre Party and Alliance of Liberals and Democrats for Europe and the Vice-Chair of the Parliament's Committee for Culture and Education. The project's sole formal objective and obligation was to deliver what was then called a narrative 'manifesto' for 'Europe', which was treated as equivalent to the EU.

Having offered its support, the Commission undertook the project's implementation. It formed a 'Cultural Committee' charged with delivering the 'New Narrative' text. This committee of some 20 'artists, intellectuals and scientists' was chaired by Paul Dujardin, the Artistic Director of the Centre for Fine Arts (Bozar) in Brussels. After the project launch in Brussels in April 2013, the Commission organized three 'general assemblies' with larger plenary audiences in Warsaw in June 2013, in Milan in November 2013 and in Berlin at the beginning of March 2014. At this last assembly the Cultural Committee presented its declaration 'New Narrative for Europe: The Mind and Body of Europe' (European Commission, 2014b) in the presence of Commission President José-Manuel Barroso and German Chancellor Angela Merkel.

The Commission followed up on the declaration's publication with a social media campaign in the late summer of 2014. The final project report (New Narrative, 2014) claims that the information dissemination via Facebook and Linkedin reached seven million people and generated 75,000 visits on the project website. The Commission also created a separate space on the project website for longer comments. Some 450 citizens used the opportunity of making such comments between 13 September and 16 October 2014. This provided the basis for a short presentation on the results of the social media campaign at the final project event in Brussels, a few days before Barroso left office.

Drawing on non-participant observation at the general assemblies and some Cultural Committee meetings, which was facilitated upon the request of the author by Dujardin after consultation with the responsible European Commission officials, as well as semi-structured interviews and qualitative discourse analysis, this article analyses the process of drafting the declaration. It argues that it was characterized by a clash of different elite cultures. This clash resulted in a chaotic process in which the declaration in the end was written by a single person, Nicola Setari, who was able to bridge the cultural divide.

The article goes on to analyze the 'New Narrative' structure and content and to contrast it with the citizens' web comments. These were overwhelmingly focused on the EU, not the 'New Narrative' text. While more extreme views were likely overrepresented, these comments nonetheless provide a kaleidoscope of opinions on the EU and desirable key objectives for the future. The article shows that the participating citizens demanded more open bottom-up debate. Their contributions also reflected much greater narrative pluralism between more federalist and strongly Eurosceptic positions than the Commission in particular favours. Finally, those citizens who commented on this aspect of the declaration very predominantly demanded that the EU focus more on Europe's own socio-economic problems than its global role in spreading norms and values, which the declaration forcefully demanded.

The analysis shows that the Commission preferred, and the Cultural Committee was complicit in, defining the 'New Narrative' in an elite-driven process. This process at times became almost surreal in ignoring critical debates about the EU outside of the Brussels bubble and when a single person ended up drafting the text in what was very much an ad hoc manner. Citizen participation, when it was finally enabled, would suggest, however, that popular attitudes to European integration embrace pluralist debate and multiple narratives of Europe – something that could actually be a much greater source of legitimacy for the EU than the Commission's continued attempts at top-down social engineering (Shore, 2000).

Clash of cultures

Cultural elites have contributed to promoting the idea of European integration. Their varied narratives have drawn on the idea of an allegedly unified medieval Occidental Europe or the Renaissance as the breakthrough of European values. They have sometimes presented the time between 1914 and 1945 as a European 'civil war', which was followed by the golden age of European integration inspired by the 'founding fathers' (Kaiser, 2011). The EU regularly draws on the 'founding fathers' trope in its own self-representation (Joly, 2007; Kølvraa, 2010). The European Commission has also sought to foster more aligned narratives of European history through various funding mechanisms, including support during the 1980s and 1990s for research into the history of European integration (Calligaro, 2013, pp. 38–78; Varsori, 2010).

When Løkkegaard initiated the 'New Narrative' project, however, he sought greater public support for the EU by cultural elites. His objective was to mobilize cultural elites to come out much more strongly in support of the EU during its severe socio-economic and political legitimacy crisis (Løkkegaard, 2013). It is not entirely clear how the project acquired the 'narrative' terminology, however. As Richard McMahon highlights in his article in this special issue, European commissioners, officials and MEPs can have a general notion of academic fashions, even when they do not have a related academic background or strong links to academia. Thus, Commission deliberation and policies clearly interacted with academic discourses about the 'democratic deficit' and the EU as a 'normative power' in the 1990s and 2000s, even if this interaction may sometimes have amounted to a dialogue of the deaf.

In this case, however, with Løkkegaard having no close connections with academia, the use of the term 'narrative' is unlikely to have been inspired by incipient academic debates. Rather, the Danish journalist was preoccupied with his own professional experience of analyzing and telling stories about political issues, and with the pronounced weakness and lack of resilience and salience of positive stories about European integration and the EU in Denmark in particular, especially in view of the then upcoming 2014 European Parliament elections. In fact, Løkkegaard also used the project to tell a narrative about himself as MEP to the Danish electorate, in the (vain) hope of accumulating enough personal votes to become reelected to the European Parliament.

Løkkegaard may have been broadly aware of the project on European 'narratives' run by the European Cultural Foundation (ECF) in Amsterdam during 2010–2012, however. In this project the ECF had organized a variety of events with artists from across Europe. Towards its end, the project produced a publication on its website and in book form

(Chenal & Snelders, 2012), which brought together 19 shorter stories about 'Europe' including 2 (Kaiser, 2012; Sassatelli, 2012) with a strong focus on the role of narratives in European political integration and the EU. The Commission definitely followed this project, and most likely took its cue from there. Although the Commission never formally consulted with the ECF over its project (Chenal, 2013), it invited ECF representatives and several of the ECF authors to the 'New Narrative' launch in Brussels in April 2013. The Commission appropriated the 'narrative' terminology, but it never collaborated with the ECF during the implementation of its own 'New Narrative' project. Whereas the ECF project had a primarily cultural focus and bottom-up orientation, the Commission's approach was top-down and geared towards culture as a support mechanism for European integration and the EU.

When the Commission took control of the project's implementation it drew on existing contacts between Barroso and his staff with Dujardin and his team. In 'bureaucratic and complex' negotiations (Dujardin, 2013), the Commission and the Bozar director agreed the Cultural Committee's composition. In line with its general practice, the Commission sought a balanced representation by gender, age and nationality. In the end however, the committee was biased in favour of the (performing) arts, reflecting Barroso's and Dujardin's interests and networks. Of the 17 full members only György Konrád, the Hungarian writer, qualified as an 'intellectual'; Michał Kleiber, the President of the Polish Academy of Sciences, was the only scientist; Tomáš Sedláček, a Czech economist, the only academic with a social science background and the Danish journalist Per Nyholm did not fall into any of the categories mentioned in the project's typology of cultural elites. None of the members had a background in European and EU history, and the project deliberately made no attempt at drawing on academic expertise.

During the project it became clear that the Commission and the Cultural Committee members had different agendas and incompatible operational modes. The resulting clash of two cultures severely endangered the project success, measured in terms of the drafting and timely delivery of the declaration (Kaiser, 2015). Three competing and very different texts written by Konrad, Sedláček and Nyholm were circulated in November 2013. Not even a first draft existed by the end of January 2014, one month before the planned event in Berlin. In these circumstances, the Bozar team charged Nicola Setari, a multilingual Italian curator with broad European experience and close connections with the Commission, who had worked for the Bozar before, with writing the declaration. He then circulated several drafts to committee members before the final version was sent out on 26 February 2014.

The 'New Narrative' project saw the EU's political-bureaucratic milieu mainly interested in enhancing the legitimacy of European integration and increasing the public visibility of the 2014 European Parliament elections. It turned out that Barroso's personal interest and full participation in all major 'New Narrative' events, combined with the bureaucratic culture of the Commission Directorate-General for Communication (DG COM), resulted in an initially extremely rigid organization of public events to make sure that they would be reported positively by the media. Thus, the opening event in Brussels supposedly included a long 'open debate'. However, Nyholm, who moderated the event attended by three commissioners, only called upon pre-selected members of the Cultural Committee and the audience to make pre-prepared statements (Nyholm, 2014; Sassatelli, 2013). While the Commission relaxed its control over the 'general assemblies' somewhat in the course of 2013 due to the widespread discontent with the format, the forum was only for invited guests from diverse cultural elites.

In contrast, the two officials who represented the Commission in the private Cultural Committee meetings limited themselves to commenting on administrative issues and reminding the committee members of the looming deadline for the compulsory declaration. Chaired by Dujardin, the committee meetings were only very loosely organized. Several members only turned up occasionally, and those who did often refused to follow a clear agenda for the discussion. In Milan in November 2013, for example, some members spontaneously organized a message of support for the Ukrainian Maidan movement during the committee meeting, which made a meaningful discussion of the drafting process of the declaration impossible.

The Commission's bureaucratic culture was goal-oriented and driven by the need to deliver a declaration of reasonable quality on time so as not to embarrass the institution and Barroso in the member states, especially in Germany, where the Commission President was keen to get Merkel to attend its public presentation. The Commission had limited interest in the actual process of developing the required narrative document. As the project was managed by DG COM, its primary concern was to influence the media reporting of the project events. The Commission allowed Dujardin so much space for managing the Cultural Committee itself because they were interested in what they saw as the cultural elites' legitimacy resources. The committee was a mixed group, however, not only in terms of their professional background, but also their political views on European integration and the EU. The committee members were also not very interested in delivering the declaration, but in using the forums created by the project as a platform for networking among themselves and with representatives of EU institutions – in some cases to enhance their possibilities of obtaining support for their initiatives and projects through other funding lines. Only certain committee members, who worked as lobbyists for European cultural organizations, to some extent succeeded in bridging the divide between the political-bureaucratic and cultural milieus that clashed in the 'New Narrative' project (Kaiser, 2015).

On message? The 'New Narrative'

The 'New Narrative' declaration raises questions about the text's objectives, structure and content. When it took charge of the project, the European Commission adopted Løkkegaard's phrase 'a new narrative for Europe'. Actually, the first version of the Commission-hosted website (European Commission, 2014a) then stipulated that the project would develop

> a new all-encompassing narrative [that] should take into account the evolving reality of the European continent and highlight that the EU is not solely about the economy and growth, but also about cultural unity and common values in a globalized world.

Far from envisaging any narrative 'unity in diversity', a slogan habitually used by the Commission, DG COM thus started on a hegemonic quest to replace existing narratives of European integration with *one* new narrative. It was clear from the project's origins and the composition of the Cultural Committee that such a narrative would not primarily emphasise the strengthening of a European identity over time, but rather the EU's alleged contemporary 'cultural unity and common values'.

Two points quickly became clear as the project progressed, however. First, members of the Cultural Committee and other participants in key project events rejected the Commission's hyperbolic objective as either unrealistic or undesirable in a pluralistic EU. Responding to these objections, the Commission, first, changed its informal terminology from 'a new narrative' to just 'new narrative for Europe' in the declaration. This choice left the option open that the committee had only produced one among several possible narratives. Second, neither DG COM nor the Cultural Committee were clear about what existing narrative or narratives they wished to revise or replace. In fact, the project website and several speakers at the general assemblies, including Barroso himself, frequently referred to key elements of traditional narratives. They included integration as 'peace through a common market' (European Commission, 2014a) or the protection of human rights invoked by Barroso in his speech in Warsaw on 11 July 2013, a trope that also features prominently in visions of the EU as a 'normative power' (Manners, 2002) and the 'progressive' Promethean narrative analyzed by Nikola Petrović in his contribution to this special issue.

Not surprisingly, therefore, the declaration's eclectic structure to some extent already reflects existing historical and contemporary justifications of European integration. In the first section, the declaration talks about numerous challenges to Europe as 'a state of mind'. It goes on to discuss lessons of past experience, starting with the First World War. In the section 'The Renaissance meets Cosmopolitanism', the declaration then demands that the arts and sciences make a major contribution to tackling shared problems, which in turn can help 'Europe' shape global politics based on its own values and vision for the future.

The narrative's content evolves around common values, 'lessons of history', a need to reinvent the EU in times of crisis through a European 'cosmopolitanism' building on the Renaissance experience, and a resulting shared commitment to improving 'humanity's well-being'. The declaration claims, to begin with, that Europe's 'spiritual, philosophical, artistic and scientific inheritance' has largely shaped Europe as 'a state of mind'. These shared traditions could help Europe address contemporary challenges 'from youth unemployment to climate change, from immigration to data security'. Tackling such challenges requires 'a genuine and effective political body', however. The declaration goes on to emphasize the importance for addressing these challenges of 'shared values of peace, freedom, democracy and the rule of law' which have to be 're-activated and made relevant for the European citizens of today and tomorrow and defended against internal and external pressures'.

Despite the project's original emphasis on the importance of historical experience for a common narrative of European integration, the subsequent section is quite short. This clearly reflects the absence of historians from the Cultural Committee and, with one exception in Rome, from all major project forums. It is probably also due to the author's own professional background in art and art history. The section recapitulates in just two sentences the experience of the two world wars, only to claim in quasi-religious language that European integration after 1945 'has brought redemption'. The 'fall of the iron curtain' then led to the pan-European breakthrough of democracy and the market economy inaugurating 'a new era of interconnectedness and interaction amongst people and countries', with the EU providing 'the visionary framework and the sense of purpose that was necessary in responding to the tremendous challenge of reunifying Europe'. The economic and financial crisis since 2008, the section concludes, demonstrated the flaws of an insufficiently regulated financial system. Supposedly, the EU stepped in to improve the 'political governance of the financial systems' and address the resulting problems.

The next section of the declaration draws on the experience of the Renaissance as a European breakthrough to modernity to argue that the arts and sciences are once more needed to play a key role in developing what is called a cosmopolitan approach to contemporary issues. Why not, the section asks rhetorically, 'imagine Europe as a great mega-city interconnected by means of transportation and communication?' This reinvigorated Europe would then 'deploy its "soft power" … also beyond its borders … , promoting a new global model of society based on ethical, aesthetic and sustainable values'. References to these values are scattered throughout the declaration, but with particular emphasis on the quite recent notion of sustainability.

Three key aspects of the declaration are especially notable. First, European history receives short shrift. Even the twentieth century experience is treated only very briefly, with more space devoted to the ongoing crisis than the two world wars. Crucially, the declaration avoids all potentially controversial references that have featured in more recent debates about European remembrance and the EU. These include, for example, the notion of an allegedly unified (Christian-Catholic) medieval Europe; the importance of the Holocaust (Littoz-Monnet, 2013); the idea of the 'founding fathers' (Kaiser, 2011), which the author may have regarded as too closely associated with the continental Western European post-war foundation myth; and demands by East-Central European memory entrepreneurs to prioritize remembrance of Stalinist and communist crimes (Neumeyer, 2015; see also Radonic in this issue). Moreover, in line with a recent trend in European memory politics and museum practice (Kaiser, Krankenhagen, & Poehls, 2014), the declaration studiously avoids any reference to perpetrators and their nationality. Hitler and the Germans are not mentioned explicitly nor are Stalin and the Soviet occupation of Eastern Europe. In the First World War, Europe 'lost its soul in the battle fields and the trenches' and then 'it damned itself within [sic!] the concentration camps and the totalitarian systems'. Possibly inadvertently, then, the declaration heavily contributes to de-historicizing European integration narratives.

The marginal role of historical experience goes hand in hand with the heavy emphasis on contemporary European values. This focus is reflective of and entirely in line with established Commission rhetoric. It also chimes with more recent attempts by supporters of European integration and the EU during the economic and financial crisis to reactivate post-war emotive appeals to European unity in supporting common values that allegedly also mark the EU and its domestic and external policies (Wellings & Parker, 2016). The declaration strongly emphasizes what might be called 'progressive' notions of the inherent limits of capitalism (requiring EU regulation) and 'participatory democracy and sustainability, which point to a new horizon of hope, solidarity and responsibility for all Europeans'. These values and the associated quasi-religious messianic language arguably befit the predominantly left-wing and left-liberal cultural elite milieu. As such, it was acceptable to all Cultural Committee members except for the Danish journalist Nyholm. He distanced himself from the final version of the text mainly because he wanted a stronger commitment to the further deepening of the EU, including in defence matters (Nyholm, 2014).

Finally, the declaration never actually mentions the EU. Firstly, this is because EU elites now tend to equate it with 'Europe'. Secondly, however, the Commission was keen in the run-up to the 2014 European Parliament elections to avoid antagonizing Eurosceptic sections of national publics with an overtly federalist statement – something that would also not have gone down well with some members of the Cultural Committee from countries like the United Kingdom where all EU issues were and, after the Brexit vote in the 2016 referendum, remain extremely divisive. Nevertheless, the declaration's demands and language effectively adopt the Commission's preferences and rhetoric, especially concerning the role of 'Europe' as a role model for the rest of the world. This narrative may well exaggerate the EU's capacity to solve national and transnational issues within Europe, such as 'unemployment levels unimaginable in European countries', or its ability to make the world a better and safer place, only to exacerbate the EU's legitimacy crisis. In any case, as the next section demonstrates, the claim that the EU can and should play a leading role in addressing global issues based on its norms and values turned out to be unpopular with the public. It was a focal point of criticism from citizens who contributed to the project's website in the wake of the social media campaign that the Commission launched to publicise the declaration.

A European world? Citizens' narratives

The 'New Narrative' project never sought to involve EU citizens in any systematic manner until the publication of the declaration in the presence of Merkel and Barroso in Berlin. For the project launch in April 2013, the Commission invited some 70 selected academics, artists and intellectuals. The following three general assemblies were attended by somewhat larger, but similarly selected elite audiences. Their taking place in conjunction with 'Dialogue with Citizens' events merely created organizational synergies for the DG COM. They did not allow for any actual input by citizens into the discussion of elements of the planned declaration, however. Until the declaration's publication, moreover, the project only had a rudimentary website with limited information about its objectives and the general assemblies.

At the concluding public event in Berlin in March 2014, the German chancellor actually declared her allegiance to established narratives of European integration with their emphasis on the EU as a project that has ensured peace, enhanced the welfare of citizens, and secured a voice for Europe in a globalizing world. Merkel also asked whether citizens in the EU really needed a 'new' narrative, as the Commission and the Cultural Committee suggested; or whether it would not be a better idea to invite them to contribute their own stories about European experiences in a pluralistic dialogue. Merkel's direct public criticism of the project's objectives and structure visibly came as something of a shock to Barroso and the Commission officials. It encouraged them to come up with the idea of combining a web-based consultation with the planned dissemination strategy for the declaration. This web-based consultation was eventually scheduled to take place prior to the final project event – the publication of a traditional book with multiple narratives by project participants and some other members of cultural elites. This was presented to Barroso on 28 October 2014 as a gift on leaving office a few days later (Battista & Setari, 2014).

Responding to promptings by the Commission, between 13 September and 16 October 2014 some 450 individuals eventually contributed to the 'New Narrative' website. These contributions resulted from some 75,000 clicks on the project website after the Commission had disseminated the declaration and additional information via Facebook and

Linkedin prior to starting the web-based consultation. Even when compared to prevalent degrees of virtual mobilization on EU-related topics, as opposed to highly topical general political issues, the 450 comments hardly constitute a great communicative success. In comparison, for example, nearly 10 years earlier a Commission e-democracy consultation on the revision of the EU's animal welfare legislation generated some 45,000 email inputs from citizens (Weller, 2012). The relatively low number of comments was probably due to the short time span of one month for the consultation and the low political salience of the topic of narratives of European integration compared to 'hard' issues of politics and policy-making.

Some of the email comments were composed in languages like French, German, Spanish and Slovak. However, most were in English, written by both native and non-native speakers. The prevalence of English on the website may have discouraged non-native speakers from contributing. In any case, British citizens were heavily overrepresented, and among them, supporters of Brexit with political affiliations with the United Kingdom Independence Party (UKIP) or the right of the Conservative Party were especially active. However, the responses do not allow their clear categorization by nationality or residence. Moreover, for data protection reasons, the website collected no personal information on gender, age etc., thus making a systematic statistical analysis of the comments impossible.

Analyzing the website comments, three points need to be kept in mind. First, enthusiasm in the 1990s for the potential of all forms of e-democracy to facilitate democratic participation and to rejuvenate democratic procedures and processes has become much more muted (Loader & Mercea, 2011). Hopes that the internet would create virtual Habermasian forums and public spheres free of social power relations and lead to open discursive exchanges (cf. Eriksen & Fossum, 2000; Hague & Loader, 1999) have often been disappointed even within Western-style democracies. This holds especially for directive, goal-oriented, consultations, which are initiated and controlled by a state actor like the Commission. While it is clear that internet forums of all kinds have strong disruptive potential in undermining established forms of discussion and the hegemonic narratives transmitted by more traditional media, it is less clear whether they actually change prevailing social power relations in any significant way (Loader & Mercea, 2011; Margetts, John, Hale, & Yasseri, 2016). Certainly, 450 email comments can neither overcome the EU's alleged democratic deficit nor put the last nail in its coffin.

Second, internet forums easily develop into echo chambers (Sunstein, 2009) where anonymity facilitates the radicalized expression of political views. They tend to replicate views that can also be found in more traditional media. However, they often amplify the more extreme views of individuals who do not feel that their preferences are sufficiently well represented and supported by mainstream political parties and more traditional media. Thus, UKIP has actively and very effectively, to judge by the outcome of the 2016 referendum (Jensen & Snaith, 2016), used social media to communicate its ideas, including its demand for a British exit from the EU (Southern, 2015). These citizens holding more radical views will be especially motivated to advertise them via social media. Due to the internet's anonymity, moreover, they frequently do so using harsh aggressive language, in order to discredit opposed views and their proponents.

Third, linked to this issue is the question of authenticity. In other words, those writing the comments may use a pseudonym to disguise their true identity. It appears in particular that Russian services under the control of President Putin have recently sought to influence or even highjack virtual debates within the EU, for example about the war in Eastern Ukraine and Western sanction policy and the future of the EU, trying to undermine the EU's cohesion as much as possible (AFP, 2015; Walker, 2015). Due to language challenges, however, most of this Russian activity for the moment seems targeted at Russian language websites. In any case, there is no evidence that state-controlled Russian 'trolls' sought to influence the Commission's online consultation for the New Narrative project.

A qualitative discourse analysis of the 450 comments reveals several influential tropes. The identification of these tropes, moreover, allows some general conclusions to be drawn about popular attitudes to the EU and to some extent, the elite-driven 'New Narrative' discourse. The most striking is how few comments support the 'New Narrative' text explicitly. In fact, a large number of them reflect attitudes diametrically opposed to the EU and the desirability of further integration.

Hostility towards the EU and elites at national and EU level informs Eurosceptic attitudes to a large degree and is also an influential trope found in many comments. Few citizens make concrete comments about the EU's political organization or individual institutions. Not one citizen among the 450 actually notes the fact, or comments on it, that the 'New Narrative' was (apparently) prepared by a group of individuals from the cultural sphere, not 'official Europe' – something that demonstrates how difficult it is for EU institutions to create the impression of independence and impartiality for groups like the Cultural Committee, especially when the European Parliament actually initiated the project, and the Commission put it together, secured the actual declaration and conducted the consultation on its website.

The main target of severe criticism is European elites, however, who apparently seem to be the only social group to profit from integration in the EU. Roughly one half of the EU-skeptic website comments are clearly associated with values of the nationalist Right and the other half with those of the radical Left. Nationalist right-wing perspectives on the EU are very predominantly advanced by British citizens who openly identify with UKIP or with right-wing Conservatism. Both political groups advocated 'Brexit' in the campaign leading up to the 2016 referendum on British membership. The criticism in these comments focuses on two points in particular. One is the claim that 'they' never chose European integration in the form that it has now taken, that is, highly institutionalized with common policies including monetary integration and closer foreign policy coordination. One citizen claims, for example (erroneously, as the European Communities were already much more than that in 1973, when the United Kingdom joined), 'We only signed up for a trade community'.[2] The bottom line of many similar comments is that 'we' may like Europe as a continent, but we don't want to partake in its political integration.

The second nationalist right-wing trope, which has antecedents in 1960s Gaullist narratives, is the notion that the EU has destroyed democracy and erected a kind of dictatorship of unelected Brussels bureaucrats. One contributor talks about an 'oppressive, undemocratic mess' in the shape of a 'wasteful organization'.[3] Another complains about the waste of taxpayers' money on 'insane wages, benefits and diets'.[4] Yet another contributor actually calls for a popular and violent uprising against the EU, 'an undemocratic, unelected and unaccountable organization that is setting up a dictatorship to rule ... It is time we took [this monster] on, and begin to take back control of our countries. If this means violent uprising, then so be it.'[5]

In contrast to this focus on preserving national independence and democracy against an overbearing EU, mostly radical Left supporters from Mediterranean member states criticize the EU (in one extreme case of a Spanish commentator) as a 'dictadura fascista / capitalista'.[6] Or, as a Greek citizen puts it, 'Europe was our dream and is our nightmare here in Greece'.[7] The main claim here is that the EU is entirely dominated by powerful business elites who make common cause with political elites to secure their own interests. Thus, one citizen claims that 'The Europe that the corporations are building right now is one of very rich lords and very poor serfs, of rich and powerful nations of owners and poor and weak nations of servants.'[8] Another contributor laments that

> the big business owners and their corrupt allies in politics are enjoying peace, freedom and the rule of (their) law while the rest of us, the 99%, get to 'enjoy' unemployment, forced emigration, endless austerity, bank and bondholder bailouts. The EU is a disaster for all but the most wealthy within it.[9]

Similarly, one citizen writes that 'Europe has become a state of "money" where financial war is raging, oppressing people's lives by making them live in grinding poverty and insecurity.'[10]

These predominantly radical Left perspectives on the EU of course reflect dominant political fault-lines in national and EU politics over the most appropriate response to the economic and financial crisis in Europe since 2008. Very often the EU as such is not the main target of criticism or derogatory comments. Economic and political elites are instead accused of creating or at least usurping the EU to advance their own self-interest at the expense of the rest of the population. It is in this criticism of European elites that nationalist right-wing and radical Left views of the EU overlap in the comments on the 'New Narrative' website, as they also do in election campaigns, referendums and in the EP. Where they usually differ radically is in their diametrically opposed demands (Usherwood, Startin, & Guerra, 2013). The Right crave withdrawal into the nation-state while the Left want to expand the EU into a European welfare state to improve the lot of the disadvantaged, unemployed and poor. They demand policies of redistribution, geographically from the North to the South and vertically within European society, from the rich to the poor.

Even many comments from the pro-EU end of a continuum of political preferences for membership in the EU and its future constitutional development diverge from the 'New Narrative' project's message. These comments offer the kind of federalist and patriotic sentiments that were still more common especially among elites in 'core Europe' – the six founding member states of what is now the EU – until well into the 1990s. However, these sentiments are no longer forcefully advocated by mainstream political parties or the very much weakened federalist movement, let alone the Commission, which tries to navigate carefully between different preferences of member state governments.

Some comments explicitly propose the creation of a federal Europe. Thus, one citizen demands that 'Europe should develop into a federal state to [sic] a brighter future. Unity leads to progress.'[11] Another contributor exclaims that 'I hope in my lifetime, we can celebrate a European Federation.'[12] Pro-federalist citizens frequently associate such a federal order with values such as 'democracy', 'freedom' and 'tolerance'. Other contributors vent their commitment to a united Europe in much more emotive 'patriotic' than political or constitutional language. Thus, one of them talks about Europe as his 'Heimat', or homeland,[13] and another simply states 'I love Europa'.[14] One British citizen, who grew up in

Australia until 1969, recounts at length his childhood experiences in continental Europe including a primary school excursion to French Normandy. He concludes that

> I never once felt as 'foreign' as I did as a young boy Down Under. Why? And why do I love Europe so much? Because, ultimately, we're the same, you and I, ultimately the same people ... – which is why we're so much better 'together' within the EEC, as brothers in arms, rather than apart. And why I, for one, will be moving to live in France if the UK should ever leave our European brothers.[15]

There is, finally, one more influential trope that can be identified in the comments on the project website. This is fairly widespread criticism of the EU's apparent desire – also strongly reflected in the 'New Narrative' declaration – to export 'European' values like democracy and human rights to other countries and continents to make the world a better and safer place. Whether the EU actually behaves like a 'normative power' or not, has been subjected to intense academic debate. In fact, in prevalent external perceptions the EU features mainly as a powerful economic actor (Larsen, 2014). Interestingly however, many citizens who contributed to the project website at least think that the EU *should not* act as a normative power. Only one contributor demands that 'Europe must use its influence in the world to help promote a global society based on shared, ethical and sustainable humanitarian values'.[16] Others are highly skeptical and advocate an isolationist cause on the question of the export of values. One advocates, for example, that

> we would gain a lot more to stand to our values and our standards and let other countries decide whether they want to follow the example or not ... Let's first care about Europe, improve it and then we'll think about the rest of the world.[17]

Another citizen says that 'we cannot help [other countries] if we don't even have money and resources to solve our own problems (unemployment, poverty).'[18] A Polish contributor claims that values are not universal:

> Let's stop exporting values please. Most of the world lives in a very different way ... and is governed by totally different values. ... Imposing democracy on people who are not used to it ends in disaster. Mentalities evolve over long time, we cannot speed this process up by our intervention.[19]

Taken together, the comments on the website reflect the diversity of views among those European citizens who chose to participate. Most likely those who held stronger views were more motivated to submit their comments. These range from leaving the EU to advocating a federal union. Similarly, they show that citizens have very different ideas about how to overcome Europe's and the EU's problems with democracy or welfare policies. Interestingly, even contributors who severely criticize the EU often embed their criticism in positive language about Europe as a continent, which probably reflects the prevalence of a more widespread and deeper civilizational identity than political identity as EU citizens (Risse, 2010).

The analysis of the comments also shows that no-one actually understood or commented on the 'New Narrative' declaration on the project website hosted by the Commission as anything other than an official EU project. Apart from the limited dissemination of the declaration among national publics, this point highlights how difficult it is for EU institutions to support and fund such initiatives in the hope of strengthening a collective European identity and generating political legitimacy. Their interlocutors – here the Cultural

Committee – effectively appear as little more than agents of EU institutions, even if they behaved quite autonomously during the course of the project.

Conclusion

The 'New Narrative' project is only one of several initiatives recently developed by EU institutions to align collective memory (see e.g. Littoz-Monnet, 2012) and strengthen European identity. These initiatives seek to shape shared stories about Europe's past, present and future, in the hope that this will re-legitimize European integration and the EU. The 'New Narrative' project tried to contribute to the quest for greater cultural cohesion and political legitimacy at a time when the EU's 'input' and 'output' legitimacy seem to be in decline and its future is unclear. It explicitly attempted to mobilize cultural elites for the EU. It fostered networking among some members of these elites, a process that was dominated by representatives of European cultural organizations in Brussels who could mediate between the political-bureaucratic and the cultural milieus. Resulting from the cultural milieu's inability to organize itself properly and produce a coherent text, however, the declaration as the project's main output was largely drafted by one person with close ties to both the Commission and the Bozar.

The general assemblies and the declaration were only reported in European media to a limited extent and mostly in the countries where the events took place. To have long-term impact on processes of identity formation, narratives have to be communicated far more consistently across time and space. Moreover, as the Hungarian writer Konrad pointed out (Konrád, 2014), 'it is perfectly impossible to write a narrative on three or four pages'. The format of the manifesto or declaration from the beginning narrowly circumscribed what the Cultural Committee could do to contribute to converging story-telling about European integration. Crucially, the EU not only funded the project, but the text drafted by Setari was also far too closely aligned with the Commission's political preferences and habitual rhetoric to stand alone as an independent statement by cultural elites.

The declaration's narrative is strongly normative and in places uses quasi-religious messianic language. It lacks a *longue durée* perspective, except for the strong reference to the Renaissance. It treats the twentieth century until 1989 in only two sentences, avoiding any potentially controversial explicit references to occupation, perpetrators, collaboration or even the Holocaust, which others have advocated as a suitable foundation myth for the EU (e.g. Leggewie, 2011). The references to European norms and values strongly resemble Commission rhetoric, as does the emphasis on Europe's crucial contribution to fostering democracy, human rights, and sustainable development globally.

Citizens' web-based comments on the declaration's content vary widely. Demands extend from leaving the EU to further European integration in a federalist direction. Interestingly, many online comments reflect widespread skepticism about the declaration's ambition of shaping the world in Europe's image. These comments highlight the need to tackle domestic European problems first or point to cultural heterogeneity that may make it difficult or impossible to spread 'European' values like democracy and human rights.

The comments reveal pronounced irritation – not just among British UKIP supporters – with the Commission's top-down approach to writing a 'new narrative'. The contributors do not engage with the actual text. Instead, their comments focus more generally on the EU and specifically, its alleged control by self-interested elites at the expense of ordinary citizens, a trope that unites radical Left and nationalist right-wing commentators. The fact that cultural elites apparently collaborated with political and administrative elites in producing the 'New Narrative' text only aggravated the complaints about European integration as an elite-driven process. Thus, in the prevailing political climate of aggressively populist radical Left and nationalist right-wing discourses about national and European elites, top-down attempts at shaping European identity and legitimizing the EU can perhaps only be shambolic and ineffective. In contrast, fostering transnational inter-cultural experiences may have much greater potential to foster feelings of cultural commonality and social community (Kuhn, 2015; Logemann, 2013).

The citizens' comments on the declaration reveal the pluralistic nature of conceiving of and narrating European integration in contemporary Europe. Elites in the contemporary EU with its very pluralistic media landscape and social media communication find it extremely difficult to develop consistent discourses about European identity and integration and to marginalize alternative voices. The Commission's original idea of drafting a 'new all-encompassing narrative', which reflected its own institutional obsession with speaking 'with one voice' in its external communication (Altides, 2008, p. 207), appears outright absurd in these circumstances, as many Cultural Committee members and other participants at the general assemblies were also quick to point out. Thus, the Commission's conduct of the project invites further research into its institutional nature and the character of its communication strategy. To judge by the 'New Narrative' project, in some ways the Commission's attitude almost resembles desperate bureaucratic and ineffective attempts by authoritarian regimes to shore up public support. Instead, EU institutions and actors should perhaps consider whether Europe's ability to tolerate the pluralism of narratives as a mark of any developed modern democratic polity could not actually help sustain the EU's legitimacy in times of crisis.

Notes

1. 13 September 2014, 1:31 pm.
2. 16 September 2014, 9:46 pm.
3. 16 September 2014, 9:46 pm.
4. 16 September 2014, 9:50 pm.
5. 23 September 2014, 9:36 pm.
6. 18 September 2014, 9:51 pm.
7. 18 September 2014, 10:13 pm.
8. 19 September 2014, 7:17 am.
9. 20 September 2014, 6:19 pm.
10. 30 September 2014, 12:58 pm.
11. 17 September 2014, 3:24 pm.
12. 5 October 2014, 2:25 am.
13. 17 September 2014, 7:55 am.
14. 23 September 2014, 5:39 pm.
15. 6 October 2014, 9:20 pm.
16. 30 September 2014, 1:08 am.
17. 17 September 2014, 2:54 pm.
18. 21 September 2014, 8:31 pm.
19. 9 October 2014, 11:09 am.

Disclosure statement

No potential conflict of interest was reported by the author.

References

AFP. (2015, August 18). Woman who sued pro-Putin Russian 'troll factory' gets one rouble in damages. *The Guardian*. Retrieved November 2, 2016, from http://www.theguardian.com/world/2015/aug/18/woman-who-sued-pro-putin-russian-troll-factory-gets-one-rouble-in-damages

Altides, C. (2008). *Making EU politics public: How the EU institutions develop public communication*. Baden-Baden: Nomos.

Anderson, B. (1991). *Imagined communities: Reflections on the origins and spread of nationalism*, Revised and extended edition. London: Verso.

Battista, E., & Setari, N. (Eds.). (2014). *The mind and body of Europe: A new narrative*. Brussels: Centre for Fine Arts.

Calligaro, O. (2013). *Negotiating Europe: EU Promotion of Europeanness since the 1950s*. Basingstoke: Palgrave.

Chenal, O. (2013, April 23). Deputy Director, European Cultural Foundation, Amsterdam, interview, Brussels.

Chenal, O., & Snelders, B. (2012). *Remappings: The making of European narratives*. Amsterdam: European Cultural Foundation.

Dujardin, P. (2013, November 6). CEO and Artistic Director, Centre for Fine Arts, Brussels, interview, Brussels.

Eriksen, E. O., & J. E. Fossum (Eds.). (2000). *Democracy in the European Union: Integration through deliberation?* Abingdon: Routledge.

European Commission. (2014a). *New narrative for Europe*. Retrieved November 9, 2013, from http://ec.europa.eu/debate-future-europe/new-narrative/ (old website version)

European Commission. (2014b). *New narrative for Europe: The mind and body of Europe*. Retrieved November 2, 2016, from http://ec.europa.eu/culture/policy/new-narrative/documents/declaration_en.pdf

Hague, B., & Loader, B. D. (1999). *Digital democracy: Discourse and decision-making in the information age*. London: Routledge.

Hobsbawm, E., & Ranger, T. (Eds.). (1983). *The invention of tradition*. Cambridge: CUP.

Jensen, M. D., & Snaith, H. (2016). When politics prevails: The political economy of a Brexit. *Journal of European Public Policy, 23*(9), 1302–1310.

Joly, M. (2007). *Le mythe Jean Monnet: Contribution à une sociologie historique de la construction européenne*. Paris: CNRS Éd.

Kaiser, W. (2011). From great men to ordinary citizens? The biographical approach to narrating European integration in museums. *Culture Unbound. Journal of Current Cultural Research, 3*, 385–400. Retrieved November 2, 2016, from http://www.cultureunbound.ep.liu.se/v3/a25/

Kaiser, W. (2012). No new DIN-norm, please: Narrating contemporary European history. In O. Chenal & B. Snelders (Eds.), *Remappings: The making of European Narratives* (pp. 75–82). Amsterdam: European Cultural Foundation.

Kaiser, W. (2015). Clash of cultures: Two milieus in the European Union's 'A new narrative for Europe' Project. *Journal of Contemporary European Studies, 23*(3), 364–377.

Kaiser, W. (2016). Limits of cultural engineering: Actors and narratives in the European Parliament's House of European History project. *Journal of Common Market Studies*. doi:10.1111/jcms.12475

Kaiser, W., Krankenhagen, S., & Poehls, K. (2014). *Exhibiting Europe in museums: Transnational networks, collections, narratives, and representations*. New York, NY: Berghahn.

Kølvraa, C. L. (2010). Political paternity and the construction of Europe. *Kontur: Tijdskrift for Kulturstudier, 19*, 6–12.

Konrád, G. (2014, October 28). Hungarian writer, interview, Brussels.

Kuhn, T. (2015). *European integration, individual transnationalism and public orientation towards European integration*. Oxford: OUP.

Larsen, H. (2014). The EU as a normative power and the research on external perceptions: The missing link. *Journal of Common Market Studies, 52*(4), 896–910.

Leggewie, K. (2011). *Der Kampf um die europäische Erinnerung: Ein Schlachtfeld wird besichtigt*. Munich: Beck.

Littoz-Monnet, A. (2012). The EU politics of commemoration: Can Europeans remember together? *West European Politics, 35*(5), 1182–1202.

Littoz-Monnet, A. (2013). Explaining policy conflict across institutional venues: EU-level struggles over the memory of the Holocaust. *Journal of Common Market Studies, 51*(3), 489–504.

Loader, B. D., & Mercea, D. (2011). Networking democracy? Social media innovation and participatory politics. *Information, Communication & Society, 14*(6), 757–769.

Logemann, J. (2013). Europe – migration – identity: Connections between migration experiences and Europeanness. *National Identities, 15*(1), 1–8.

Løkkegaard, M. (2013, October 16). MEP, interview, Brussels.

Manners, I. (2002). Normative power Europe: A contradiction in terms? *Journal of Common Market Studies, 40*(2), 235–258.

Margetts, H., John, P., Hale, S., & Yasseri, T. (2016). *Political turbulence: How social media shape collective action*. Princeton, NJ: Princeton University Press.

Neumeyer, L. (2015). Integrating the Central European past into a common narrative: The mobilizations around the 'crimes of communism' in the European Parliament. *Journal of Contemporary European Studies, 23*(3), 344–363.

New Narrative for Europe. (2014, October 24). *Draft Final Report*. Cultural Committee.

Nyholm, P. (2014, April 22). Journalist, Jyllands-Posten, interview, Vienna.

Risse, T. (2010). *A Community of Europeans? Transnational identities and public spheres*. Ithaca, NY: Cornell University Press.

Sassatelli, M. (2012). Has Europe lost the plot? In O. Chenal & B. Snelders (Eds.), *Remappings: The making of European narratives* (pp. 55–63). Amsterdam: European Cultural Foundation.

Sassatelli, M. (2013, April 23). Lecturer, Goldsmiths, University of London, interview, Brussels.

Settele, V. (2015). Including exclusion in European memory? Politics of remembrance in the House of European History. *Journal of Contemporary European Studies, 23*(3), 405–416.

Shore, C. (2000). *Building Europe: The cultural politics of European integration*. London: Routledge.

Southern, R. (2015). Is web 2.0 providing a voice for outsiders? A comparison of personal web site and social media use by Candidates at the 2010 UK general election. *Journal of Information Technology & Politics, 12*(1), 1–17.

Sunstein, C. R. (2009). *Republic.com 2.0*. Princeton, NJ: Princeton University Press.

Usherwood, S., Startin, N., & Guerra, S. (Eds.). (2013). Confronting euroscepticism. *Journal of Common Market Studies* special issue, *51*(1), 153–168.

Varsori, A. (2010). From normative impetus to professionalization: Origins and operation of research networks. In W. Kaiser & A. Varsori (Eds.), *European Union history: Themes and debates* (pp. 6–25). Basingstoke: Palgrave.

Walker, S. (2015, April 2). Salutin' Putin: Inside a Russian troll house. *The Guardian*. Retrieved November 2, 2016, from http://www.theguardian.com/world/2015/apr/02/putin-kremlin-inside-russian-troll-house

Weller, J. (2012). *Democratic legitimacy? The online consultations of the European Commission* (PhD). University of Portsmouth, Portsmouth.

Wellings, B., & Parker, B. (2016). Euro-myth: Nationalism, war and the legitimacy of the European Union. *National Identities, 18*(2), 157–177.

Progress, democracy, efficiency: normative narratives in political science EU studies

Richard McMahon

ABSTRACT
This article identifies influential political narratives in the 73 currently most highly cited political science articles on the EU. It is based on systematic analysis of expressions of normativity, which signal that European integration, or its institutions or policies, are bad, good, flourishing or declining. A normative narrative of continuous progress in integration, connected with a 1990s grand theoretical debate in EU studies, accounts for much of the positive tone of EU studies until about 1998. Narratives about the EU's democratic deficit and its impact beyond its borders help explain the subsequent negative turn in EU studies normativity.

Sociologists of knowledge and historians of science stress that scholars produce narratives that have a vital role in interpreting and legitimising major political developments. The modern social sciences emerged to a great extent as the intellectual infrastructure of nineteenth-century nation states. Stephanie Mudge and Antoine Vauchez thus see 'knowledge-bearing elites', linking academia with politics, as equally central to both 'Western state-building processes' and European integration (2012, p. 450). Despite episodes like European Commission President José Manuel Barroso's references since 2008 to the political scientist Ian Manner's normative power thesis (Manners, 2015, p. 330), scholars disagree about whether academics have directly influenced European integration politics, and in particular, 1960s Commission strategy (Cohen & Weisbein, 2005, pp. 354–360; Kaiser, 2010, p. 52; Mudge & Vauchez, 2012, p. 459; Rosamond, 2015, p. 186; White, 2003, p. 126). There is more consensus however on the continuing importance of indirect academic influence on European integration politics, through factors like networks, press-reporting, the university education of political leaders, and the academic professional background of some of them, including Barroso (Kaiser, 2010; White, 2003, p. 131).

Despite these important influences, only one existing work expressly identifies influential political narratives in current EU studies. The historian Mark Gilbert argues that scholars of the EU have always systematically 'generated … narrative accounts' of its inexorable progress towards supranational integration (2008, p. 649). Until the 1990s for example, theoretical debate in political science EU Studies (PS-EUS) revolved around neo-functionalism. This theory provided a mechanism for progressive (i.e. continuously intensifying) integration and was very close to the European Commission's own understanding of integration as a process (White, 2003, p. 114).

This article explores and analyses the presence and use of narratives by scholars in Political Science, which is a central discipline within the multi- or interdisciplinary field of European Studies. It confirms that the progressive narrative identified by Gilbert remains important in the most highly cited PS-EUS journal articles, but that narratives of democratic deficit and efficiency are also significant. In addition, the article relates currently dominant narratives to an increasingly negative tone towards European integration in PS-EUS articles since about 1998.

The research for this article systematically analyses expressions of normativity, which signal that European integration, or its functioning, institutions or policies, are bad, good, flourishing or declining, in the 73 most cited PS-EUS peer-reviewed articles (see the appendix). This corpus, or canon, was defined by searching Google Scholar on 29 April 2015 for the terms 'European Union', 'European integration', their French and German equivalents and 'EU' and selecting political science articles. These articles are referenced in the text with a # followed by their ranking in the canon (e.g. Scharpf, #3). Normative expressions, which appeared to some extent in the texts of 85% of the 73 articles and quite assertively in more than 75% of them, are treated as the building blocks from which politically useful narratives are constructed.

Three trends should be expected to draw scholarly attention to practices of normativity in EUS writing. First, a large post-positivist constructivist and critical studies literature has, since the 1990s, increasingly challenged the previously dominant positivist approach to political science (Bevir, 2006, pp. 591 and 600). This has 'warmly embraced' 'a reflection on the relation between political science and politics', including normativity in public, elite and official discourse on European integration (Berling & Bueger, 2013, p. 116). The normative power thesis constitutes a prominent example. Second, questions about the democratic legitimacy of EU governance stimulated what is often labelled a 'normative turn' in EUS in the 1990s, placing issues of justice on the disciplinary agenda (Bellamy & Attucci, 2009, p. 198). Third, since the millennium, some EUS scholars, especially in France, have turned a reflexive eye to the organisation and practices of their own field (e.g. Mudge & Vauchez, 2012; Rosamond, 2007). Parallel developments in International Relations (IR), drawing particular inspiration from Bourdieu's key concept of reflexivity, meanwhile suggest this is part of a broader opening in political science to the sociology of knowledge (Berling & Bueger, 2013, p. 116; Eagleton-Pierce, 2011, pp. 805–806 and 815). Elements of this trend, such as the autobiographical reflexivity of feminist and critical scholars, offer avenues for reflection about scholarly normativity (Eagleton-Pierce, 2011, pp. 808–809).

Nevertheless, scholarly practices of normativity, impartiality, objectivity, value neutrality, etc. have so far been a Cinderella topic in political science. Several historians and legal scholars of the EU identify strong pro-European political agendas in their fields, but they focus heavily on early scholarship (Robert & Vauchez, 2010, pp. 15–16; Varsori, 2010, p. 6). Even self-described critical scholars are accused of using reflexivity to attack the positivist mainstream, rather than reflecting on their own practices (Berling & Bueger, 2013, p. 116). Scholars struggle with contradictions within reflexivity and especially with the still powerful grip of the positivist stricture that "good' scholarship' and 'rigour' require 'an objectivist gaze free from personality' (Berling & Bueger, 2013; Eagleton-Pierce, 2011, p. 809). This positivist scientific ideology of neutral, objective and apolitical discovery and analysis of real facts about the world remains a 'prevailing convention' in science, despite sociologists of knowledge having criticised it for decades as a social construct (Berling & Bueger, 2013, pp. 115–116; Harding, 1992, pp. 567–570). EUS scholars, like political scientists more widely, therefore still often assume that they and the politics they study constitute separate spheres (Adler-Nissen & Kropp, 2015, p. 156; Oren, 2003, p. 20; see also Kaiser, 2010, p. 53).

This scholarship-politics dichotomy imposes subtle, implicit rules, governing the habitual practices of writing, into which academic disciplines socialise scholars. The presence of the author, their emotions or viewpoint is, for example, acceptable in so-called mainstream political science, and in fact ubiquitous, when it discusses what can be called 'internal' academic issues such as theory and methodology. PS-EUS articles regularly express forceful opinions about theory (e.g. Stone Sweet & Sandholz, #24, p. 314) and speak about their authors having a hunch, something sparking their interest or surprising results (e.g. Hooghe, Marks & Wilson, #9, p. 985). However, unlike openly political genres such as hustings speeches or tabloid editorials, scholarship frowns on this normativity when it is applied to the object of study (Berling & Bueger, 2013, p. 116).

In part, these practices of normativity go unrecognised because outside of the sociologically oriented French discipline, political science has been slow to develop a disciplinary 'sociology of itself' (Eagleton-Pierce, 2011, pp. 805–806). Even where this has emerged in PS-EUS, it focusses on more conspicuous issues such as the subfield's transatlantic and theoretical cleavages and has only very recently begun to engage with sociology of knowledge literature (Adler-Nissen & Kropp, 2015).

Against this background, the first section explains in detail the selection of the 73 chosen texts, including the use of Google Scholar, journal articles, highly cited texts, political science and the introductions and conclusions of texts. The section also addresses the canon's distinct Anglophone bias. The second section then sets out how expressions of political normativity, including implicitly through scholars' use of language and evidence, were identified. This is an intensely complex issue. Expressions of normativity can frame narratives in positive, negative or neutral terms. Whether they are accidental or deliberate, they can express a scholar's ideological commitments, such as to European federalism or social democracy, or be generated 'coincidentally' in the reader's perception, regardless of the author's intention (Gilbert, 2008, p. 649). This section also draws on the key sociology of knowledge insight that issues 'external' and 'internal' to academia interpenetrate and influence one another (Adler-Nissen & Kropp, 2015, pp. 156 and 160–165). Developments in European integration and academic theories and disciplinary organisation both shape scientific practices of expressing normativity and creating narratives. Some apparently political normativity is, for example, a mere by-product of arguments about theory.

The subsequent sections examine three important sets of narratives, concerning progressive integration, the democratic deficit and efficiency. Narratives of progress in grand theoretical debates explain much of the positive tone in canonical PS-EUS articles up to 1998. In contrast, discussion of the democratic deficit and the EU's external effects account for much of the negative, critical turn since then. In part, these factors reflect the EU's 'sea of troubles' since the millennium. However, they also mark a transformation in the agenda of EUS, from trying to define European integration, to an often critical assessment of its politics and policies.

Selecting the canon

The canon was selected using Google Scholar, which for the purposes of this research, is less flawed than other citation databases (Harzing & van der Wal, 2008, pp. 63–65). All available databases are, for example, heavily weighted towards English-language work,[1] but Google Scholar at least indexes post-1993 sources in German and French. Nevertheless, all but one of the 73 canonical articles are in English. This reflects linguistic and disciplinary relations within EUS as well as Google's linguistic bias. Political scientists formed the majority in 'barely 10%' of national ECSAs in 2006, but dominated the huge American (78% political scientists) and British (50%) societies, which together accounted for 59% of the world's ECSA members (Rosamond, 2007, p. 10). For historical reasons, moreover, English speaking and especially American political scientists were largely responsible for prominent early theories of integration. Scholars of law and economics dominated EUS in continental countries because political science there developed later as an entirely autonomous discipline (Waever, 1998, pp. 704–707).

The Google search was limited in three ways. First, only peer-reviewed journal articles were chosen, leaving out books, reports, etc., which might have different conventions of normativity. Citations of books outnumber those of articles by more than two to one among all EUS works cited over 500 times. As Wæver notes, however, for 'practitioners', an academic field 'exists mostly in the journals', and they constitute its 'crucial institution' (1998, p. 697). The total citations of the canonical writers above 100 cites were also checked, including their books. It turned out that there was a strong match between their ranking in both lists. Of the 17 authors in the top ten articles of my canon, for example, 78% were also in the top 10 of the longer list.

Second, to get a sense of the narratives preoccupying PS-EUS at present, its most highly cited texts were chosen, but a series of progressively lower inclusion thresholds (see table below) were also used to include well-cited recent texts (since 2003). These have simply not had time to be cited as often as older works have been. These lower thresholds brought citations in 2003–2010 up to an average of 3.5 per year, which is comparable with the 3.86 annual average in 1995–2001. The same attempt to compensate was not made for the period since 2010, however, in which only one article has been cited over 100 times. These low numbers make the genuine preoccupations of EUS relatively uncertain.

Threshold no. of citations	Period	No. articles	No. articles 2003–2006	No. articles 2007–2013
400	All articles	52	7	1
300	Since 2003	8	7	1
200	Since 2007	4		4
100	Since 2008	9		9
Total		73	22	11

Canons of authoritative texts, repeatedly read and cited, are a key institution in any academic community. The hope is that the PS-EUS canon offers a model for normative practices in general. The canon is not necessarily a typical sample of PS-EUS literature, however. Political science requires authors to locate their work within the major theoretical debates that structure the disciplinary literature. This may create an overrepresentation of works on what are known as theoretical grand debates (11 articles), which receive an average of 751 cites each, compared to 468 for other articles, and literature reviews (five articles).

By contrast, most writing on the EU is probably much more empirical (Andrews, 2012, p. 757; Katzenstein, Keohane, & Krasner, 1998, p. 655).

Third, only political science articles were chosen for the canon. Interdisciplinary articles were included or excluded on the basis of the balance of the authors' training and current departmental affiliations, the article's subject matter and the journal's declared disciplinary affiliation.

Finally, in order to review a large number of articles efficiently, only their introductions and conclusions were examined. These sections are the most likely to contain normative language because this is where authors present their project and sum up the more technical analysis in the main body of the article. For example, authors quite often use their first paragraphs to make broad and eye-catching framing statements that are not necessarily very closely related to the article's main argument. The first four sentences of the single most cited PS-EUS article therefore enthusiastically sets out the essence of the progressive narrative, It calls the EU 'an extraordinary political experiment ... [p]rogressing ... in a consistent direction', pooling 'increasing areas of political authority' through 'prominent' institutions which have 'transformed the nature of European politics' (Pierson, 1996, p. 123). Conclusions often attempt a high-level synthesis of the evidence that the body of an article closely analyses. This greater distance from the evidence gives freer rein to the author to interpret it imaginatively and link it with broader political or theoretical concerns that they feel strongly about and therefore discuss in normative terms.

Identifying normativity

The empirical research centres on how building blocks of narratives represent integration or its works favourably or unfavourably. Normativity towards supranational integration is particularly important. Whereas the neo-functionalist progressive narrative insisted that supranational institutions like the European Commission and Parliament would grow in power, the rival intergovernmentalist theory claimed that member state governments remained in control. Normative expressions therefore include statements which contrast supranational integration and institutions with intergovernmentalism, nationalism and member states. Individual canonical articles frequently contain multiple normative expressions, which can support different narratives and take positive and negative stances towards different aspects of integration.

As Figure 1 demonstrates, normative expressions can take several different forms. The most straightforward is an explicit opinion, criticising or praising some aspect of integration. Ernst Haas considers integration 'most satisfying' (#15, pp. 366 and 389). Fritz Scharpf by contrast describes the EU's Common Agricultural Policy as 'almost universally considered a grandiose failure' (#3, p. 241). However, this explicit normativity is relatively rare. Figure 1 therefore shows three more common types of normative expression, which imply praise or criticism more indirectly. First, several articles assert that some aspect of integration is failing or succeeding, whether now or in a predicted future. This implies that the integration project is well or ill-founded in some way, with particular implications for the progressive narrative. A common example is the opinion that the democratic deficit constitutes a serious problem for the EU. However, a surprising number of EUS authors contest this, illustrating the extent to which this opinion is a normative choice. The degree of normativity of such opinions depends strongly on how they are expressed

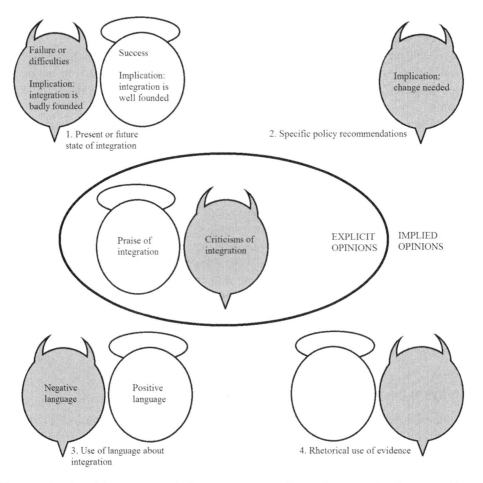

Figure 1. Angels and demons, respectively, represent types of normative expression that are positive or negative towards integration.

and the extent that they are relatively gratuitous, rather than being critical to the author's broader argument or emerging from the evidence.

Second, a few articles explicitly recommend policy change, implicitly criticising present policy. Thomas Risse, for example, advocates informal networks and institutionalised 'communicative processes' as more efficient decision-making mechanisms than 'slow-moving' intergovernmental bargaining, which produces 'nothing more than the lowest common denominator' (e.g. #16, p. 73).

Third, a very common form of normative expression is the choice of words and phrases such as 'fortunately', 'improve', 'optimistic', 'succeed', 'good', 'should' and their antonyms, especially if such language is repeated or extreme, or if more neutral synonyms are available. Scharpf for example describes some 'beneficial programmes' as 'ridiculously underfinanced' (#3, p. 241). Chadwick and May meanwhile use inverted commas to delegitimise managerial e-government's emphasis on '"efficient"' '"service delivery"' to '"customers"' or '"users"' (#21, p. 272). These 'scare-quotes' ostentatiously disapprove of practitioners' claims of efficiency and representations of citizens as customers. A very common variant of normative phraseology associates or disassociates integration with ideas such as progress, innovation, creativity, democracy, peace, fairness, efficiency, reform, idealism, solidarity, compromise and rationality, which Western culture or liberal scholars generally load with positive meaning. When Ian Manners describes the EU's 'creative efforts and long-term vision' as encouraging 'a more just, cosmopolitan world', for example, he references values of creativity, foresight, justice and cosmopolitanism which all have positive connotations for Western liberals (Manners, #58, p. 60).

Fourth, a very occasional form of normative expression is the selective presentation of evidence for rhetorical effect. Peter Mair, for example, uses the French and Dutch referendum votes against the EU constitution in 2005, and the lukewarm Luxembourg yes, as examples of 'ebbing' support for the EU, but never mentions the 77% yes vote in Spain's referendum (#64, p. 2). Literature reviews can also be a rhetorical strategy for using evidence, in which it is not always entirely clear whether the author is endorsing or merely reporting the views of cited scholars (e.g. Wessels, #31, pp. 291–292).

These are all ways of judging individual normative expressions within articles rather than the overall stances of articles or authors. Risse's policy recommendation above, for example, implicitly criticises the existing EU for not being supranational enough, so he is using a negative expression of normativity to advocate for greater integration. The very pro-integrationist Ernst Haas meanwhile despairs of integration's prospects outside Europe (#15, p. 389).

The assessment of individual normative expressions was then used to rate the overall tone of each canonical article on a scale of positivity. Scoring was based on (1), a judgement of the explicitness, forcefulness (e.g. strong language) and gratuitousness of individual normative expressions and (2), the degree to which they were repeated and consistently negative or positive across the article as a whole. Though this two stage process helped ensure consistency, the judgements nevertheless involved some subjectivity. A finely graduated scale for a simple judgement of articles as neutral, balanced (positive and negative statements cancel one another out) or very or slightly favourable/unfavourable towards European integration and its works was therefore eschewed. This resulted in a positivity scale running from + 2 to −2, which in turn allowed the production of quite fine-grained quantitative results for the 73 articles as a whole. Their overall average positivity score was 0.03, for example.

Two caveats are in order, the first concerning context. Clearly, normative vocabulary only counts in the analysis when it refers to European integration, but context is most crucial where it involves the relationship of statements to evidence. References to the democratic deficit are for example often presented briefly and with little supporting evidence in framing statements, sometimes to illustrate a broader European malaise. For this reason, the assertion at the start of Sean Carey's article that EU citizens 'have rarely had any direct involvement in the major political decisions made in their name' is treated as highly normative (#29, p. 388). Not only is it unsupported by his empirical survey-based study of how Europeans identify with their nation and other territorial entities, but it is only loosely related to it. He instead appears to be making a deliberate declaration of his normative political position. By contrast, Simon Hix's conclusion that political parties find it 'very difficult' to establish 'stable' pan-European alliances is treated as non-normative, because it emerges directly from his detailed empirical analysis of party alignments across the EU (#42, p. 92).

The second caveat concerns author's intention. The concern here is with narratives as a form of political communication which shapes opinion. Particular expressions as normative are therefore judged on the basis of whether readers, including relatively unsophisticated readers, such as undergraduates, are likely consciously or unconsciously to interpret them as such. This defines normativity very broadly. It can include assertions that, for example, a treaty is 'ambitious' or the EU is a 'unique laboratory', which others might interpret as simple non-normative statements of fact.

This broad definition means that normativity is attributed to authors with very different degrees of commitment to political persuasion, apolitical science or reflection on their own normative writing practices. Some of the normative expressions identified are ambiguously and perhaps accidentally normative (e.g. Dür, #66, p. 1213; Hay & Rosamond, #30, p. 163), whereas certain other authors use strong language in canonical articles and are identified in their own writing or secondary sources as politically engaged. Fritz Scharpf (#3, p. 241) is thus firmly committed to the national welfare state, for example, and refers to the EC's 'pervasive sense of disappointment, frustration and general malaise' and 'the perversities of CAP'. The critical theorist Ian Manners meanwhile speaks about the EU's 'creative efforts', promotion of 'universally applicable' normative principles and 'ability to normalize a more just, cosmopolitan world' (#58, pp. 45–47).

Normative internal academic agendas add a crucial complication. As examples in the following section demonstrate, authors sometimes make what readers can interpret as normative statements about the EU in order to make arguments about academic theories or the disciplinary organisation of EU studies. The analysis therefore pays attention to differences between surface meaning and, to the extent it can be reconstructed, the author's agenda.

The progressive narrative

Representations of a progressive process of European integration and of its failure to create adequate institutions for democratic representation constitute quite coherent narratives. Three elements of these narratives appear to explain a key pattern detected in the canon. Positivity dropped from an average of 0.39 among the 17 articles published before 1998, to −0.11 among the 56 later articles (see Figure 2). More diverse sets of arguments reject the democratic deficit thesis and emphasise the importance of efficiency.

Discussing the progressive narrative Gilbert identifies a systematic use in EUS of terms such as 'Europe's 'path', 'march', 'advance', 'progress'', re-launch, revival or, conversely, 'stagnation' and 'set-backs'. He argues that they turn progressive integration 'into a creature with a vital life of its own' (2008, p. 645). Judgements by authors of the success or failure of measures, he adds, depend 'almost always [on] whether they augmented or reduced' supranationality, describing reforms as 'limited', 'tinkering' or 'piecemeal' if they do not. This is a longstanding criticism of EUS. In 1971, Donald Puchala complained that it focussed on what integration 'should be and ... be leading towards' rather than on 'what it really is' (#51, p. 268). Two decades later, Alan Milward and Vibeke Sørensen described EUS's central theory of neo-functionalism, which since the 1960s represented integration as self-reinforcing progress towards supranationalism, as a creature of America's Cold War foreign policy and European policy-making (1994, pp. 2–3). Gilbert agrees that '[a]lmost all scholars of European integration', have 'blithe confidence in the

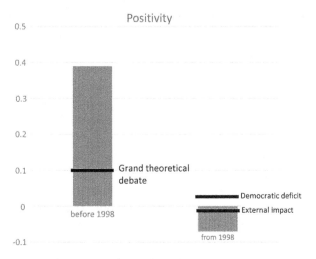

Figure 2. The dark lines show how positivity before 1998 is reduced if grand theoretical debate articles are removed and positivity from 1998 increases if democratic deficit or external impact articles are removed.

inevitability' of 'profoundly desirable' progress towards 'ever more complex forms of supranational government' and 'gradual erosion of national sovereignty' (Gilbert, 2008, pp. 641–642, 649–650). Even Stanley Hoffmann's intergovernmentalist critique opposed neo-functionalism 'gloomily', recognising its 'optimism' (Cafruny & Ryner, 2009, p. 223).

The issue of whether the EU has been, will be or should be becoming more deeply integrated and transferring power from member states to supranational institutions, is a key issue in the canon, mentioned normatively (and mostly positively) in 26 of the 73 articles. Richard Eichenberg and Russell Dalton (#12, p. 507) reproduce Gilbert's narrative most faithfully, describing the Single European Act and Maastricht Treaty as an 'ambitious' 'historic threshold' following 'a decade of stagnation'. James Caporaso's description of integration's 'incoherent path ... disjointed, moves forward (and backward) in fits and starts' (#11, p. 30) meanwhile exemplifies the negative language that Gilbert says is used about non-progressive change.

The inherently teleological nature of the progressive narrative, perhaps combined with positivist ambitions for the predictive power of science, leads PS-EUS scholars to make normative statements about the future of integration. Alec Stone Sweet and Wayne Sandholz predict that integration will continue to deepen and become more supranational because 'the long-term interests of member state governments will be increasingly biased towards the long-term interests of transnational society' (#24, pp. 314–315). A consoling perspective for pro-integrationists compares the 'historical process of state building' of the EU and the pre-Civil War USA, implying that the present uncertain and halting integration process may ultimately culminate in close unity (Caporaso, #11, p. 30). Eight canonical texts reference innovation and creativity, a key element of Europe's progressive narrative. Jachtenfuchs describes the 'exciting' and 'important' 'transformation' of nation-states into 'a new transnational political system', where 'fundamental developments are probably transforming the possibilities of effective and responsible governance' (#23, pp. 256 and 260). Marks, Liesbet Hooghe and Kermit Blank praise the EU's 'innovative jurisprudence' (#2, p. 372).

Canonical narratives frequently represent integration as the EU's power struggle against its member nation states. Burkard Eberlein and Dieter Kerwer say the EU 'has overcome' member-state interests to move into new policy fields (#60, p. 122). Nation-states are commonly portrayed as the violent, selfish, Machiavellian antitheses of European peace, justice and openness. Five canonical articles link the EU with cooperation, negotiation, decentralisation and peace and 12 refer to selfish, anti-democratic, cynical, hierarchical and violent nation states. Critical scholars argue that key theoretical frameworks, including neo-functionalism, transactionalism and neo-institutionalism, 'idealized' integration 'as the 'rational' and 'general'', in contrast to the 'irrational', 'special interests' and 'power politics' of states and their international system (Cafruny & Ryner, 2009, pp. 222–223). Jeffrey Lewis identifies the practice of 'appeals to fairness or principled debate' as part of the socialisation of EU officials into EU norms, based on his empirical observations (#59, p. 969). However when he adds they can 'revert to more egoistic and instrumental' national stances under certain circumstances, it is Lewis who chooses to use terms with negative normative connotations. Substituting national interest, democratic representativeness or patriotism for egoism would leave his basic point largely intact but dramatically change its normative tone. Gary Marks et al. discuss state power and control in the emotionally charged language of loss; it has 'slipped away', been 'diluted'; states 'lose their grip' and 'weaken' (#2, pp. 342–343). The authors then however hint that this is a civilising process. States are 'extremely powerful … capable of crushing' threats and 'systematically wielding violence' but, weakened by mutual 'mistrust', are 'melded gently' into the EU, with its more attractive characteristics of 'mutual dependence' and 'complementary functions' (Marks et al., #2, pp. 371–372).

Several authors contrast historical 'national rulers', who 'reinforced national solidarity by impelling their populations' into war and 'great suffering', with European integration 'thankfully' not using 'coercion' (Hooghe & Marks, #10, p. 23; Zürn, #40, p. 212). Hooghe and Marks present current member state leaders as irresponsible cynics, stimulating Euroscepticism among the less 'cognitively sophisticated' general public through an 'elitist style' of negotiating EU institutional change (#10, p. 22; Marks et al., #2, pp. 371–373). Member governments 'purport' incorrectly to represent all their citizens by intensifying 'national stubbornness in European negotiations', while trying to preserve 'log-rolling and side-payments' (Hooghe & Marks, #10, p. 22). These and other authors argue that member governments use 'strategic' European integration rhetoric to push through 'unpalatable reforms', shifting decisions to the EU level 'to shed responsibility' for them (Hay & Rosamond, #30, p. 163; Marks et al., #2, p. 371). This argument is only normative however, to the extent that authors or readers may decry government strategies to sell reforms as manipulative and sneaky.

More than half of the eleven articles that address theoretical grand debates over neo-functionalism, intergovernmentalism, etc. also reference the progressive narrative. Though recognising difficulties in integration, many were critical of nation states and stressed the progress of integration, plus sometimes its innovation and necessity. The average positivity score for grand debate articles was a very high 1.11. Grand debate texts leaning towards supranationalism, with an even higher positivity score of 1.125, outnumbered intergovernmentalist articles by four to one. Grand debate articles are thus an important factor accounting for the high level of positivity before 1998. Without the eight grand debate articles (positivity 0.75), the positivity of the nine other articles before 1998 is just 0.1 (see Figure 1).

The clustering of eight grand debate articles in 1995–1998 was however due less to EUS's traditional intergovernmentalist-neo-functionalist debate, than to a new Comparative Politics (CP) challenge to both IR, its disciplinary rival, and intergovernmentalism (Diez & Wiener, 2009, p. 9). For intergovernmentalists, the pre-integration landscape of state-dominated IR remained central and essentially intact. Moravcsik argues that 'bargaining and delegation by explicit governmental agreement better explains most important decisions in EU history than the supranationalist alternative' (#37, p. 625). By contrast, CP scholars turned towards the EU following the Maastricht Treaty because they believed integration had become 'so advanced' (Bulmer, #31, p. 352; Christiansen, Jorgensen & Wiener #43, p. 528). Their analyses of the EU's day-to-day functioning minimised the role of member states and their occasional grand bargains (Pierson, #1, p. 124). Gilbert therefore characterises neo-institutionalist CP scholars like Paul Pierson as sharing the supranationalist enthusiasm and faith of neo-functionalism (Gilbert, 2008, pp. 641–642, 649–650). In 1999, the CP scholar Hix explicitly challenged IR's traditional leadership of PS-EUS, insisting that 'the EU is now more a 'political system' than an international organisation' (#42, p. 69).

If CP contributions to grand debates account for much of the positivity in 1995–1998, why did positivity then decline? After all, articles of empirical CP research on governance, policy-making, institutional design, political parties, Europeanisation and lobbying soared from 23% of my canon prior to 1998 to 53% thereafter. The 32 articles of empirical CP research have an unremarkable positivity score of −0.125 and are not particularly normative. The answer appears to be that Hix and others specifically emphasised supranational progress in grand debate articles in order to advance their disciplinary claim to priority in EUS. This is therefore an example of how the internal academic agendas of academics can produce language which a reader can interpret as politically normative.

Intensifying integration is the main preoccupation of the progressive narrative but 13 articles (5 on enlargement and 8 on the EU's global influence) deal with the expanding geographical impact of European integration, and at least 10 focus exclusively on this. Almost all external impact articles were published in 2000–2008. Manners's piece on the EU's normative power (2007) celebrates Europe's potential to encourage a new, peaceful form of new, peaceful system of relations between states and promote liberal norms outside Europe. However external impact texts are relatively negative in tone (positivity: −0.33). In their absence, positivity for the period since 1998 rises from −0.11 to −0.05 (see Figure 2). About eight texts criticise the EU's double standards, incoherent external relations and harmful effects. The two on migration policy are especially critical (Guiraudon, #50; Huysmans, #13). Texts that portray the EU as 'a unique laboratory', implicitly suggest that its innovations can be copied elsewhere (Jachtenfuchs, #23, p. 260), but articles that focus on external impact highlight problems with exporting Europe's model. Ernst Haas believes integration contributes to world peace but is deeply pessimistic about the 'pleasant' prospect of its development outside Europe (#15, pp. 366 and 389). Wolfgang Wessels suggests that widening and deepening may be incompatible, as eastern enlargement might require 'bold' and difficult constitutional reforms (#31, p. 292).

Democratic deficit narratives

Worries about democracy are central to three canonical articles and raised in normative terms by 32 others, often linked with normative turn issues of elitism and technocracy. Rejections and near-rejections of EU treaties since 1993 have made the so-called 'democratic deficit' between the EU's increased powers and its insufficiently democratic political system a core issue for even pro-European PS-EUS scholars (Bellamy & Attucci, 2009, pp. 198–199; Gilbert, 2008, pp. 648–649). Thomas Risse for example considers 'the consequences of ignoring' this problem 'disastrous' (# 16, p. 74) and along with Matthew Gabel and Harvey Palmer (#36, p. 13), offers policy recommendations to address it. Democratic deficit worries are sometimes expressed in strongly normative terms. One article for example complains that although member states '[n]ot surprisingly' resist 'the EU interfering with national production and welfare regimes', 'European elites' show an 'alarming tendency' not to take' the public's 'growing unease … seriously enough' (Höpner & Schäfer, #67, p. 364). Many other references to democracy are only normative however, in the sense that they recognise it as a serious problem for European integration and its progress (e.g. Hix, #42, p. 70).

Democracy concerns are the third major explanation for falling positivity. Since 1998, articles normatively referencing democracy have a positivity of −0.41 while the remaining articles score 0.13 (see Figure 2). Negativity is concentrated in the five texts which warn that the democracy problem is worsening (positivity −1.6), and also in the 13 articles from 2002 to 2007 (positivity −0.8). In this period, Irish, French and Dutch voters rejected proposed treaties to reform the EU in four separate referenda. Other articles referencing democracy are slightly positive on average. A surprising portion of theorists are therefore quite sanguine on the subject (Schmidt, #70, p. 2). Jonas Tallberg identifies a synergistic 'mutual empowerment' of supranational EU institutions and the 'citizens and companies' who use them to complain about infringements of European law (#38, p. 638). Andreas Dür cites studies of EU lobbying that aim to counter the 'simplistic … popular' view of 'all-powerful interest groups', implying that EU governance is somewhat better than its stereotype suggests (#66, p. 1213).

Andrew Moravcsik's exceptionally clear and comprehensive rejection of democratic deficit worries as 'unsupported by the existing empirical evidence' may offer a second example of academic agendas influencing normative narratives of integration (#4, p. 605). Andreas Føllesdal and Hix (#6, p. 541) describe his arguments on the democratic deficit as 'extensions' of his liberal-intergovernmental theory of European integration, around which he constructed his entire career. Some elements of Moravcsik's argument, such as describing EU democracy as 'very much in line with the general practice of most modern democracies' (#4, pp. 621–622) do not necessarily support this accusation. Other key elements, such as insisting that the EU is 'restricted by treaty and practice to a modest subset of the substantive activities' of modern states (#4, p. 607), certainly do however. Moravcsik's quest for liberal-intergovernmentalist explanations for practically all major developments in EU politics (e.g. Moravcsik & Vachudova, 2003) suggest his democracy article was part of a campaign to demonstrate its comprehensiveness as a grand theory, and therefore, as theoretical rivals complain, 'aggressively' demonstrate 'its superiority' (Stone Sweet & Sandholz, #24, p. 298). Moravcsik thus boasted that 'many critics now concede' that his theory 'remains indispensable and fundamental to any account of regional integration' (#37, p. 625).

The progressive and democratic deficit narratives interact in complex ways. Hix describes concerns about democracy as a 'bi-product' of enhanced and increasingly politicised integration (1999, p. 70). Føllesdal and Hix disagree with Moravcsik's 'optimistic conclusions' about EU democracy but predict a brighter future (#6, pp. 556–557). 'All is not lost … change is on its way' in transnational political alignments and institutions, which 'may not even require fundamental reform', while democratic contestation has 'started to emerge'. Some critical EUS scholars since the early 1990s have denounced the 'imperialist', 'neo-liberal' EU but others placed their hopes in its 'post-national and cosmopolitan democracy', implying progress beyond the nation-state era (Manners, 2007, pp. 77–78). Other theorists offer very conditional hope for progress. Sandra Lavenex qualifies her rather negative assessment of EU external governance by leaving open the 'long run' possibility that adaptation by the EU and its member states, 'if successful', could create greater 'politics of inclusion' (#35, p. 695). Simon Bulmer meanwhile states that European institutions developed 'ahead of a popular, democratic groundswell of support' and 'in advance of the structures for ensuring democratic legitimation' (#31, p. 353). The phrases 'ahead of' and 'in advance of' suggest that he expects these developments to occur. Some leading rational choice scholars in the canon reverse the causal relationship; democracy might 'slow down the pace' of integration (Gabel & Palmer, #36, p. 13; Tsebelis & Garrett, #28, p. 32; #46, p. 384). They argue that once those citizens 'least able to benefit from EC membership' realise that the European Parliament has increased its powers, they may demand that MEPs 'act more as delegates' than as 'pro-integrationist coconspirators with the Commission and Court'.

Efficiency narratives

For scholars of institutional design in particular, efficiency and effectiveness are key normative considerations, expressed in normative language in 14 canonical articles. Tallberg repeats the adjective 'effective' for the EU's compliance mechanisms four times in the first three paragraphs of his conclusion (#38, pp. 637–638). In four paragraphs of their introduction, tracing the history of European institutions, Tsebelis and Garrett use the terms 'remarkably effective', 'legislative gridlock' (twice), 'ineffective', 'hamstrung', 'effective' and 'gridlock' (#46, pp. 358–359). In contrast to other articles, those referencing efficiency became much more positive after the millennium. Far from explaining the drop in positivity therefore, it becomes wider if these articles are removed.

The broadest efficiency narrative is that integration is a practical necessity to provide 'benefits' and address 'real problems', which member states cannot handle singly (Eichenberg & Dalton, #12, p. 508; Scharpf, #3, p. 270). Three articles for example argue that globalisation requires international political organisation. Linking efficiency and democracy, Eichenberg and Dalton say 'elites must convince their domestic audiences that the benefits of further integration are worth their costs'. This might just be an objective analysis of political strategy, but by adding that 'active public support' is needed for the EU 'to deal forcefully' with issues confronting it (#12, p. 508), they hint that they also normatively believe the benefits of integration outweigh its costs.

Five articles on 'new governance' techniques, such as the open method of coordination, multi-level governance and policy networks, tightly link narratives of efficiency, innovation and democracy. Schimmelfennig and Sedelmeier (#8, pp. 674–675) distinguish between the 'hierarchical' 'old governance', involving 'command, control, and steering by the state', and the ''new' or 'network governance' … based on horizontal co-ordination and co-operation, negotiated in decentralized settings'. Their normative language about 'bureaucratic actors' and 'a top-down process' imposing rules, even where 'societal actors should have played an important role', suggests that they see the new governance as more socially representative. Whereas scholars are largely positive about governance innovations, many recognise that they may pose problems of elitism and opacity. John Peterson for example suggests that democracy and efficiency may not be entirely reconcilable. He says policy networks 'bring advantages' for 'policy innovation', allow 'affected interests to participate directly' and 'curb the excesses of public power' but may have 'sinister' implications for democracy (#19, p. 88). He quotes both a national official complaining about 'real decisions' being taken in 'cosy chats' with EU officials and EU officials praising these 'useful and 'important' 'informal conciliations' (Peterson, #19, p. 87). Moravcsik meanwhile insists that certain public institutions work better when insulated from democratic control (#4, p. 614).

Conclusion

Identifying normativity in scholarly writing is challenging and necessarily subjective. In view of this this article has sought to clarify its interpretative process as much as possible. The vast majority of canonical PS-EUS texts were found to contain some normative commentary on European integration, its institutions and policies. The main pattern in the degree of positivity of articles towards European integration and its works is greater negativity from 1998 on. Three explanatory factors account for this. One is that in a batch of highly cited grand debate articles, clustered in 1995–1998, CP scholars successfully presented an alternative to IR-centred intergovernmentalist EUS. By arguing that the advanced state of supranational integration necessitated their research on the EU's day-to-day operations, they contributed to the progressive narrative, one of the longest-standing and most powerful narrative traditions in EUS, including in the canon for this research.

This teleological narrative sometimes takes such forms as predictions and hopes. It celebrates supranational integration as an innovative force for peace and rationality, gradually but successfully supplanting the cynical and brutal old nation state system. This grand debate episode illustrates however the difficulty in neatly separating normative language about integration and about theoretical or disciplinary agendas. Hix's perhaps spoke of the EU's 'enormous' or 'increasing impact' to advocate for CP's role in studying it. Still, readers, particularly if unfamiliar with intra-disciplinary agendas of this kind, could be forgiven for understanding a normative endorsement of the progressive narrative.

The negative tone of writing on two subject matters which became particularly prominent after the millennium, the EU's external impact and its democratic deficit, both help account for falling positivity after 1998. Democratic deficit articles were much more numerous and had a more significant effect, though surprising numbers of them were relatively relaxed about the EU's democratic legitimacy. The democratic deficit and progressive narratives interacted in complex ways. Ten authors believed more effective democracy was on the way, though one rational choice article thought more democracy would empower opponents of further integration.

The third major group of narratives of integration, concerning the EU's efficiency in functioning, delivering benefits and addressing Europe's problems, were also entangled with the other narratives. Innovative new forms of governance and the technocratic threat they posed to democracy were, for example, major concerns. Coping with the evolving (e.g. progressive) problem of globalisation was meanwhile more prominent than escaping the past problem of war among European states.

Factors external to academia, such as the EU's constitutional crisis and its new responsibilities for difficult external impact issues such as migration, help explain why PS-EUS scholars are increasingly pessimistic and critical about integration. Deepening integration has meanwhile assured the triumph of the CP agenda of studying EU politics and policy, side-lining the grand ontological debates, around which PS-EUS revolved in the twentieth century. This internal academic upheaval then made CP preoccupations, such as the democratic deficit, external impact and efficiency, prominent in the PS-EUS canon. It also ended the grand debate practice of rhetorical use of normative language about the EU, to further disciplinary or theoretical arguments.

If EUS indeed influences policy-makers' narratives of European integration, EUS scholars should be aware of how their practices of normative writing construct these narratives. Even without political influence however, scholars need reflexivity about practices like normative expression, in order to avoid reproducing unconscious biases. Did different national narratives about European identity, for example, shape EUS debate about the specific geography of EU enlargement? As Pierre Bourdieu argues, continuous awareness of 'the implications and presuppositions of the routine operations of scientific practice' is 'a particularly effective means' for scholars to improve our 'chances of attaining truth' (2004, p. 89).

Note

1. Thomas Diez (personal communication, July 10, 2015) also noted that my harvesting software failed to find certain highly cited articles. Google refuses to explain how its searches work, but the problem probably stems from how its algorithm lists results in order of 'relevance'.

Funding

This work was supported by the Marie Curie Intra-European Fellowships (IEF) [FP7-PEOPLE-2013-625508].

References

Adler-Nissen, R., & Kropp, K. (2015). A sociology of knowledge approach to European integration: Four analytical principles. *Journal of European Integration*, *37*, 155–173. doi:10.1080/07036337

Andrews, D. M. (2012). The rise and fall of EU studies in the USA. *Journal of European Public Policy*, *19*, 755–775. doi:10.1080/13501763.2011.646794

Bellamy, R., & Attucci, C. (2009). Normative theory and the EU: Between contract and community. In A. Wiener & T. Diez (Eds.), *European integration theory* (pp. 198–220). Oxford: Oxford University Press.

Berling, T. V., & Bueger, C. (2013). Practical reflexivity and political science: Strategies for relating scholarship and political practice. *PS: Political Science & Politics*, *46*, 115–119. doi:10.1017/S1049096512001278

Bevir, M. (2006). Political studies as narrative and science, 1880–2000. *Political Studies*, *54*, 583–606. doi:10.1111/j.1467-9248.2006.00616.x

Bourdieu, P. (2004). *Science of science and reflexivity*. Cambridge: Polity.

Cafruny, A., & Ryner M. (2009) Critical political economy. In A. Wiener & T. Diez (Eds.), *European integration theory* (pp. 221–240). Oxford: Oxford University Press.

Cohen, A., & Weisbein, J. (2005). Laboratoires du constitutionnalisme européen. Expertises académiques et mobilisations politiques dans la promotion d'une Constitution européenne. *Droit et société*, *60*, 353–369.

Diez, T., & Wiener, A. (2009). Introducing the mosaic of integration theory. In A. Wiener & T. Diez (Eds.), *European integration theory* (pp. 1–22). Oxford: Oxford University Press.

Eagleton-Pierce, M. (2011). Advancing a reflexive international relations. *Millennium-Journal of International Studies*, *39*, 805–823. doi:10.1177/0305829811402709

Gilbert, M. (2008). Narrating the process: Questioning the progressive story of European integration. *JCMS: Journal of Common Market Studies*, *46*, 641–662. doi:10.1111/j.1468-5965.2008.00795.x

Harding, S. (1992). After the neutrality ideal: Science, politics, and" strong objectivity". *Social Research*, *59*(3), 567–587.

Harzing, A. W. K., & van der Wal, R. (2008). Google scholar as a new source for citation analysis. *Ethics in Science and Environmental Politics*, *8*(1), 61–73. doi:10.3354/esep00076

Kaiser, W. (2010). From isolation to centrality: Contemporary history meets European studies. In W. Kaiser & A. Varsori (Eds.), *European Union history: Themes and debates* (pp. 45–65). Houndsmills: Palgrave.

Katzenstein, P. J., Keohane, R. O., & Krasner, S. D. (1998). International organization and the study of world politics. *International Organization*, *52*(4), 645–685.

Manners, I. (2007). Another Europe is possible: Critical perspectives on European Union politics. In K. E. Jørgensen, M. Pollack, & B. Rosamond (Eds.), *Handbook of European Union politics* (pp. 77–95). London: Sage.

Manners, I. (2015). Sociology of knowledge and production of normative power in the European Union's external actions. *Journal of European Integration*, *37*, 299–318. doi:10.1080/07036337.2014.990141

Milward, A. S., & Sørensen, V. (1994). Interdependence or integration? A national choice. In Alan S. Milward, Frances Lynch, Federico Romero, Ruggero Ranieri, and Vibeke Sorensen. *The frontier of national sovereignty: History and theory 1945–1992* (pp. 1–32). London: Routledge.

Moravcsik, A. & Vachudova, M.A. (2003). National interests, state power, and EU enlargement. *East European Politics and Societies, 17*, 42–57. doi:10.1177/0888325402239682

Mudge, S. L., & Vauchez, A. (2012). Building Europe on a weak field: Law, economics, and scholarly avatars in transnational politics. *American Journal of Sociology, 118*, 449–492. doi:10.1086/666382

Oren, I. (2003). *Our enemies and US: America's rivalries and the making of political science*. Ithaca: Cornell University Press.

Robert, C., & Vauchez, A. (2010). L'Académie européenne. *Politix, 89*(1), 9–34. doi:10.3917/pox.089.0009

Rosamond, B. (2007). European integration and the social science of EU studies: The disciplinary politics of a subfield. *International Affairs, 83*, 231–252. doi:10.1111/j.1468-2346.2007.00616.x

Rosamond, B. (2015). Performing theory/theorizing performance in emergent supranational governance: The 'live' knowledge archive of European integration and the early European Commission. *Journal of European Integration, 37*(2), 175–191. doi:10.1080/07036337.2014.990134

Varsori, A. (2010). From normative impetus to professionalization: Origins and operation of research networks. In Wolfram Kaiser & Antonio Varsori (Eds.), *European union history. Themes and debates* (pp. 6–25). Basingstoke: Palgrave.

Waever, O. (1998). The sociology of a not so international discipline: American and European developments in international relations. *International Organization, 52*, 687–727. doi:org/10.1162/002081898550725

White, J. P. (2003). Theory guiding practice: The neofunctionalists and the Hallstein EEC Commission. *Journal of European Integration History, 9*, 111–132.

Appendix. Canonical texts.

Key: *CPS: Comparative Political Studies, EJPR: European Journal of Political Research, EUP: European Union Politics, IO: International Organization, JEI: Journal of European integration, JEPP: Journal of European Public Policy, JCMS: Journal of Common Market Studies, JoP: Journal of Politics, WEP: West European Politics.*

Number of citations, Rank in canon, Authors, Year of publication, Title, Journal

1765, 1, P Pierson, 1996, The Path to European Integration, *CPS*

1610, 2, G Marks et al., 1996, European Integration from the 1980s, *JCMS*

1563, 3, FW Scharpf, 1988, The joint-decision trap, Public Administration

1204, 4, A Moravcsik, 2002, In Defence of the 'Democratic Deficit', *JCMS*

1101, 5, F Schimmelfennig, 2001, The community trap, *IO*

965, 6, A Føllesdal, S Hix, 2006, Why there is a democratic deficit, *JCMS*

935, 7, FW Scharpf, 1985, Die Politikverflechtungs-Falle, Politische Vierteljahresschrift

829, 8, F Schimmelfennig, U Sedelmeier, 2004, Governance by conditionality, *JEPP*

794, 9, L Hooghe et al., 2002, Does left/right structure party positions, *CPS*

704, 10, L Hooghe, G Marks, 2009, A postfunctionalist theory, *British Journal of Political Science*

701, 11, JA Caporaso, 1996, The European Union and forms of state, *JCMS*

655, 12, RC Eichenberg, RJ Dalton, 1993, Europeans and the European Community, *IO*

623, 13, J Huysmans, 2000, securitization of migration, *JCMS*

619, 15, EB Haas, 1961, International integration, *IO*

619, 14, M Gabel, 1998, Public support, *JoP*

612, 16, T Risse-Kappen, 1996, Exploring the nature of the beast, *JCMS*

602, 17, E Meehan, 1993, Citizenship and the European community, *Political Quarterly*

586, 18, P Taggart, 1998, A touchstone of dissent, *EJPR*

571, 19, J Peterson, 1995, Decision-making in the European Union, *JEPP*

550, 20, S Borrás, K Jacobsson, 2004, The open method of co-ordination, *JEPP*

544, 21, A Chadwick, C May, 2003, Interaction between States and Citizens, *Governance*

543, 22, C Knill, D Lehmkuhl, 1999, How Europe Matters, European Integration online Papers (EIoP)

539, 23, M Jachtenfuchs, 2001, The governance approach, *JCMS*

529, 25, CM Radaelli, 2000, Policy transfer, *Governance*

529, 24, AS Sweet, W Sandholtz, 1997, supranational governance, *JEPP*

524, 26, S Hix, 1998, The study of the European Union II, *JEPP*

501, 27, P Bouwen, 2002, Corporate lobbying, *JEPP*

501, 28, G Tsebelis, G Garrett, 2000, Legislative politics, *EUP*

498, 29, S Carey, 2002, Undivided Loyalties, *EUP*

494, 30, C Hay, B Rosamond, 2002, discursive construction of economic imperatives, *JEPP*

492, 31, W Wessels, 1997, An ever closer fusion? *JCMS*

487, 32, SJ Bulmer, 1993, The governance of the European Union, *Journal of Public Policy*

483, 33, L Hooghe, G Marks, 2005, Calculation, community and cues, *EUP*

478, 34, LM McLaren, 2002, Public support for the European Union, *JoP*

478, 35, S Lavenex, 2004, EU external governance in 'wider Europe', *JEPP*

474, 36, M Gabel, HD Palmer, 1995, Understanding variation in public support, *EJPR*

472, 37, A Moravcsik, 1995, Liberal intergovernmentalism and integration, *JCMS*

471, 38, J Tallberg, 2002, Paths to compliance, *IO*

454, 39, CJ Anderson, 1998, When in Doubt, Use Proxies, *CPS*

450, 40, M Zürn, 2000, Democratic governance beyond the nation-state, *European Journal of International Relations*

448, 41, L Ray, 1999, Measuring party orientations, *EJPR*

444, 42, S Hix, 1999, Dimensions and alignments, *EJPR*

441, 44, C Knill, D Lehmkuhl, 2002, The national impact, *EJPR*

441, 43, Christiansen, Thomas et al., 1999, The social construction, *JEPP*

429, 45, G Marks, D McAdam, 1996, Social movements, *WEP*

422, 46, G Tsebelis, G Garrett, 2001, The institutional foundations, *IO*

418, 47, FW Scharpf, 1994, Community and autonomy, *JEPP*

417, 48, G Majone, 2001, Two Logics of Delegation, *EUP*

409, 49, P Kopecký, C Mudde, 2002, The two sides of Euroscepticism, *EUP*

405, 51, DJ Puchala, 1971, Of Blind Men, Elephants and International Integration, *JCMS*

405, 50, V Guiraudon, 2000, European integration and migration policy, *JCMS*

400, 52, F Schimmelfennig et al., 2003, Costs, commitment and compliance, *JCMS*

363, 53, M Verloo, 2006, Multiple inequalities, *European Journal of Women's Studies*

343, 54, A Alesina et al., 2005, What does the European Union do? *Public Choice*

341, 55, G Marks et al., 2006, Party Competition, *CPS*

341, 56, L Hooghe, G Marks, 2004, identity or economic rationality, *Political Science and Politics*

335, 57, KE Smith, 2005, The outsiders, *International affairs*

311, 58, Ian Manners, 2008, The normative ethics, *International affairs*

309, 59, J Lewis, 2005, The Janus face of Brussels, *IO*

306, 60, B Eberlein, D Kerwer, 2004, New governance, *JCMS*

220, 61, MA Schreurs, Y Tiberghien, 2007, Multi-level reinforcement, *Global Environmental Politics*

210, 62, Hooghe, Liesbet et al., 2010, Reliability and validity of measuring party positions, *EJPR*

208, 63, RC Eichenberg, RJ Dalton, 2007, Post-Maastricht blues, *Acta Politica*

201, 64, P Mair, 2007, Political Opposition, *Government and Opposition*

163, 65, FW Scharpf, 2009, The asymmetry of European integration, *Socio-Economic Review*

148, 66, A Dür, 2008, Interest groups, *WEP*

137, 67, M Höpner, A Schäfer, 2010, A new phase, *WEP*

135, 68, B Eberlein, AL Newman, 2008, Escaping the international governance dilemma? *Governance*

120, 69, C Boswell, 2008, The political functions of expert knowledge, *JEPP*

118, 70, VA Schmidt, 2013, Democracy and legitimacy, *Political Studies*

113, 71, M Carbone, 2008, Mission impossible, *JEI*

107, 72, T Raunio, 2009, National parliaments, *Journal of Legislative Studies*

100, 73, S Piattoni, 2009, Multi-level governance, *JEI*

European Union or Kingdom of the Antichrist? Protestant apocalyptic narratives and European unity

Brent F. Nelsen and James L. Guth

ABSTRACT
This article examines Protestant Euroscepticism in its purest form by focusing on the apocalyptic narratives of conservative Protestant dispensationalists in the UK, Scandinavia and the Netherlands. It estimates the numbers of end-times Eurosceptics, summarizes their apocalyptic narrative, traces its lineage to the Reformation, and explores its use in debates on European integration. The article argues that analyzing Protestant apocalyptic narratives contributes to understanding some important roots of present-day Euroscepticism in sixteenth-century anti-Catholicism and Protestant distrust of the 'Catholic' continent.

European Protestants are more likely to be Eurosceptic than Catholics. Protestant identities and nation-states were forged in the fires of religious conflict and wars of survival. Protestantism shattered Latin Christendom by rejecting centralized religious and political authority, building new states behind protective borders, and creating new identities as people chosen by God to resist the Antichrist in Rome and the political domination of continental powers under his influence (Appelbaum, 2013; Dingley, 2011).

Efforts to unify Europe after 1945 originated in Catholic countries or those with politically influential Catholic communities, such as West Germany and the Netherlands, whose elites had long thought of Europe as a cultural whole, unified spiritually by a supranational institution, the Roman Catholic Church. Protestants were often mystified by the almost spiritual commitment to European federalism that many continental European leaders demonstrated after the Second World War. Protestant elites predominately favoured deeper cooperation among sovereign states to solve common problems within a larger Western Europe. Many Protestants distrusted the emerging apparently Catholic-dominated continental Western 'core Europe' – a place many Protestants in Britain and Scandinavia considered 'over there' – preferring a more intergovernmental design for cooperation among nation-states with well-defined borders.

When Protestant countries joined the European Community (EC) for pragmatic reasons, they did so purely for the expected economic or political benefits of membership and not for ideational reasons (Kaiser, 1999; Milward, 2002). They brought with them a different vision of unity, echoing the theological and political struggles of the sixteenth and seventeenth centuries, a vision which clashed with the dominant ethos in the informal 'core

Europe' capitals of Luxembourg, Strasbourg and Brussels. Protestant-dominated countries have tended to be less enthusiastic in joining and expanding integrative efforts. At the individual level, moreover, Protestant citizens are less likely than Catholics to support integration or think of themselves as 'European', taking all other factors such as gender, age and ideological orientation into account (Nelsen & Guth, 2014, 2016a). Thus, Protestants have been Europe's reluctant partners.

Protestantism, however, is not monolithic. The majority of European Protestants are only loosely connected to their religious tradition – whether Lutheran, Reformed, Anglican, Anabaptist or non-conformist. Such 'cultural' Protestants have been socialized in a Protestant confessional culture, especially if they live in a majority Protestant country, but may never cross a church threshold as an adult. They also however tend to have more negative attitudes than other Europeans towards the EU and its symbols.

Other Protestants belong to the established theologically liberal denominations such as the Church of England and the Protestant Church in the Netherlands (PKN) and exhibit more religious commitment. These churches have usually joined with other denominations in ecumenical efforts to minimize or eliminate theological and organizational boundaries. This ecumenical spirit has extended to the integration project. Although these Protestants were wary of early efforts at European unity, since the 1989 fall of the Berlin Wall their leaders and active members have demonstrated a more positive view of integration (Nelsen & Guth, 2015).

Our focus here is on a third group: conservative Protestants. They are distinctive in several ways. Many remain in established churches, but others are non-conformists or members of free churches. They believe the Bible is literally true and take traditional Protestant positions on theology, ecclesiology and ethics. They attend religious services frequently and orient their lives around the church. A substantial subset of believers, however, distrusts the European Union (EU) because they see it playing a destructive role in an imminent global apocalypse. This article seeks to estimate the numbers of such end-times Euroskeptics, summarize the apocalyptic narrative, trace its lineage to the Reformation, and explore its use in debates on integration. The article argues that analyzing Protestant apocalyptic narratives contributes to understanding the roots of present-day Euroscepticism in sixteenth-century anti-Catholicism and Protestant distrust of the 'Catholic' continent.

Europeans and the apocalyptic narrative: estimating group size

The number of Europeans consciously adhering to an apocalyptic narrative of the EU – 'apocalyptic evangelicals' according to Ruane and Todd (2009) – is difficult to determine but certainly small. Unlike North America where large numbers can be found in fundamentalist denominations, including independent Baptist groups, most Pentecostals and many African-American and Hispanic churches, the numbers are smaller in Europe. These believers are largely confined to the UK (especially Northern Ireland), the Nordic countries and the Netherlands where they attend small non-conformist or Evangelical chapels (UK), revivalist or free-church congregations (Nordic countries), fundamentalist Reformed churches (the Netherlands and Northern Ireland) or Pentecostal congregations (everywhere). No EU-wide polling of these groups exists, as *Eurobarometer* and *European Values Survey* do not have sufficiently granular religious measures to identify with confidence end-times Christians. Hence, we must rely on cruder measures.

As we shall see below, most of these believers are highly religious and socially conservative. They identify with Christian political parties, which include the Nordic Christian parties, the small religious parties in the Netherlands, and the Democratic Unionist Party (DUP) in Northern Ireland. In the UK most end-times Christians side with the Conservative Party or, more recently, the United Kingdom Independence Party (UKIP). Even in these parties, only some supporters focus on biblical prophecy. Thus, taking denominational and party membership into account, we can safely assume that the number of end-times Christians is fewer than 5% in each of the Protestant European countries. The exception, however, might be Northern Ireland where the DUP is strong and anti-EU rhetoric caustic.

The EU and the end times: the apocalyptic narrative

Religious apocalyptic narratives sound strange to modern ears, but resonate deeply with people steeped in Biblical language and imagery. Since the first-century crucifixion of Jesus of Nazareth, many Christians have anticipated his return – as stated in the *Apostles' Creed* – 'to judge the living and the dead'. Christian traditions have interpreted the utterances of the Jewish prophets, the author of Revelation and Jesus himself in their own particular ways – often arriving at very different views of the end of history. But orthodox Christians of all sorts have agreed that history will conclude dramatically with Jesus Christ returning to set things right.

For some conservative European and North American Protestants, the 'imminent return of Christ' is central to their faith. They believe that the Bible's prophetic works contain specific predictions of Jesus' physical return in the very near future. For them, the Scriptural apocalyptic narrative is unfolding before their eyes – and the EU is on the wrong side of a cosmic struggle, contributing to the world's subjugation by the forces of evil.

'Prophecy writers' tell slightly different stories about the 'end times', but most envision the following scenario (Franklin, 2002). First, political, economic and social changes will make societies, particularly in the West, more immoral and less hospitable to true Christians. At the same time, an apostate church will emerge to serve a rising world government. The EU itself will be a testing ground for that regime and the political vehicle of the Antichrist – the future world dictator. Second, after watching in horror as the world spirals toward the abyss, true Christians will be rescued from the earth, meeting Christ in the air in 'the rapture'. Third, with the righteous now removed from earth, evil will rule: the Antichrist will declare a one-world government with its capital in Jerusalem, the pope will unite the one-world church, headquartered in Rome, and the government will issue a universal currency. Fourth, a seven-year 'tribulation' then ensues, plunging the world into wars, plagues, natural disasters and persecutions. Fifth, after those seven years a great battle will be fought at Armageddon, during which Christ will return and defeat the Antichrist and his armies of darkness, establishing his own capital at Jerusalem and reigning for a thousand years. Finally, at the end of this millennium, the dead are raised and Christ pronounces judgment on all human beings who have ever lived. The blessed rise to heaven; the damned are cast into hell. Then God shapes a new heaven and new earth to be populated by his saved people.

For end-times Christians the EU paves the way for the Antichrist. Supranational institutions constitute a proto-world government; European federalism leads to global union. The euro begets a global currency. Europol presages a global police force. EU battle groups comprise an embryonic global military force, and so on. Thus, the Antichrist uses European integration to create an irresistible world power capable of dominating the planet. Put another way, the EU's process of enlargement will extend to every state in the international system, but the resulting Global Union will be far from democratic. No wonder these conservative European Christians are some of the most vociferous Eurosceptics.

Anti-Catholicism, premillennialism and evangelicalism: the roots of apocalyptic narratives

Protestant apocalyptic narratives are rooted in Reformation theology. The Catholic Church considered itself the single, universal representation of Christ on earth. To be 'Catholic' was to be committed to the visible universal Church headed by the pope in Rome. Baptism into the One True Church meant membership in the chosen people of God. But for the reformers – Martin Luther, John Calvin, Huldrych Zwingli – the corrupt sixteenth-century Roman Church could not possibly be the pure Body of Christ. Instead they suggested that God elects some to salvation while others refuse the gift of grace. The *visible* Church, they offered, was the church gathered for worship, but some standing in the congregation would be hypocrites. According to Protestants, the church of God's elect remained universal and undivided, but it was *invisible,* known only to God. The reformers could, therefore, 'tear asunder' the corrupt *visible* church while maintaining the unity of the pure *invisible* church.

Protestants thus legitimated the fragmentation of the Church by arguing that the true Church was the invisible Body of Christ comprising true believers wherever they were, even outside the Roman Church. In addition, they undermined the authority of the Roman Church by shifting the source of truth away from priests and popes to the Scriptures alone as read by followers of Jesus, clerical and lay alike. If all believers were priests, the Church hierarchy had no special standing and the pope did not speak for God.

Protestant leaders set out to reform the Catholic Church, but the Church refused reform on both theological and political grounds (Greengrass, 2014, pp. 352–386). Thus the conflict very early took on a harsh tone as each side tried to convince Latin Christendom of the rightness of its cause. For the reformers, the pure Christian faith, derived from Scripture and affirmed in the great creeds, had been obscured by man-made practices of an evil hierarchy. Thus Rome, and particularly the pope, became the focus of their increasingly harsh rhetoric. Luther called the papacy 'an institution of the devil' and Pope Paul III the 'Most Hellish Father' (Luther, trans. 1966a, p. 263). Calvin lamented that

> the world today is flooded with so many perverse and impious doctrines, full of so many kinds of superstitions, blinded by so many errors, drowned in such great idolatry – there is none of these evils anywhere that does not flow from the Roman see, or at least draw strength there. (Calvin, trans. 1960, pp. 1143–1144)

The pope was the human face of evil, the embodiment of all that was corrupt, false and destructive in the church, an enemy bent on destroying 'the reviving doctrine of the gospel' (Calvin, trans. 1960, p. 1144).

The early reformers' anti-papalism, couched in the venomous language of vernacular books and pamphlets, drew on their personal experience of the Roman Church as well as fourteenth- and fifteenth-century reform efforts. The sixteenth-century Council of Trent later addressed many of their charges, especially concerning simony and other overt corruptions, but hatred of the pope as the source of spiritual deception and material corruption entered the heart of Protestant confessional culture, even as Protestants lost contact with actual Catholics. Exaggeration and distortion became the currency of Protestant propagandists. Catholic military pressures in Germany, France and the Low Countries and persecution by Catholic rulers on the continent and in Britain also hardened anti-papalism. Protestants feared that the pope's 'greatest ambition was to root out Protestantism with the maximum of bloodshed and cruelty' (Miller, 1973, p. 67). Anti-papalism and a more general opposition to Catholics as an enemy community became less and less distinguishable as the Reformation spiralled into religious warfare. As the Counter-Reformation pushed embattled Protestantism to Europe's northern periphery, deep-seated anti-Catholicism emerged there, vilifying the pope as the feared enemy of the kingdom of God – indeed, the 'Antichrist'.

The identification of Rome as Antichrist illustrates the depth of anti-Catholic sentiment. The Bible itself speaks of the 'Antichrist' in two senses. In one sense, Antichrist is anyone opposed to Christ and his kingdom, whether they are outsiders attacking the church, or church leaders promoting false teachings (II John 7). Both Luther and Calvin applied 'Antichrist' to the popes and their defenders in this first sense. 'Antichrist', however, also appears in the New Testament in a second, apocalyptic sense. Thus Paul wrote of a 'man of lawlessness' who would appear just before Christ's return, a man who 'will oppose and will exalt himself over everything that is called God or worshiped, so that he sets himself up in God's temple, proclaiming himself to be God' (II Thess. 2:1–4). To many interpreters this seemed to be the same figure that Revelation calls the 'beast' who will receive the worship of the whole world (13:8) and John's first epistle calls *the* antichrist who is to appear at the 'last hour' (2:18). Identifying this last great Antichrist, therefore, was key to unlocking the mystery of the Apocalypse and the Day of Judgment.

The reformers were cautious about such prophecy. They usually refrained from calling a particular pope the Antichrist or the beast of the last days, but drew heavily on these apocalyptic concepts to argue that it was from the papacy that the final Antichrist would emerge, perhaps quite soon. The pope's claim to divine authority and the pomp of his court deeply offended the reformers, who charged that the pope had done just what the Scriptures foretold of the Antichrist: elevating himself to a status equal with God (Luther, trans. 1966b, pp. 194–195; Calvin, p. 1145). In sum, the reformers spiced their critique with hints that their struggle with Papal Rome might anticipate the long-awaited Apocalypse – a view that subsequent Protestant generations would periodically elaborate.

One such elaboration had an extraordinary impact on conservative Protestants for nearly 200 years, emerging from British Evangelicalism in the early nineteenth century. The French Revolution encouraged Evangelicals to reconsider biblical prophecy as they sensed that this cataclysmic political event might presage the imminent return of Christ (Sandeen, 1970). In the decades after the Revolution, numerous Evangelicals – usually Anglicans and often prominent scholars – returned to the books of Daniel (Chapters 2, 7–8) and Revelation (Chapter 13) to read the signs of the times and predict the future. They speculated at length on exactly when Christ would return, a question downplayed by earlier exegetes. The Roman Church, following Augustine, viewed itself as the embodiment of Christ's present reign and abjured speculation as to when he might return in the flesh (*amillennialism*). The early reformers did not challenge such thinking, although some argued that the struggle with Rome signalled the imminence of Christ's return. Protestants who did speculate on the Apocalypse usually assumed that at some point the world would be Christianized and an age of peace would settle on humanity for a 1000 years, after which Christ would return to reign (*postmillennialism*). The new nineteenth-century prophecy teachers, however, rediscovered a neglected reading of Revelation 20 that called for Christ's return *before* the millennial peace. This *pre*millennial view envisioned a time of general spiritual, moral and material decline in Christendom, ending in a series of divine judgments and the glorious return of Christ as supreme judge of all, visibly and in the flesh. After the final judgment, his reign of peace would last a 1000 years (Sandeen, 1970).

The British 'premillennial shift' in the early 1800s had profound effects on Evangelical Protestantism. It added a sense of urgency to preaching the gospel that fuelled Evangelicalism's frenetic activism. If judgment was near and Christ's return imminent – literally 'at any moment' – preachers must traverse the globe to warn of impending doom and map the way of escape (Beegle, 1978, p. 160). Heightening the urgency was the emphasis placed by some premillennialist teachers, most notably the Anglo-Irish clergyman John Nelson Darby, on the 'secret rapture' of the saints – a literal flight to heaven of Christians – that would come before the worst of the predicted suffering. Many responded in faith for fear of being 'left behind' and having to endure the horrors of sinful society's death throes. Premillennialism also encouraged Evangelicals to watch closely for signs of social decay, divine judgment and fulfilled prophecy, a propensity that made them profoundly pessimistic about the course of human history, believing that the times had to get worse before Christ's return would make all things right. Finally, premillennialists remained staunch anti-Catholics, but for somewhat different reasons. The pope was still Antichrist, but represented more the decadence of the present age than the reformers' 'Great Evil' (Sandeen, 1970).

Premillennialism, with John Nelson Darby as its most influential promoter, steadily gained ground among Evangelicals in the nineteenth and early twentieth centuries (Bebbington, 1989; Sandeen, 1968). Not only did Darby preach the secret rapture, but he also developed a system of biblical interpretation called 'dispensationalism' that divided God's actions in human history into 'ages' or 'dispensations'. Darby disseminated his doctrine widely through extensive writings and many travels, including seven lengthy tours of North America in the late nineteenth century.

By the First World War dispensationalism dominated Evangelical circles. The horrors of the war silenced the postmillennialists, who could no longer expect the Kingdom of God to appear on earth before Christ's return, leaving premillennial dispensationalism as the obvious alternative for conservative Christians across North America and Europe. The nineteenth century, for instance, saw revivals everywhere in Scandinavia, beginning in Norway, followed by Denmark and Sweden. The revivals, however, were not always appreciated by state officials or established Lutheran clergy. Mass migrations to America encouraged by pressure put on revivalists by the Swedish and Norwegian states soon connected the revivals in Europe and North America. Revivalists across the two continents shared a belief in personal salvation by faith in Jesus Christ, reliance on the Bible for guidance in doctrine and practice, and in many cases, premillennial interpretations of biblical eschatology. Dispensationalism reached Scandinavia by mid-century and took hold of revivalist movements. For instance, in 1871 a dispute over school textbooks in Jarlsberg, Norway led an Evangelical congregation to charge that the State Church's unwillingness to fight the new texts revealed the power of the Antichrist and pointed to Christ's imminent return (Hale, 1980). One of the most influential evangelists of the late nineteenth century, Fredrik Franson, a Swedish immigrant to America, carried the message of the imminent Second Coming back to Scandinavia in several evangelistic forays (Woodward, 1966). Premillennialism did not influence most Scandinavian Lutherans, but for the revivalists, both in and outside the state churches, end-times thinking with its strong dose of anti-Catholicism remained a central article of faith well into the twentieth century.

In the Netherlands, conservative Dutch Reformed Protestants were not as influenced by English dispensationalism as the Nordics, but they were still interested in biblical prophecy. Abraham Kuyper, the nineteenth- and early twentieth-century Dutch journalist, theologian and prime minister, believed with British premillennialists that the French Revolution fitted well with prophetic passages that foresaw an 'anti-Christian power [that] will manifest itself in all its naked brutality only *toward the end* ... ' (Kuyper, 'Maranatha', p. 212). Along with many other Dutch Protestants, Kuyper believed events were hurtling the world toward the end times and return of Christ.

Differences among dispensationalists in the twentieth century fragmented the movement. Many actively looked for signs of fulfilled prophecy in both past and current events, but others thought all prophecy was yet to be fulfilled. Some remained virulently anti-Catholic, others less so. Many believed that cosmic events were unfolding as tyrants rose to power and war loomed. These certainly looked like the 'end times'. Neither the First nor the Second World War ushered in the Apocalypse, but prophecy teachers anxiously searched for signs of fulfilled Scripture, while incessantly squabbling about the details.

Dispensationalism retained a strong hold on conservative Evangelicals after 1945. Surprisingly, however, just as secularization loomed in North America and Europe, dispensationalism burst into American popular culture and soon made its way across the Atlantic (Boyer, 1992; Sutton, 2014). In 1970 Hal Lindsey published *The Late Great Planet Earth*, which rocketed to the top of bestseller lists, eventually selling more than 35 million copies in over 50 languages (ABC News, 6 June 2006). The book offered a detailed history of the future that put European integration in the centre of the apocalyptic narrative. In the 1977 edition, for instance, Lindsey stated: 'We believe that the Common Market and the trend toward unification of Europe may well be the beginning of the ten-nation confederacy predicted by Daniel and the Book of Revelation' (Lindsey, 1994a, p. 76). This confederacy, he argued, was a revived Roman Empire perfectly suited for the coming Antichrist.

The United States will not hold its present position of leadership in the western world; financially, the future leader will be Western Europe (...). As the United States loses power, Western Europe will be forced to unite and become the standard-bearer of the western world. Look for the emergence of a 'United States of Europe' composed of ten inner member nations. The Common Market is laying the groundwork for this political confederacy which will become the mightiest coalition on earth. It will stop the Communist take-over of the world and will for a short while control both Russia and Red China through the personal genius of the

Antichrist who will become the ruler of the European confederacy. Look for the papacy to become even more involved in world politics, especially in proposals for bringing world peace and world-wide economic prosperity. (Lindsey, 1994b, p. 150)

Lindsey underlined this same point in later books: *There's a New World Coming* (1973), *Planet Earth – 2000 A.D.: Will Mankind Survive?* (1994), *The Final Battle* (1995), *Apocalypse Code* (1997), and *Planet Earth: The Final Chapter* (1998). All identify the EU as the Antichrist's vehicle to achieve global control. Indeed, Lindsey's view quickly became the 'common sense' of the subject among American dispensationalists, and among their international counterparts. According to Rapture Ready, a popular Internet site, for instance, 'The Bible predicts that someday a world leader will emerge from a revived Roman Empire. The EU is clearly the fulfilment of this prophetic event' (Rapture Ready, 2015; see also Rema Marketing, 2015). Popular American teachings on the EU have combined with traditional anti-Catholicism to undergird the anti-EU stance of conservative Christians in Protestant areas of Europe.

The EU and the last days in the European North: apocalyptic narratives in contemporary Europe

Protestants' instinctive anti-Catholicism, sense of national chosen-ness, and distrust of transnational authority made them suspicious of the idea of a single European polity. Postwar leaders of predominantly Protestant countries found Jean Monnet's vision of a politically and economically united Europe unattractive, even threatening. They favoured deep, pragmatic cooperation with their European partners to solve common problems, but the semi-religious belief in a federal Europe held by many Continental leaders struck them as idealistic, mystical and frightening. Thus Protestant-majority countries worked to preserve national vetoes in postwar organizations such as the Council of Europe. They were reluctant to cede sovereignty to supranational institutions as in the European Coal and Steel Community (ECSC), formed in 1951–1952. The Dutch government joined the negotiations leading up to the ECSC late and then insisted on the creation of a Council of Ministers not originally foreseen in the Schuman Plan drafted by Monnet and his co-workers. When other Protestant countries found it necessary to join the EC in 1973 and 1995, they did so reluctantly, to gain economic or political benefits of membership, while insisting on restraining federalist efforts.

British distrust of the 'Continent' (a sometimes pejorative term for the land across the Channel) spanned the political spectrum, taking several different forms (Kaiser, 1999; Ludlow, 2002). Religious prejudice was one. Both the socialist left and the traditional right at times emitted a strong scent of historic British anti-Catholicism (Wilkes, 1997, p. 15). Talk in Europe of recreating Charlemagne's empire, the open Catholic piety of major European leaders, and the perceived centrality of the Church to the European project set many Britons on edge. For the postwar British, 'the Catholic nature of "Europe" was a generous source of prejudice against it. (…) Britain in 1950 was still an emphatically Protestant country, in which Catholicism was something foreign and therefore suspect. (…) Anti-Catholic prejudice was instinctive (…)' (Young, 1998, p. 50).

The Labour party's left wing, which opposed integration, was deeply suspicious of a Europe dominated by Christian Democrats resistant to international planning for full employment (Bullock, 1983; Mullen, 2007). They saw the Christian Democrats, who drew heavily on the votes of practicing Catholics, as the political arm of the Roman Church. Denis Healey, for instance, was deeply troubled by the *Mandement* (letter of admonition) issued by Dutch bishops in 1954 that listed penalties, including excommunication, for those participating in socialist political activities (Young, 1998). Christian socialists were also suspicious of the '"Roman" flavour of European integration' and often expressed their distrust in anti-Catholic terms (Coupland, 2004). More moderate Labourites were less likely to write off Europe as hopelessly clerical, but were acutely aware of pressure from the left.

Similarly, more theologically extreme perspectives could be found on the evangelical and nationalist right. The National Union of Protestants, for instance, warned, 'Romanism is trying to knock out, not only Protestantism, but any suspected [rival] to world domination' (Coupland, 2004, p. 390). Not all anti-Catholic rhetoric was quite so direct, but 'suspicion of Catholicism remained, and it continued to be seen as a definite threat – "the Roman menace"' (2004, p. 390). Many dispensationalist British Protestants had come to see some good in the Catholic Church, but they still found much of its ecclesiology, doctrine, theology and worship repellant. They also objected to its reactionary politics, corruption and worldly intrigue, which made it a 'terrible menace to freedom and even in many places to true religion itself' (Coupland, 2004, p. 391).

For some Protestants the distrust precluded even battles against a common foe. Protestants and Catholics, for instance, could agree that communism must be resisted, but some evangelicals rejected co-belligerency with Catholics as a cure worse than the disease. As one writer in *The English Churchman and St. James Chronicle* put it, 'The choice is not between Communism and Vaticanism, both are from a common source and are characterized by the same spirit and practices'. This anti-Catholic view was applied effortlessly to the Common Market when the *English Churchman* warned that, 'Rome is endeavouring to create a Rome-sponsored bloc of nations', and later opined, 'By all means co-operate, but not amalgamate. For England to surrender her sovereign power to a super-state would be yet another step towards our downfall' (Coupland, 2004, p. 390). Mainstream British Protestantism remained suspicious of Catholicism and by extension an EC popularly associated with the Vatican. Anti-Catholicism did begin to mellow in British mainstream Protestantism during the 1960s, however, making it less central to the debate over 1973 EC accession and the 1975 referendum about continued membership.

That mellowing, however, did not extend to Northern Ireland, where bitter confessional divisions, dating from the Reformation, spilled over into violence in 1966 (Dingley, 2009, 2013). Hardline Ulster Protestants led by Reverend Ian Paisley still brought seventeenth-century Protestant passion to bear on the question of membership. Paisley's conservative Presbyterianism drew its premillennialism from nineteenth-century British Evangelicals, but shared this theological ancestry with American fundamentalists, with whom he had strong ties (Bruce, 1986). Paisley's premillennialism, unlike that of most Anglo-American dispensationalists, did not include a belief in the rapture, and focused almost exclusively on the papal Antichrist and the Roman church. For Paisley's movement the Roman Catholic Church was the only institution with 'the power, influence, and reach to be the sort of comprehensive anti-Christian force suggested in prophecy', the evil 'Babylon' of Scripture (Bruce, 1986).

Paisley, for whom the world had entered 'the final unfolding of the great drama of world empires of history', saw the Common Market as the 'final manifestation' of the evil Roman Empire, the kingdom of the Antichrist, and Irish and Northern Irish Catholics as its servants. As Paisley interpreted the books of Daniel and Revelation, when history drew to a close there would be

> ten kingdoms in Europe and at the head of those kingdoms there will be the beast and in association with the beast there will be a church, and that church will be the Church of Rome in her final manifestation (Paisley, 1975).

The Common Market, established by the Treaty of *Rome*, where it was signed, was dominated and controlled by the Roman Catholic Church, which Revelation 17 depicts as a woman representing the city of Rome ('Mystery, Babylon the Great, the Mother of Harlots'). Paisley was convinced that the EC was the seat of evil and the last thing he wanted was to see the UK aid and abet the forces of darkness (Paisley, 'Common Market', 1975; see also Coakley, 2009). Joining 'Europe' would also weaken Protestantism and undermine the liberty of Protestant peoples. Paisley lamented that Britain had joined 'the greatest Catholic super State the world has ever known'. Not surprisingly, Paisley urged his followers to vote 'no' to British accession and later, continued EC membership: 'I trust that every man and woman (...) across our Province will take their stand against what is nothing less than the kingdom of the Anti-christ' (Paisley, 'Common Market', 1975).

Paisley's anti-EU vitriol continued into the twenty-first century. As a member of the European Parliament from 1979 to 2004 he had ample opportunity to rail against the EU. In 1988 he famously interrupted a speech to Parliament by Pope John Paul II by repeatedly shouting, 'I renounce you as the Antichrist!' ('Ulster Protestant Interrupts Pope, Yelling "Antichrist!"' *The New York Times*, 12 October 1988). In June 2000, Paisley, who eventually served as First Minister of Northern Ireland (2007–2008), posted on the European Institute of Protestant Studies website a summary of his perspective:

> Knowing the Bible should make us realise that it is pure folly to want to join (via ecumenism) this final apostasy of Babylon which is Biblically and historically wrong. Rome is unchanging, unrepentant and arrogant without change. People are striving for unity with this beast as though it was something required as a necessity in this life and for the next. Such folly when our gracious Lord brought us out of such bondage in the Sixteenth century. (...) What folly to return. (Paisley, 2000)

Paisley's hardline British Protestantism saw a Vatican conspiracy to create a 'Roman Catholic European Superstate' as a first step to world domination. The Vatican's fingerprints, in this view, were all over the EU. In his perspective, the deep blue and 12 stars of the EU flag were symbols of the Madonna. The repeated references to Charlemagne presaged re-creation of a Catholic Carolingian Empire. The depiction of Europa riding on a bull (Zeus) on a postage stamp represented the whore of the Book of Revelation. The creation of an EU Common Foreign and Security Policy anticipated a military take-over by the Vatican. The European Parliament building in Strasbourg eerily re-created Bruegel's *The Tower of Babel* (Noble, 1999; Gillis, 2000). For such Northern Irish Protestants, however, the central issue was identity. As God's chosen people they had to resist the coming Antichrist. To join Catholics in building Europe would mean the end of their sacred mission and the loss of their identity as a separate people.

Northern Irish Protestants were not the only UK Protestants to resist the EU on biblical grounds. British author Alan Franklin, for instance, called the EU the 'final world empire' and, like Lindsey, saw the EU birthing the Antichrist:

> As a Christian versed in prophecy I cannot help but see in the emerging European superstate the foundations of a one-world government with a one-world dictator at its head – the man whose biblical names include the Beast, the Man of Sin, and Antichrist. (Franklin, *EU*, 2002)

Likewise, Adrian Hilton, in his very popular 1997 book, *The Principality and the Power: Britain and the Emerging Holy European Empire,* critiqued the EU as a papal-dominated, re-created Holy Roman Empire: 'If European federalism triumphs, the EC will indeed be an empire. It will lack an emperor: but it will have the Pope' (Hilton, 1997, p. 18). Thus Britain, the home of dispensational theology and vitriolic anti-papalism, still contains citizens who combine these two cultural currents into a sincere hatred of the EU and Britain's membership.

The presence of apocalyptic Eurosceptics would be an interesting sideshow were it not for the fact that prominent British end-times activists have been gravitating toward the UKIP, which gained 12.6% of the vote (although only one seat) in the 2015 national elections. Alan Franklin, for instance, declared on his 4 May 2009 blog post, 'I vote UKIP, which has the right idea of getting us out of the superstate'. And before the 2014 European Parliament elections he observed, 'people are casting around for alternatives. UKIP is their choice: a patriotic but non-racist party, one that stands for the nation state, against the sinister anti-democratic EU dictatorship' (Franklin, 'Electoral Earthquake', 2014). In addition, recent survey results indicate that UKIP supporters believe that the Apocalypse will occur in their lifetimes in far greater proportions than among backers of other parties. According to YouGov (2015), 31% of UKIP voters believe the end of the world – 'an apocalyptic disaster' in the words of the polling question – is around the corner compared to an average of 23% in Britain. Not all UKIP supporters, of course, are Protestant dispensationalists, but some do put their pessimism in religious terms. Former Tory turned UKIP councilor David Silvester, for instance, claimed that the winter 2014 storms in Britain were caused by the Government's legalization of same-sex marriage: 'The scriptures make it abundantly clear that a Christian nation that abandons its faith and acts contrary to the Gospel (…) will be beset by natural disasters such as storms, disease, pestilence and war' (Best, 2014). UKIP first defended Silvester's right to express his religious beliefs but later suspended his party membership after taking a beating in the press. UKIP leaders acknowledge the presence of 'fundamentalists' but seek to distance the party from Apocalyptic perspectives (Personal Communication with a UKIP leader, 9 November 2015). That has not stopped prophecy teachers, however, from glorifying UKIP leader Nigel Farage as a politician willing to stand up to 'the United States of Europe' (The EU Anti-Christ, 2015).

Most recently, the 'Brexit' referendum reminds us of the continuing importance of historic Protestant beliefs in secular Europe. In June 2016 a solid majority of Protestants voted to 'leave' the EU, while Catholics, secular people and ethnoreligious minorities voted to remain. This Protestant tendency certainly represents in part a continuation of the ancient religious identification with British nationalism, although most Anglican leaders cautiously backed the 'remain' camp. As we would expect, however, the staunchest antipathy to the EU was shown by non-conformist Protestants (often captured by the 'other Christian' rubric in opinion polls) (Nelsen & Guth, 2016b). More detailed religious surveys confirm this suspicion, without actually probing the theological basis for Euroskeptic votes (Fox, 2016). Nevertheless, the press observed several evangelical congregations where clergy and lay leaders invoked 'end times' rationales for supporting 'Brexit'

(Farley, 2016). Indeed, the prevalence of such rhetoric was lamented by mainstream Protestant leaders, frustrated in knowing how to respond (Bell, 2016). Given the narrow margin in the referendum, Protestant apocalyptic perspectives may have played a critical role in the result.

Turning to postwar Scandinavia, the continental Christian Democrats' Catholicism stirred the embers of Nordic anti-papalism and religious stereotypes. It also influenced the mostly secular or nominally religious Social Democrats. The Christian Democrats' tendency to ground political thinking in Christian concepts and religious rhetoric struck Social Democrats as archaic and coercive. The Nordic Social Democrats, like the left wing of the British Labour party, saw continental Europe as a bastion of capitalism and Catholic traditionalism. In Sweden, Social Democrats, indeed most Swedes, could summarize the threat of Europe using four C's (or K's in Swedish): 'capitalism, Catholicism, conservatism and colonialism' (Trägårdh , 'Welfare State Nationalism', 1999). Socialists of the north found the EEC insufficiently progressive. According to Judt (2005), Swedish Prime Minister Tage Erlander (1948–1968), 'ascribed his own ambivalence about joining [the EEC] to the overwhelming Catholic majority in the new Community' (p. 158). Niels Matthiasen, the secretary of the Danish Social Democrats in the late 1950s, articulated the party line: 'As a member of the Common Market we would become the seventh country in a union dominated by the Catholic church and Right-Wing movements' (Laursen & Olesen, 2000, p. 229). Even Gunnar Myrdal described the EC members as states 'with a more primitive form of social organization than ours', arguing that, 'it is above all the securely Protestant countries that have progressed economically and in all other ways' (Trägårdh, 'Sweden', 2002, p. 154). Another leading Social Democrat, Enn Kokk, put it even more starkly. His description of a Europe ruled by capitalism and papism ended with a dismal assessment: 'Today's Franco-German combination, an alliance between General de Gaulle and Dr. Adenauer at the forefront of a Catholic, conservative and capitalist western Europe is a disquieting creation (…). a politically dead landscape' (Trägårdh, 'Sweden', 2002, p. 156).

The animosity that Social Democrats felt for continental Christian Democrats sat atop an iceberg of popular cultural distrust. Rural populations in all the Nordic countries feared the cultural changes that integration might bring. Religiously conservative Scandinavians, heirs of the nineteenth-century revivals, were quite willing to express those concerns. Free-Church partisans in the Swedish Riksdag parliament in 1951 'saw the threat of Catholic monasteries as being almost as dangerous as secularization and de-Christianization'. For them, 'Europe' was 'synonymous with Catholicism' (Stråth, 2002, p. 137). During the 1962 Norwegian Storting parliament debate over applying for Common Market membership, religious conservatives from the Liberal and Christian People's parties, with some help from Labour, rejected membership 'on the basis that the Protestant religion in Norway would be weakened', that EEC countries would exert a 'conservative influence, as a result of the strong position of the Catholic church in these countries', and that in general, 'full membership would constitute a threat to Norwegian culture' (Heradstveit, 1972, p. 189). Such arguments disappeared from the Storting in the 1970s, but not from campaigns. During the 1972 membership referendum 'a number of people were worried about the EC closing down the Protestant Norwegian state church, and also feared (…) a "Catholic invasion"' (Neumann, 2002, p. 114). More generally, foes of Community membership claimed that 'The country would be invaded by foreign workers, catholic ideas, continental drinking habits, and foreigners buying up their mountain huts, lakes and forests' (Allen, 1979, 107). The state alcohol monopoly was possibly in danger, which greatly bothered teetotalers, among others.

Well into the 2000s conservative Christians in Norway denounced the EC as the Vatican-dominated kingdom of the Antichrist (Nelsen, 1993). Norwegian prophecy teachers Bente and Abel Struksnæs, for example, predicted on their website a Vatican take-over of the EU in a 'quest for European unity and world dominion' (Struksnæs & Struksnæs, 2014). One Norwegian bishop grew so concerned by such rhetoric in the early 1990s that he warned 'believers against indulging too much in demonising the EEC' (Willaime, 1994, p. 97). Other Nordic states saw similar expressions. During the Maastricht Treaty debate in Denmark, for instance, conservative Christians debated in *Idé Politik* whether or not the EC was the resurrected Roman Empire of biblical prophecy (Mathieu, 1999).

Dispensationalism and prophecy teaching have influenced conservative Dutch and German Protestants less than their counterparts elsewhere. While such thinking can be found in the Netherlands (Baptistengemeente Immanuël te Hoogeveen, 2015; Wereld van Morgen, 2016) and Germany (Gassmann, 2015) it has no discernable impact on Dutch or Germany political discussion, even within the most conservative Christian parties (Staatkundig Gereformeerde Partij, 2015). While the small Reformed parties in the Netherlands, for instance, rejected the Constitutional Treaty in the 2005 referendum (as Wolf Schünemann discusses in his article in this special issue) and remain skeptical of European integration on Biblical grounds (Van Campen, 2010), they have not adopted the harsh, apocalyptic rhetoric of the theologically similar DUP in Northern Ireland (Vollaard, 2006). Fewer ties to American dispensationalists and a more tolerant pluralistic Dutch context most likely account for the difference.

Conclusion

End-times narratives do not fit well with modernity. They are conspiratorial, non-empirical, intolerant and often authoritarian. In other words, they are the antithesis of rational, scientific, tolerant and democratic contemporary Europe. But they are not alien to Europe. They are the leftover bits of the Reformation that have survived into the current liberal age and serve as windows to the Protestant past, helping us to understand the contemporary Euroscepticism of many Protestants, whether or not they are conscious of its sources.

Beneath the apocalyptic overlay of these narratives rests a primitive Protestantism and a rhetorical style that Martin Luther might recognize. These conservative Protestants display in their passionate oratory anti-Catholicism untempered by secularism and ecumenism. Furthermore, they express a deep belief in their personal divine chosen-ness and in the chosen-ness of their nations. In their estimation they and their fellow citizens are right with God. Above all they demonstrate a distrust of all earthly centralized power, believing that only God, through a returned Jesus Christ, can institute a government of justice and peace. This is an ideology that naturally opposes attempts to unify Europe and helps explain Protestant Euroscepticism in its purest form.

Few in Europe believe dispensational apocalyptic EU narratives. However, many Eurosceptics with nominal Protestant backgrounds espouse similar views, if somewhat milder and certainly more secularized. Many of these citizens in culturally Protestant countries take a skeptical view of the Catholic Church, which they perceive as reactionary, undemocratic, corrupt and restrictive of personal liberties, especially regarding moral issues such as abortion and same-sex marriage. This view, of course, is shared by many Europeans in culturally Catholic countries too, but in Protestant Europe this anti-Catholicism is instinctual and takes a rather different political form than what is typically found in Catholic countries. For some cultural Protestants it is easy to project their anti-Catholic sentiments onto that other continental supranational organization that seeks to unify Europe. In their view an overbearing EU is intent on destroying national differences and the liberties of European nations just as the Roman Church is intent on limiting the freedoms of individuals. Such a Eurosceptical narrative, stripped of its religious language, is certainly more acceptable in modern Europe. Nevertheless, like the stories told by apocalyptic Eurosceptics, secular Protestant Euroscepticism reflects a similar deep distrust of unity efforts and supranational centralization. That should not be surprising because they share common roots.

Acknowledgements

The authors would like to thank Joseph Biedlingmeier, John Bleed and Christopher Schoen for their research assistance.

References

Allen, H. (1979). *Norway and Europe in the 1970s.* Oslo: Universitetsforlaget.

Appelbaum, D. M. (2013). Biblical nationalism and the sixteenth-century states. *National Identities, 15* (4), 317–332.

Baptistengemeente Immanuël te Hoogeveen. (2015). *Antichrist.* Retrieved from http://bgimmanuel. nl/encyclopedia-of-the-bible/encyclopedia-of-the-bible/english-index-on-a/antichrist/

Bebbington, D. (1989). *Evangelicalism in modern Britain: A history from the 1730s to the 1980s.* Grand Rapids, MI: Baker Book House.

Beegle, D. M. (1978). *Prophecy and prediction.* Ann Arbor, MI: Pryor Pettegill, 160.

Bell, I. (2016) *Why I Will Be Voting for the UK to Remain Part of the European Union.* We Do God: Revelation TV. Retrieved from http://www.revelationtv.com/rnews/entry/why-i-will-be-voting-for-the-uk-to-remain-part-of-the-european-union

Best, J. (2014, January 18). *UKIP councilor claims gay marriage laws are to blame for recent storms and floods.* Mirror. Retrieved from http://www.mirror.co.uk/news/uk-news/ukip-councillor-david-silvester-claims-3035201

Boyer, P. (1992). *When time shall be no more: Prophecy belief in modern American culture.* Cambridge, MA: The Belknap Press.

Bruce, S. (1986). *God save ulster! The religion and politics of paisleyism.* Oxford: Oxford University Press.

Bullock, A. (1983). *Ernest bevin: Foreign secretary, 1945–1951.* New York, NY: W. W. Norton.

Calvin, J. (1960). *Calvin: Institutes of the Christian Religion,* Vol. 2, (F. L. Battles, Trans.). McNeill, J. T. (Ed.). The Library of Christian Classics, Vol. 21. Louisville: Westminster John Knox Press.

Coakley, J. (2009). A political profile of protestant minorities in Europe. *National Identities, 11*(1), 9–30.

Coupland, P. M. (2004, July). Western union, 'spiritual union', and European integration, 1948–1951. *Journal of British Studies, 43*, 366–394.

Dingley, J. (2009). Religion, truth, national identity and social meaning: The example of Northern Ireland. *National Identities, 11*(4), 367–383.

Dingley, J. (2011). Sacred communities: Religion and national identities. *National Identities, 11*(4), 389–402.

Dingley, J. (2013). Religion, protestants and national identity: A response to the March 2009 issue. *National Identities, 15*(2), 101–124.

The EU Anti-Christ. (2015). *The Ron Paul of Europe stands up to the United States of Europe!* Retrieved from http://www.theeuantichrist.com

Farley, H. (2016). *Christians and Brexit: Did God command the UK to leave the EU?* Retrieved from http://www.christiantoday.com/article/christians.and.brexit.did.god.command.the.uk.to.leave.the.eu/89427.htm

Fox, S. (2016). *Religion and the EU referendum: After the poll.* Retrieved from: http://blogs.cardiff.ac.uk/wiserd/2016/07/11/religion-and-the-eu-referendum-after-the-poll/

Franklin, P. (2002). The great commission. In A. Franklin (Ed.), *EU: The final world empire* (pp. 205–221). Oklahoma City, OK: Hearthstone

Franklin, A. (2014, May 21). *Expect an electoral earthquake in the United Kingdom tomorrow*, Thursday [Blog post]. Retrieved from http://nevrapture.blogspot.com/2014/05/the-always-well-informed-alan-franklin.html

Gassmann, L. (2015). *Nähert sich das Reich des Antichristen? (Dr. theol. Lothar Gassmann)/Kommentar.* Retrieved from http://neue-weltordnung.info/nahert-sich-das-reich-des-antichristen-dr-theol-lothar-gassmann-kommentar/

Gillis, C. (2000, October 21). *The Popes at war and the fall of the Papal States.* Retrieved from http://www.ianpaisley.org/article.asp?ArtKey=papalstates

Greengrass, M. (2014). *Christendom destroyed: Europe 1517–1648.* New York, NY: Viking.

Hale, F. (1980). Anticlericalism and Norwegian society before the breakthrough of modernity. *Scandinavian Studies, 52*(3), 245–263.

Heradstveit, D. (1972). The Norwegian EEC debate. In N. Örvik (Ed.), *Fears and expectations: Norwegian attitudes toward European integration* (pp. 177–206). Oslo: Universitetsforlaget.

Hilton, A. (1997). *The principality and power of Europe: Britain and the emerging holy European empire.* Herts: Dorchester House.

Judt, T. (2005). *Postwar: A history of Europe since 1945.* New York, NY: Penguin Press.

Kaiser, W. (1999). *Using Europe, abusing the Europeans. Britain and European integration 1945-1963.* Basingstoke: Palgrave.

Laursen, J. N., & Olesen, T. B. (2000). A nordic alternative to Europe? The interdependence of Denmark's Nordic and European policies. In H. Branner & M. Kelstrup (Ed.), *Denmark's policy towards Europe after 1945: History, theory and options* (pp. 223–259). Odense: Odense University Press.

Lindsey, H. (1973). *There's a new world coming: A prophetic Odyssey.* Santa Ana, CA: Vision House.

Lindsey, H. (1994a). *The greatest works of Hal lindsey: The late great planet earth; satan is alive and well on planet earth.* New York, NY: Inspirational Press.

Lindsey, H. (1994b). *Planet earth – 2000 A.D.: Will mankind survive?* Palos Verdes, CA: Western Front.

Lindsey, H. (1995). *The final battle.* Palos Verdes, CA: Western Front.

Lindsey, H. (1997). *Apocalypse code.* Palos Verdes, CA: Western Front.

Lindsey, H. (1998). *Planet earth: The final chapter.* Beverly Hills, CA: Western Front.

Ludlow, P. (2002). Us or them? The meaning of Europe in British political discourse. In M. af Malmborg & B. Stråth (Ed.), *The meaning of Europe: Variety and contention within and among nations* (pp. 101–124). Oxford: Berg.

Luther, M. (1966a). Against the roman papacy an institution of the devil (E. W. Gritsch, Trans.). In E. W. Gritsch (Ed.), *Luther's works* (Vol. 41, pp. 257–376). Philadelphia, PA: Fortress Press.

Luther, M. (1966b). To the Christian nobility of the German nation concerning the reform of the Christian estate (Jacobs, C. M. Trans.). In J. James Atkinson (Ed.), *Luther's works* (Vol. 44, pp. 115–217). Philadelphia, PA: Fortress Press.

Mathieu, C. (1999). *The moral life of the party: Moral argumentation and the creation of meaning in the Europe policy debates of the christian and left-socialist parties in Denmark and Sweden 1990–1996*. Lund: Dept. of Sociology, Lund University.

Miller, J. (1973). *Popery and politics in England, 1660–1688*. Cambridge: Cambridge University Press.

Milward, A. S. (2002). *The rise and fall of a national strategy: The UK and The European community: Volume 1*. London: Frank Cass.

Mullen, A. (2007). *The British left's 'great debate' on Europe*. New York, NY: Continuum.

Nelsen, B. F. (1993). The European community debate in Norway: The periphery revolts, again. In B. F. Nelsen (Ed.), *Norway and the European community: The political economy of integration* (pp. 41–62). Westport, CT: Praeger.

Nelsen, B. F., & Guth, J. L. (2014, December 8–10). *Religion in the creation of European and national identities: An empirical test of identity construction*. Oxford Symposium on Religious Studies at the University Church of St. Mary, Oxford, England.

Nelsen, B. F., & Guth, J. L. (2015). *Religion and the struggle for European Union: Confessional culture and the limits of integration*. Washington, DC: Georgetown University Press.

Nelsen, B. F., & Guth, J. L. (2016a). Religion and the creation of European identity: The message of the flags. *Review of Faith & International Affairs, 14*(1), 80–88.

Nelsen, B. F., & Guth J. L. (2016b, September 13). *Prelude to Brexit: Euroscepticism in Great Britain, 2014*. Presented at the 9th International Conference on Social Science Methodology, University of Leicester.

Neumann, J. B. (2002). This little piggy stayed at home: Why Norway is not a member of the EU. In L. Hansen & O. Wæver (Ed.), *European integration and national identity: The challenge of the Nordic States* (pp. 88–129). London: Routledge.

Noble, A. (1999, April 30). *The conspiracy behind the European Union: What every Christian should know*. A lecture delivered at the annual Autumn Conference of the United Protestant Council in London on Saturday, November 7, 1998. Retrieved from European Institute of Protestant Studies, http://www.ianpaisley.org/article.asp?ArtKey=conspiracy

Paisley, I. (1975, June). The Common Market, the Kingdom of the Anti-christ, Why It Must Be Resisted. *The Revivalist*. Retrieved from http://www.ianpaisley.org/revivalist/1975/Rev75jun.htm

Paisley, I. R. K. (2000, December 6). *May God Save Us From Coming Under This Dictatorship Once Again*. Retrieved from European Institute of Protestant Studies, http://www.ianpaisley.org/article.asp?ArtKey=soul

Rapture Ready. (2015). *Frequently Asked Questions*. Retrieved from https://www.raptureready.com/faq/faq179.html

Rema Marketing. (2015). *The EU Antichrist*. Retrieved from http://www.theeuantichrist.com

Ruane, J., & Todd, J. (2009). Protestant minorities in European states and nations. *National Identities, 11*(1), 1–8.

Sandeen, E. R. (1968). *The origins of fundamentalism: Toward a historical interpretation*. Philadelphia, PA: Fortress Press.

Sandeen, E. R. (1970). *The roots of fundamentalism: British and American millenarianism*. Chicago, IL: University of Chicago Press.

Staatkundig Gereformeerde Partij. (2015). *Standpunten*. Retrieved from https://www.sgp.nl/Standpunten/Standpunten/Standpunten_ABC?letter=E&standid=77

Stråth, B. (2002). The Swedish demarcation from Europe. In M. af Malmborg & B. Stråth (Ed.), *The meaning of Europe: Variety and contention within and among nations* (pp. 148–225). Oxford: Berg.

Struksnæs, B., & Struksnæs, A. (2014). *Watch Out for a Catholic European Union!* Retrieved from Christian Information Service, http://www.endtime.net/engelsk/KEU.htm

Sutton, M. A. (2014). *American apocalypse: A history of modern evangelicalism*. Cambridge, MA: The Belknap Press.

Trägårdh, L. (1999). Welfare state nationalism: Sweden and the specter of the European Union. *Scandinavian Review, 87*(1), 18–23.

Trägårdh, L. (2002). Sweden and the EU: Welfare state nationalism and the spectre of 'Europe'. In L. Hansen & O. Wæver (Eds.) *European integration and national identity: The challenge of the Nordic States* (pp. 130–181). London: Routledge.

Van Campen, M. M. (2010). *Oorlog tegen Israël*. Retreived from http://www.refoweb.nl/vragenrubriek/16329/oorlog-tegen-israel/

Vollaard, H. (2006). Protestantism and Euro-scepticism in the Netherlands. *Perspectives on European Politics & Society*, *7*(3), 276–297.

Wereld van Morgen. (2016). Retreived from http://www.wereldvanmorgen.nl

Wilkes, G. (1997). The first failure to steer Britain into the European communities: An introduction. In G. Wilkes (Ed.), *Britain's failure to enter the European community, 1961-63: The enlargement negotiations and crises in European, Atlantic and commonwealth relations* (pp. 1–32). London: Frank Cass.

Willaime, J.-P. (1994). Protestant approaches to European unification. In J. Fulton & P. Gee (Eds.), *Religion in contemporary Europe* (pp. 96–103). Lewiston, NY: Edwin Mellon Press.

Woodward, D. B. (1966). *Aflame for God: Biography of Fredrik Franson*. Chicago, IL: Moody Press.

YouGov, (2015, March 10). *UKIP voters most likely to think the apocalypse is coming*. Retrieved from https://yougov.co.uk/news/2015/03/10/apocalypse/

Young, H. (1998). *This blessed plot: Britain and Europe from Churchill to blair*. Woodstock, NY: Overlook Press.

Post-communist invocation of Europe: memorial museums' narratives and the Europeanization of memory

Ljiljana Radonić 🆔

ABSTRACT
How do post-communist memorial museums in East-Central Europe tell stories about double occupation (by Nazi Germany and the Soviet Union), collaboration, the Holocaust and victim narratives, and how have these narratives been influenced by accession to the European Union? How do the museums reference trends set by Holocaust memorial museums? The article shows that one group of museums invokes Europe and the Europeanization of the Holocaust. Other museums seek to contain certain aspects of the memory of Nazism so that it cannot compete with stories of Soviet crimes. Both incorporate elements from Holocaust memorial museums, indicating how universalized Holocaust remembrance is.

This article examines how state-owned or state-funded post-communist memorial museums dealing with the Second World War and/or the communist period address Europe and the Europeanization of memory. The first section introduces the actors who produce the museum narratives. The second section discusses how Europe is depicted in the museums and to what extent international musealization trends are reflected in the narratives and aesthetics of the museums. This article is based on analysis of the permanent exhibitions, guidebooks, audio guides and websites of six post-communist memorial museums from the Baltics to former Yugoslavia. It also draws on publications by museum officials and (with the help of native speaker assistants where necessary) the reporting of two daily newspapers from each country from the time of major debates or events in the respective museum's recent history.

Representations of cultural memory, particularly of the traumatic experiences of the twentieth century, became battlefields in the process of reconstructing and renegotiating the past in both post-communist and Western European countries after 1989. Those 'wars of memory' (Welzer, 2007) about interpretative authority between different social and political groups have included attempts to re-narrate the past as shared European history. Three international remembrance trends are crucial for understanding such Europeanization of remembrance: the universalization of the Holocaust, the Europeanization of the Holocaust and divided memory in Eastern and Western Europe.

The memory boom in the West after the Cold War emphasized the Holocaust as a 'negative icon' (Diner, 2007, p. 7) of the twentieth century. This 'universalization of the

Holocaust' (Eckel & Moisel, 2008) implies that the Holocaust has become a universal imperative for the respect of human rights in general and a 'container' (Levy & Sznaider, 2005, p. 195) for the memory of different victims and victim groups. This development brought about a change in the focus of remembrance: the figure of the hero-martyr, formerly associated with those who resisted the Nazis, has been replaced by the victim (Rousso, 2011, p. 32). This transformation has had a strong impact on memorial museums. Although the term 'memorial museum' was developed for institutions that were not at the site of an atrocity (especially the US Holocaust Memorial Museum (USHMM) in Washington and *Yad Vashem* in Jerusalem), these institutions' approach (and the term) have become archetypical for many other museums. The Washington and Jerusalem museums became role models for individualizing the victims by displaying their 'ordinary life before' (Köhr, 2007), evoking empathy with the individual victim instead of showing heaps of anonymous corpses.

The aesthetics of dark exhibition rooms and the focus on individual victims have been copied in many museums. Sometimes, however, the victim is represented as part of a collective, as an emotionalizing symbol for national suffering. In other cases, universalization means that museums tell individualized victim stories with the help of objects and historical photographs. Yet, this strategy is applied only to 'our' victims, members of the majority society in the respective post-communist country, while 'their' victims, which is how, for example, Jews are conceived, as I will show, are depicted in a reserved de-individualized manner – for example, by using only few often humiliating photographs taken by perpetrators as in the *Museum of Occupation of Latvia* in Riga.

In the European Union (EU), this universalization includes another dimension: the Holocaust has become a 'negative European founding myth' (Leggewie & Lang, 2011, p. 15). Although European integration after 1945 was in no way a reaction to the Holocaust, Judt (2005) has argued that 'the recovered memory of Europe's dead Jews has become the very definition and guarantee of the continent's restored humanity' (p. 804) since it 'seemed so important to build a certain sort of Europe out of the crematoria of Auschwitz' (pp. 831–832). Post-war Europe is understood as a collective that developed shared structures and institutions in order to avoid a recurrence of the catastrophe of the Holocaust.

In the European search for an identity that goes beyond economic and monetary union, this founding myth provides a compelling common narrative that is otherwise lacking. This is one of the reasons why the *Task Force for International Cooperation on Holocaust Education, Remembrance, and Research* (renamed *International Holocaust Remembrance Alliance*) attracts such interest and includes 31 countries (2016), most of them European. The 'suggestion' that – especially post-communist – countries join the Task Force and implement a Holocaust Memorial Day was the first step towards some kind of European standard. While no official political pressure was applied during the EU's eastern enlargement in 2004, these standards nevertheless seem to have been internalized by the new member countries, not in the sense of implementing defined policies or guidelines, rather a set of conventions around depicting certain subjects in a similar vein to Western policies and in our particular case Western museums. Thus, Hungary's *Holocaust Memorial Centre* opened in Budapest a few weeks before EU accession – despite no permanent exhibition having been installed at that point.

Several post-communist memorial museums invoke Europe. This article will show that they claim they have implemented vaguely defined international standards, understood as copying aesthetical standards established by Western Holocaust memorial museums. The article argues that this Europeanization process has involved a limited formal adoption of aesthetical standards. Only in a few cases has this been accompanied by a shift from a narrative of collective suffering to 'negative memory' (Knigge, 2008, p. 157) focusing on the crimes committed by the country's own (national) collective. Most museums instrumentalize Western Holocaust remembrance aesthetics and a European narrative for nationalist purposes, resulting in a 'national-European narrative' (Sniegon, 2008).

Finally, since 1989 East-Central European countries have experienced, in parallel with the Europeanization of the Holocaust, a re-narration of national history, in particular the invention of a golden era before Communist rule. The narrative of the heroic anti-fascist struggle has been delegitimized along with the communist regimes, and the trauma of communist crimes is placed at the core of remembrance strategies. The resulting divided memory between East and West has prompted representatives of post-communist EU member states to demand that communist crimes be condemned to the same extent as those of the Holocaust. Narratives of Nazi occupation are often used to frame an anti-communist interpretation of history that even depicts Communism as the greater evil.

The article aims to show that one group of museums invokes Europe and tries to prove its European-ness. Yet, another group of museums demands from Europe or the West even more generally, that they acknowledge the East European experience of communist crimes and seeks to contain certain aspects of the memory of Nazism, so that it cannot compete with stories of Soviet crimes.

Actors producing museum narratives

Memorial museums are not neutral spaces of knowledge transfer. Rather, they are core sites for the negotiation of historical narratives and contested spaces for the manifestation of cultural patterns, inclusion and exclusion mechanisms as well as social, ethnic and religious in- and out-groups (Sommer-Sieghart, 2006, p. 159). Memorial museums spell an inherent contradiction. While a memorial is seen to be safe in the refuge of history, a history museum is presumed to be concerned with interpretation, contextualization and critique.

> The coalescing of the two suggests that there is an increasing desire to add both a moral framework to the narration of terrible historical events and more in-depth contextual explanations to commemorative acts. That so many recent memorial museums ... find themselves instantly politicized itself reflects the uneasy conceptual coexistence of reverent remembrance and critical interpretation. (Williams, 2007, p. 8)

Thus, memorial museums represent identity, canonize official memory and make visible the dominant historical narrative.

The directors of the East-Central European memorial museums are appointed by ministries of culture, as is the case with the *Museum of the Slovak National Uprising* (SNU) in Banská Bystrica, Slovakia, the *Jasenovac Memorial Museum* in Croatia, the *Museum of Genocide Victims* in Vilnius, Lithuania, and the *House of Terror* in Budapest, Hungary. In contrast, the *Museum of Occupations* in Tallinn, Estonia, and the *Museum of the Occupation of Latvia* in Riga were initiated by private foundations and co-financed by the state only later on. Still, it has become customary for foreign state representatives who visit Latvia to come to the *Museum of Occupation* (Museum of Occupation of Latvia, 2016a, 2016b), so that even those privately initiated museums have de facto acquired the status of national museums.

Two museums exemplify these museum types. Just like the *Museum of the SNU*, the *Jasenovac Memorial Museum* already existed in the socialist period. First created in 1968, it is situated at the site of the largest Ustaša-led concentration camp on the territory of the so-called Independent State of Croatia (NDH), which existed under Nazi German tutelage between 1941 and 1945. Due to the fact that the fascist Croat (and Bosnian) Ustaša had committed mass murder of Serbs, Roma and Jews there, the communist authorities could not integrate the site into its post-war narrative of 'brotherhood and unity'. As a result, no official memorial existed until the 1960s. Once created in 1966, the memorial became one of the most famous in Yugoslavia. At the same time, the Jasenovac narrative was ambiguous, as members of all Yugoslav nations were listed as victims (Radonić, 2010, pp. 116–118).

The Ustaša regime, Jasenovac and the question of how many people had been killed there during the war were key issues in the evolving nationalist conflict between Serbian and Croatian historians from the 1960s onward. The Institute of Military History in Belgrade tended to depict Croats as 'genocidal', while Franjo Tuđman relativized Ustaša crimes at that time. These nationalist tendencies peaked in the late 1980s and became a key factor in the mobilization before the Yugoslav civil wars when the issue of the number of Jasenovac victims filled the newspapers almost every day (Radonić, 2010, pp. 127–134). For the former Tito partisan, Yugoslav general and historian Tuđman, elected president of Croatia in 1990, Jasenovac played a key role in his idea of 'national reconciliation' between Ustaša and partisans. In his preferred narrative, both had fought for the Croatian cause, only in different ways. In line with this interpretation, he suggested digging up the bones of Ustaša and NDH soldiers killed by partisans near Bleiburg on the Yugoslav-Austrian border and reburying them at Jasenovac next to the victims of the concentration camp in order to create a 'national reconciliation site' (Čulić, 1999, p. 108).

Due to domestic and international protests, Tuđman could not realize his plan and the museum – devastated during the civil war in Croatia between 1991 and 1995 – remained closed until 2006. Ivo Sanader, the next prime minister from the former Tuđman party, the national-conservative Croatian Democratic Union (HDZ), understood its potential as a 'dray-horse towards Europe' (Pavelić, 2005) as one critical journalist put it, while negotiations about accession to the EU were stagnating. Thus, the Ministry of Culture appointed Nataša Jovičić as director, an art historian who had studied in the United States. She was a political appointee whom the government expected to be familiar with international trends at the same time.

In contrast, the construction of the *Museum of Occupations* in Tallinn and the opening of the permanent exhibition in 2003 were funded by the Kistler-Ritso Estonian Foundation named after the Estonian expatriate Olga Kistler-Ritso. Her mother had died while she was a toddler. Her father was deported to Siberia during his stay in Moscow in 1921, just as her uncle some time later after having taken care of her after her father's deportation. Olga Ritso fled to Germany in 1944 and to the US in 1949 (Koch, 2003). She and her husband visited Estonia in 1998. 'When the Kistler family said that they wanted to do something good for Estonia, I immediately thought of a museum', Tunne Kelam, the historian, former dissident and conservative vice-president of the parliament (Kaas, 2002) told the Estonian newspaper *Postimees* (2003, June 11).

As a result, the museum was privately funded, but always closely connected to the Estonian political establishment. Its narrative has been shaped by the shared experience by key actors of Soviet repression. Thus, Heiki Ahonen, the museum's founding director, was a dissident who was imprisoned several times by the Soviet authorities and expelled to Sweden in 1988, where he organized a Relief Committee for Estonian political prisoners. He worked for Radio Free Europe from 1989 to 1998 when he became the chairman of the Kistler-Ritso-foundation (Ahonen, 2005, p. 299). The laying of the corner stone of the museum building in 2002 was then attended by former Estonian president Lennart Meri (1992–2001), who had been deported to Siberia with his whole family in 1941 at the age of 12 and was not allowed to work in his profession as a historian during the Soviet era. The museum's anti-Soviet thrust even led to protests by the Russian foreign ministry (*Postimees*, 14 August 2013).

Narratives: invocating Europe

In the museum field, these actors' preferences and intentions are reflected in the institutions' narratives. The directors of the *Museum of the SNU* in Banská Bystrica and the *Jasenovac Memorial Museum* in Croatia strongly allude to their intended adoption of Europeanization and European standards. In Banská Bystrica, the permanent exhibition no longer presents the SNU, an armed insurrection against Nazi Germany in 1944, as an isolated historical event having 'an exclusive class (regime) or national meaning but rather in a European historical context', as an 'inseparable part of European history' (Lášticová & Findor, 2008, p. 237). The current permanent exhibition was installed in 2004, the year Slovakia joined the EU. Already in 2000, the museum's director and exhibition curator explained his plans to expand the museum's scope 'to fill empty areas in the historical memory so as to be able to correspond to a European standard' (Sniegon, 2008). It is exactly this invocation of such a standard despite the fact that the EU did not apply any pressure in this regard, which makes the analysis of how and why applicant countries addressed Europe and European-ness so interesting. In fact, Slovakia was catching up quickly with international debates in the period after its international isolation during the leadership of Vladimír Mečiar, the prime minister from 1990 to 1998 (with only brief interruptions). Rather, the concept for the new exhibition, written before EU accession, suggests that the norms were already internalized within a society seeking to become 'European'. The concept document argued that,

> even today when Slovakia is striving to take part in the European integration process the anti-fascist resistance and the SNU have significance as political capital which cannot be lost. … This will increase the chances of the Slovak Museum of the National Uprising of presenting the anti-fascist resistance and the SNU as part of the European anti-fascist resistance during the Second World War. (As cited in Sniegon, 2008)

According to the guidebook's introduction, the exhibition 'presents the decisive political, military and social events of Slovak history in the context of the history of Europe in the years 1918–1948' (Museum of the SNU, 2006). The invocation of Slovakia's European character is obvious in the titles of the chapters 'Europe and Slovakia after the year 1938' and 'SNU as a part of European antifascist resistance during the Second World War'. The museum presents the uprising as a worthy example of European integration: 'The Slovak National Uprising was an inseparable part of European antifascist movement. Inspiring for today's effort to integrate Europe was the involvement of people of 32 nations and nationalities in the Uprising.'[1]

Stressing the SNU's European dimension helps highlight the alleged 'Slovak contribution' to the 'building of Europe'. Already in 1996, the director explained why the memory of the uprising was so important for the new independent Slovak state. His comments demonstrate how the museum sought to support the official history of the increasingly authoritarian Mečiar government:

> Thanks to the uprising Slovakia returned to its place among the democratic countries, and the uprising to a great degree washed away that stain which the persistent cooperation between the Hlinka Party's political leadership with Hitler's Nazi Germany constituted. … The uprising is one of the greatest national events in our modern history, which in a sense could be called modern only after the uprising. (Stanislav & Halaj, 1996, pp. 18–19)

At the same time, the permanent exhibition shows the collaborationist regime of Jozef Tiso in an ambivalent way. His party, the Hlinka, is introduced as 'fighters for Slovak autonomy' in the interwar period and the Nazi satellite is not called a 'so-called' Republic: 'In spite of the authoritarian regime the Slovak Republic achieved many positive results in the areas of economy, science, schools and culture, owing to the war boom.' The exhibition avoids mentioning that Slovaks fought against Slovaks during the uprising and not only against Nazi Germany. The integration of the nationalist narrative about 'positive' aspects of the collaborationist regime with the claim to 'Europeanization' constitutes a 'national-European' narrative (Sniegon, 2008) trying to incorporate both dimensions to re-narrate Slovak history after 1989.

Reflecting the Europeanization of the Holocaust, the new permanent exhibition discusses the extermination of Slovak Jews for the first time in a separate section (Lášticová & Findor, 2008, p. 251). However, the explanatory text in the exhibition actually addresses the Holocaust as the '(final) solution of the Jewish question', using Nazi terminology, without adding a 'so-called' or inverted commas. Nevertheless, the section on 'The Tragedy of Slovak Jews' makes clear that in 1942 the 'Slovak Government deported by its own legal-administrative means almost 58.000 Jews from Slovakia to Nazi extermination camps' and 'the deportations were brutally organized, particularly by the members of Hlinka's Guard'. Thus, despite the questionable characterization of the Slovak collaborationist state, the exhibition does not relativize Slovak responsibility for the extermination of Slovak Jews.

The permanent exhibition is dominated by numerous medals, guns and uniforms. However, the aesthetics of the museum in the Holocaust section is more modern. It includes a pillar with portraits of victims from their lives before being sent to the death camps (Figure 1). This representation is a clear allusion to the archetypal individualization of the victim narrative at the USHMM in Washington where the three-storey 'Tower of faces' with private photographs from 1890 to 1941 shows a Jewish community from a village in what is now Lithuania, which was massacred in 1941. The term Holocaust itself is only mentioned once on the Slovak museum website in the description of the section on 'the tragedy of European Jewry and the Holocaust in Nazi occupied countries'.

Interestingly, however, the exhibition does use it as a standard expression in the permanent Slovak 'national exhibition' in Auschwitz-Birkenau, which the Museum of the

Figure 1. Private photographs of Holocaust victims at the *Museum of the SNU*. © Ljiljana Radonić.

SNU developed in 2002. In other words, the Slovaks use very different vocabulary for the domestic and international publics although both exhibitions were essentially designed by the same two curators. Just as in Jasenovac, the Slovak exhibition in Birkenau focuses on individual victim stories. In contrast, visitors in Banská Bystrica learn more about heroes and collective Slovak suffering.

At the *Jasenovac Memorial Museum*, the first permanent exhibition after Croatia's independence only opened during the EU accession talks in 2006. In the preface of the museum's publication, the Croatian Minster of Culture stresses that the *Jasenovac Memorial*'s exhibition has a 'specific architecture' – a phrase that alludes to the circumstance that it looks like other Holocaust memorial museums despite the fact that more Serbs than Jews were killed there. As such, the Minister claims, it is 'part of the European cultural heritage and symbolizes a place which requires remembering and encourages learning about the history of a nation' that has – as the Croatian version but not its English translation (Benčić-Rimay, 2006a, p. 5) continues – 'actually always communicated with the world and Europe' (Benčić-Rimay, 2006b, p. 5). As Nataša Jovičić, the director, stressed in an interview for the Croatian state-owned newspaper (Vjesnik, 2004, July 24) 'we want to be part of the modern European education and museum system and comply with the framework given by institutions dealing with these topics' (Tenžera, 2004). Once more, there were no such official guidelines for applicant countries, so external political pressure in the course of EU accession did not seem to have played a role. Rather, the need to design both a 'Western' and a 'European' exhibition appears to have been internalized by the curators.

The exhibition actually names the USHMM as its role model (Vjesnik, 2004, March 7). It also has many similarities with the permanent exhibition at the *Holocaust Memorial Center* in Budapest which also opened in 2006 (Figure 2). Here, the names of the victims are

(a)

(b)

Figure 2. (a) The permanent exhibition at the *Jasenovac Memorial Museum* in Croatia. (b) The permanent exhibition at the *Holocaust Memorial Centre* in Budapest. © Ljiljana Radonić.

written in white letters on black background. In both the cases, the survivors' interviews and a few belongings of the victims in showcases dominate the dark exhibition space. There are no direct links between the two institutions, but both reference the USHMM as their role model (Seewann & Kovács, 2006a, p. 198). The overriding narrative approach is to allow 'space for the individual victims to speak, so that their dignity is experienced', as the Jasenovac museum website puts it (http://www.jusp-jasenovac.hr). The broadsheet guidebook contains 221 photographs, most of them – in sharp contrast to the collectivist approach focusing on medals and guns at the Museum of the SNU – portraits of victims, from before the war and inside the camp.

The exhibition had been conceptualized together with experts from abroad in order to be 'recognized internationally and follow international standards' (Vjesnik, 2004, February 14). Yet, these experts only came from institutions concerned with the Holocaust, such as the USHMM, *Yad Vashem* or the *Anne Frank House* in Amsterdam. The Croatian curators did not seek to learn from memorial museums at the sites of former concentration and death camps in Nazi Germany or occupied Poland, which try to show the complex character and daily routine of a concentration camp. 'Like at the Anne Frank House', Jovičić wants to 'tell a tragic life story with the help of a few objects' (Vjesnik, 2004, May 24). The *Anne Frank House* naturally focuses on individual victims, first of all the life of the Jewish girl who hid there. In Jasenovac, however, a hyper-modern exhibition also uses new media in order to spotlight only individual victims' stories, blending out the role of Croat perpetrators (Vjesnik, 2004, March 7).

Referring directly to the 'illustration of the executioner and the victim in world museology', Nataša Jovičić did not want to show anonymous corpses and deadly weapons, as exhibitions during communist rule did. Instead, she was keen to create a 'positive message of hope' by turning Jasenovac into a 'site of life'. Criticism of the shock aesthetics used in numerous exhibitions on the Second World War in previous decades is certainly an important issue, but the director at the same time tries to make sense of mass murder by 'sending a message of light to the site of crime' (Vjesnik, 2004, March 7). In this way, Jovičić carries the idea of human rights education at the memorial sites to the extremes by depicting genocide and the Holocaust as something that teaches youth the value of life and thus gives hope for the future.

While the exhibition clearly acknowledges that 'Jews, Roma and Serbs' were deported to Jasenovac in mass transports and often killed immediately after that, the perpetrators are only vaguely identified as 'the Ustaša'. One of the first exhibition panels shows the only non-digital visual representation of perpetrators, Adolf Hitler and the Ustaša leader Ante Pavelić. It informs the visitor that during Pavelić's first visit to Hitler's Bavarian residence in June 1941, Hitler gave him 'full support' for the policy of genocide against the Serbian population. If this explanatory text argued that Hitler gave Pavelić full support for the annihilation of Croatian Jews, it would be factually correct. Yet the Ustaša repressions against Croatian Serbs, their first and greatest enemy image, had actually caused protests by the Nazis since it significantly strengthened anti-Nazi and anti-Ustaša resistance (Schmider, 2002, p. 161). The exhibition does not problematize the genuine Ustaša hatred against Serbs. In contrast to that, it at least tries to tackle the reasons why Jews were persecuted – although the curators seem very naïve when they try to fight anti-Semitism by arguing that Jews were not destructive since many of them were architects who constructed buildings in Zagreb. The exhibition also does not deal with the fact that the Ustaša camps were actually – beside the camps in Transnistria run by Romanians – the only death camps in German-controlled Europe that were operated by local collaborators (Radonić, 2013, p. 236). Thus, designing the Jasenovac site like a Holocaust memorial museum and making the focus on individual victims' stories, an explicit agenda turns out to be convenient: it allows the curators to downplay the question of perpetrators, their motivations and the daily routine at the death camp.

The Europeanization of museum narratives, as in Jasenovac, is sometimes informed by a highly instrumental approach to using the past. On the occasion of Prime Minister Sanader's visit to Jasenovac in 2005, Branko Mijić, a prominent columnist of the left-liberal daily *Novi list*, wrote: 'If this rhetoric had emerged earlier and been perpetuated longer, our image in the world would have been way more positive. This would also have facilitated our entry into the European Community' (2005, April 25). What Mijić positively refers to as rhetoric is what we critically term invocation of Europe and European standards in this article. Two months later, Mijić wrote on the occasion of Sanader's visit to Israel:

> After years of mistrust and suspicion … it is certainly a big issue to make a relatively small, but terribly [strašno] influential country like Israel take sides with us. An enemy less and a partner more is a big success, especially since our future depends on the mercy of the powerful in more than one way. (Pavelić, 2005, June 29)

His instrumental suggestion, tinted with anti-Semitism, is of a conspiracy theory about the alleged influence of Jews or Israel. This shows that advocating European-ness is by no means the same as internalized 'negative memory' of the crimes committed by one's own collective. On the contrary, the instrumental argumentation, as one critic argued, does not 'bring about Europe, reverence or the truth' (Pavelić, 2005, May 15). It becomes clear that the process of apparent Europeanization is neither the result of pressure from allegedly 'terribly' influential and powerful countries, nor of the 'internalization' of European norms in a psycho-analytical sense of the word. Rather, it is a nationalist political strategy, criticized by more liberal sections of society. These are still sceptical towards any kind of memory politics that can be traced back to the HDZ party of former president Tuđman, which initiated the new exhibition.

Why, then, are the two museums at Banská Bystrica and Jasenovac those that invoke Europe the most? There are obvious historical parallels: the first and only time the two newly independent countries had existed before the 1990s was as Nazi German satellites during the Second World War, one called a 'Republic', the other an 'Independent State'. A substantial number of Slovaks and Croats saw these satellite states as liberating them from the constraints of the interwar multi-national states of Czechoslovakia and Yugoslavia. In the 1990s, moreover, both countries were deficient democracies: Mečiar's authoritarian style manoeuvred the country into international isolation and put NATO and EU membership in jeopardy (Haughton, 2003). In Croatia, Tuđman severely limited checks and balances and the freedom of the press even after the end of the war in 1995. Together with his aggressive support for the autonomy of the Croatian part of Bosnia-Herzegovina, his domestic rule left Croatia isolated until his death in 1999 (Radonić, 2010, pp. 135–137).

Their authoritarian style went hand in hand with historical revisionism concerning the character of the Nazi German satellite states. Once Mečiar included the ultra-nationalist and revisionist party *Slovenská národná strana* (SNS) into his government in 1994, the Minister of Education from the SNS distributed Milan Ďurica's anti-Semitic book *History of Slovakia and the Slovaks* (1995) as supplementary teaching material in schools (Bútora, 2007, p. 15). Tuđman claimed that the so-called Independent State of Croatia was 'not only a "Quisling creation" or a "Fascist crime", but also an expression of the Croatian nation's historic desire for an independent homeland' (as cited in Goldstein, 2001, p. 597). Thus, both countries canonized an historical narrative after the Mečiar and Tuđman experience to prove that they had become truly European after their temporary international isolation. Yet, their staged European-ness was highly instrumental.

Narratives: Europe, accept our suffering

The museums in the Baltic countries tell a different story about the past. Paulis Lazda, the American-Latvian history professor who initiated the *Museum of the Occupation of Latvia* in 1993, wanted to ensure the recognition of the occupations of Latvia first by the Soviet Union, then Nazi Germany and then the Soviet Union again, as unjust and not as liberation (Michel & Nollendorfs, 2005, p. 118). He conceived of the acceptance of the 'okupācijas fakts' (Lazda, 2003), the fact that Latvia was occupied and not liberated by the Soviets in 1944, as the basis for the stability of the young Latvian state. According to Lazda, the museum tries to subvert misinformation that dominates nationalist Russian discourses about the Latvian occupations (as cited in Velmet, 2011, p. 192). The museum furthermore seeks to defend Latvia against 'defamation' because of its citizenship and language policies concerning the Russian-speaking population – in effect since 1991 and improved in the course of EU accession talks – and the role of the Latvians in the Holocaust in Latvia (Lazda, 2003). Instead, it should inform Latvians and other countries about the 'tragic' history of the Baltic States, which has allegedly been forgotten by the world (as cited in Blume, 2007, p. 36).

Similarly, Kelam, who proposed the Tallinn *Museum of Occupations*, expressed the hope that it would provide 'younger generations as well as foreign visitors ... [with] an understanding of the difficult path of the Estonian people, but also of their unique experience of preserving their spirit, language and culture' (as cited in Burch & Zander, 2010, p. 57).

The physical centrepiece of the Estonian museum is a massive mock-up of two trains forming a giant gateway to the back half of the museum, one train decorated with a Nazi swastika, the other with a communist red star. Although the installation at the entrance of the museum appears to equate the two symbols and regimes, the exhibition actually uses the Nazi period to show that Soviet crimes in Estonia were worse. Director Ahonen suggests that the Nazi occupation claimed 'fewer casualties' (2005, p. 110) and that the degree of oppression was not as fierce as during the earlier (1940–1941) and subsequent Soviet occupations. 'War brought hope for the re-establishment of the old life, a kind of double rule with Germans as the gents of the country and participation of Estonians in the fighting' (2008, p. 237).

This museum has no guidebook, but in its most extensive publication, *Estonia's occupation revisited. Accounts of an era*, compiled by director Ahonen (2014), the story jumps from 'the first year of occupation' to 'the return of the Soviet occupation' (p. 4) in 1944. The first two-thirds of the work, on 'destruction of the Estonian state' and 'persecution of the people', basically omit the Nazi occupation. This is only discussed in the third and last chapter titled 'Resistance', which implies that 'Estonian Citizens in the German Armed Forces' carried out 'armed and political resistance against the Soviet Union during the Second World War' (p. 2). The Estonian Legion of the Combat SS, Police Battalions formed of Estonian policemen as well as Estonians serving in the Nazi Security Police and the Security Service are mentioned, but 'alleged' crimes appear only in one sentence: 'The alleged involvement of the [36th Front Defence] Battalion in the liquidation of the Novogrudok ghetto and in the execution of Jews has not been substantiated' (p. 38). Director Ahonen instead describes the first year of Soviet occupation as a 'total extermination' of the previous way of living (2008, p. 237).

Mark (2008) has claimed that the Baltic museums use the Nazi era to frame an anti-communist reading of history. From this perspective, museums dealing with both Nazi and communist terror seek to contain two threatening aspects of the memory of Nazism so that its crimes cannot compete with stories of Soviet crimes (p. 336). The first threatening aspect is the capacity of the horrors of Nazism to justify being attracted to the communist state or to evoke sympathy for the idea of the Soviet Union as a liberator. Secondly, the memories of victims of Nazism have the potential to drown out the appeals of those who suffered under communism.

In the Estonian *Museum of Occupations*, the anti-communist framing determines what evidence is deemed meaningful. There is a documentary film for each phase of the occupations from 1941 to 1991. In the 28-minute segment on 'War and the German years', German wartime propaganda films, including the original Nazi comments, speaking of the 'red terror' and 'Bolshevik assaults', are employed as authentic evidence of Soviet atrocities. The exhibition does not use the sources to explore how the Nazis used actual atrocities to manipulate the local population. Instead, the museum lends this material greater authority by combining the Nazi shoots with contemporary witnesses recalling their experience of being shown evidence of Soviet violence as 'pupils' – this is how the captions introduce them in the documentary – under the Nazi occupation.

One of these 'pupils' elaborates in a one-minute long sequence on the 'murdered Jews' that the Klooga concentration camp had 'been described as an extermination camp, but I'd call it a labour camp instead because when the working day was over, the inmates could go to surrounding villages. ... We gave them whatever food there was'. We learn nothing about the fact that the 'Holocaust on the territory of Nazi-occupied Estonia', as the Jewish community of Estonia puts it (Katz, 2012), did not just mean the extermination of up to 1000 Estonian Jews. Jews from the Czech lands, Germany, Lithuania, France and elsewhere were also deported to its concentration camps and mass execution sites.

While the museums in Tallinn and Riga already put great emphasis on the Communist crimes, the Lithuanian *Museum of Genocide Victims* in Vilnius focused solely on the two Soviet occupations from its inauguration in 1992 until one former prison cell was dedicated to the Nazi era in 2011. The exhibition deals with the building's former use as a prison of the Soviet secret services, the NKVD and later the KGB. The fact that the building served as a Gestapo prison from 1941 to 1944 is not mentioned at all in a booklet on the 'KGB prison' and only once on a tiny text board at the exhibition on the ground floor. It reads: 'For visitors willing to get acquainted with the period of Nazi occupation in Lithuania and the Holocaust more extensively we suggest visiting the Vilna Gaon Jewish State Museum.' In the guidebook (Rudienė & Juozevičiūtė, n.d.), the German occupation only appears in the phrase 'after the three-year-long-occupation by Nazi Germany' (p. 32) and in the table with the victim numbers from both periods on the last page. It defines (exclusively) the Soviet crimes as 'physical and spiritual genocide against the Lithuanian people' (p. 3).

While the hidden communist execution chamber was discovered after great efforts, no attempt was made to preserve the obvious traces left by prisoners of the Gestapo prison during the first 18 years of the existence of the museum. In fact, evidence of the use of the prison by communists for interrogations, torture and executions was also absent in the beginning. The site had not been used for the latter purposes since the 1950s. Some cells continued to hold political dissidents, but most were converted to house the archives of the KGB. In this case, the lack of evidence of communist crimes was used to illustrate the ability of the evil Soviets to cover up their crimes and to demonstrate the capacity of post-communist reconstructions to uncover their suppression of the alleged historical truth. In contrast, the same lack of information about the Nazi terror served as a justification for not dealing with this period in the exhibition (Mark, 2008, p. 342).

Having said this, the museum did change its policy regarding one room that contains remaining signs of use as a Gestapo prison cell. Until 2011, these almost unrecognizable graffiti, of, for example, a swastika and the name and date (1943) of the imprisonment of a Polish partisan, remained unmarked. Before the tiny exhibition on the Holocaust (Figure 3) was installed, the illegible graffiti were used in guided tours to illustrate the apparent impossibility of reconstructing the Nazi past. Today, they are illuminated and protected by glass. The audio guide about the prison cells in the cellar still refers to the building as the 'NKVD prison' and 'KGB headquarters', yet eight sentences about the new exhibit in cell number five were added, saying:

> Beside the Gestapo, the troops of the Vilnius extraordinary detachment engaged in the annihilation of Jews and other Lithuanian nationals who were quartet in the building from February 1944 [sic!] till the end of 1943.... The Nazi occupation is one of the darkest periods in the history of the country when around 200.000 Jews were killed. Some Lithuanians participated in the killings.

This article argues that the fact that the exhibit was added can be seen as a sign of the museum's essentially instrumental approach the Europeanization of Holocaust remembrance. Therefore, if one searches for the term Holocaust on the museum's website (http://genocid.lt/muziejus/en) today, the only result is the description of the abovementioned cell, while the main site still invites visitors to 'the former KGB building, where the crimes of the Soviet regime were planned and executed for fifty years' without mentioning Nazi crimes or the Gestapo prison.

Figure 3. Holocaust exhibition at the *Museum of Genocide Victims* in Vilnius added in 2011. © Ljiljana Radonić.

Despite the focus in terms of content on the suffering under communism, the Baltic museums nonetheless either use or at least refer to musealization strategies of the Holocaust like the individualization of victim narratives. Even where the museums decide against adopting practices of international Holocaust museums, they still confirm them as an international standard by taking a stand against them. Thus, according to director Ahonen, the *Museum of Occupations* in Tallinn was inspired by the *Museum of Danish Resistance* in Copenhagen (2008, p. 233). It aimed to be different from Holocaust museums, which he describes as dark and plangent (2005, p. 108). In fact, he says Western Holocaust museums have limited the museum experience through their use of dark and oppressive spaces combined with a hushed reverent tone that was

> almost church-like. In Holocaust-museums, you are told not to speak loudly, have to behave, but the church atmosphere does not support learning. You are just made to act in a certain way. You are dragged into some kind of environment where there should be no doubts. It's all set. (Cited in Mark, 2008, p. 351)

Ahonen opposes importing what he sees as a Western style of representing history that is much less significant to Estonia than it is to other parts of Europe. He insists on the need to show an international audience the validity of the specific nature of an Estonian story that does not need to foreground the Holocaust. When asked what his museum contained regarding the Holocaust, he answered:

> Estonia never had a Jewish question and we just simply don't have any physical items from these people who were killed. … We are never going to do what's done in some concentration camps, let's say they built the new crematorium and said that this is original. (Cited in Mark, 2008, p. 367)

Similar to the two trains in Tallinn, the symbolic equation of the National socialist and communist regimes is also obvious at the *House of Terror* in Budapest, where the Arrow Cross, the symbol of the 'Hungarian Nazis' as they are called in the exhibition, and the red star appear next to each other everywhere, from the museum's logo to its roof and entrance hall. The *House of Terror* is located at the historical site where people were detained, interrogated, tortured or killed, both during the short-lived regime of the Arrow Cross Party (1944–1945) and the communist regime after the Second World War (Ungváry, 2010). The Arrow Cross period after the Nazi occupation in 1944 is only displayed in two and a half of more than 20 rooms. The Holocaust in essence is only represented by a few photographs shown on one of the screens and a projection of ice flowing down the Danube, symbolizing the practice of members of the Arrow Cross party of shooting Jews at the bank of the river in the winter of 1944–1945.

The Horthy era (1920–1944) is depicted as democratic, ignoring its strongly anti-Semitic and authoritarian aspects (Rév, 2008, p. 60). The fact that most Hungarian Jews were deported immediately after the Nazi German invasion, most of them in May 1944 while Horthy was still in power and before the Arrow Cross Party took control, is neglected (Seewann & Kovács, 2006b, p. 53). The responsibility for both regimes is externalized to foreign powers and just a few domestic perpetrators: the Arrow Cross Party and some (predominantly either Jewish or allegedly former Nazi) communists (Horváth, 2008, p. 271). Besides these, Hungarians are solely shown as victims. Even those responsible for atrocities during the Second World War only feature as later 'victims of communist dictatorship', as the guidebook informs us (Schmidt, 2008, p. 86). This is the case, for example, in the prison cells in the cellar, where their photographs and short biographies are exhibited and where all anti-communist fighters are depicted as heroes 'who sacrificed their lives or freedom in the fight against oppression' (Schmidt, 2008, p. 84).

This is the best-known and most visited of the museums that this article considers and also the one opened for the clearest political purposes. Prime Minister Victor Orbán inaugurated the *House of Terror* in a big rally a few weeks before the 2002 parliamentary elections (Apor, 2012, p. 233). Although the building was only used by the security police until the 1950s, the museum exhibits display events up to a speech delivered by Orbán in post-socialist Hungary and the opening of the museum. Both are shown on video screens at the end of the exhibition, surrounded by images of Soviet tanks leaving Hungary, thus suggesting that Orbán himself was involved in liberating Hungary. Nevertheless, even the *House of Terror* adopted the principle of the 'Tower of faces' from the USHMM by exhibiting portraits of the victims on a wall that ranges from the ground floor up to the roof (Figure 4). The 'Hall of Tears' in the basement in turn is strongly reminiscent of the Children's Memorial in *Yad Vashem*. Yet, these aesthetics, originating in the turn towards the individual victim in Western museology, are placed in a narrative of collective (Hungarian) suffering.

Why is it, then, that the first category of memorial museums, in Slovakia and Croatia, feel obliged to demonstrate their conformity with European standards, while the Baltic museums and the *House of Terror* implicitly or explicitly depict the Soviet regime as the

Figure 4. Wall with photographs of victims at the *House of Terror* in Budapest. © Ljiljana Radonić.

greater evil – even though this risks undermining their integration into the EU? In the case of Latvia, for example, in contrast to 1993, when the museum was founded, the country was stable by the late 2000s and independence as a sovereign state no longer needed legitimating. There was no need to correct Soviet distortions of history since the occupation was not a taboo any more. The museum, instead of clinging to a narrow Latvian nationalist perspective, could have opened up its exhibition concept (Blume, 2007, p. 66) – something that Valters Nollendorfs, the vice-director of the museum, has insisted in numerous publications that it is trying to achieve (Nollendorfs, 2008, 2011). More recently, however, the Russian annexation of the Crimea and its direct involvement in the military conflict in Eastern Ukraine highlight that the idea of 'liberating' former parts of the Soviet Union might still be on the agenda of Vladimir Putin – something that could still impact on musealization strategies in East-Central Europe, and especially in the Baltic states.

Conclusion

This research has found two forms of communication with 'Europe' in post-communist memorial museums: first, the affirmation that their own institutional practices are commensurate with European standards concerning Holocaust memory, and second, the demand that Europe must acknowledge the suffering experienced during the communist era. Slovakia and Croatia as the most prominent examples of the first group invoke Europe in the exhibitions commissioned by their respective governments. The fact that those two states had existed only as Nazi satellite states before the 1990s and that those collaborationist regimes were trivialized as 'milestones on the way to independence' by the first freely elected governments obviously made it necessary to prove that the countries were ready for 'Europe' later on.

Lithuania joined the *International Task Force for Holocaust Education, Remembrance and Research* shortly before and Latvia shortly after EU accession as well, but these links seem to have had no impact on the museum policies and practices. In fact, the Lithuanian attorney general even threatened to charge four Jewish Second World War partisans for war crimes against Lithuanian citizens, one of them being Yitzak Arad, the long-term director of the Israeli Holocaust Memorial *Yad Vashem* (Schröder, 2008). As the only ex-Soviet EU accession states, and due to their experience of being annexed by the Soviet Union in 1939 and remaining forcibly incorporated into it after 1944–1945, the Baltic republics felt free to focus to a greater extent on the demarcation from the Soviet narrative than other accession candidates did.

Yet, can Europeanization of remembrance mean depicting the Holocaust as *the* European founding myth and at the same time equating Nazi German and communist Soviet crimes? Both are contemporary developments. Some internationally established trends on how to deal with the Holocaust also have a strong impact on memorial museums in post-communist countries. Even the museums that foreground their national suffering incorporate elements from Holocaust memorial museums or take a stand regarding their aesthetics, indicating just how universalized Holocaust remembrance practices are. Holocaust musealization, aesthetics and individualization of the victim are understood as such strong universal symbols that they are copied – or indignantly refused – even by those actors who want to contain the memory of the Holocaust in order to put their own victims and collective suffering to the fore.

In contrast, the simultaneous commemoration of victims of both Nazi and communist crimes is also apparently evolving into a European standard, but only to the east of the former Iron Curtain. To the west, few have actually heard of 23 August as the 'European Day of Remembrance for Victims of Stalinism and Nazism' established by the European Parliament in 2009.

As the analysis of museums in East-Central Europe has shown, the symbolic equation of the Nazi and Stalinist regimes and their crimes amounts to a form of containment of National Socialism with the aim of depicting communism as the greater evil. This equation and the related allocation of historical responsibility to external forces contravene the concept of negative memory. The same is true for the de-historicized, symbolic Europeanization of Holocaust remembrance that focuses on 'the universal victim' and tends to detach Jews as victims and Germans (and others) as perpetrators from the discourse (Dunnage, 2010). In contrast to that, European remembrance and memory might also mean struggling to learn as much as possible about history and identity of neighbouring societies as well as critically reflecting victims' hierarchies and narratives of collective victimhood, especially in the era of rising nationalist, authoritarian and revisionist powers not only in Hungary and Poland.

Note

1. All quotations without indication of sources are from the texts or audio guides in the exhibitions.

Disclosure statement

No potential conflict of interest was reported by the author.

Funding

This work was supported by the Austrian Academy of Sciences (APART).

ORCID

Ljiljana Radonić ⓘ http://orcid.org/0000-0002-5474-318X

References

Ahonen, H. (2005). Wie gründet man ein Museum? Zur Entstehungsgeschichte des Museum der Okkupationen in Tallinn. In V. Knigge & U. Mählert (Eds.), *Der Kommunismus im Museum. Formen der Auseinandersetzung in Deutschland und Ostmitteleuropa* (pp. 107–116). Köln: Böhlau.

Ahonen, H. (2008). Das Estnische Museum der Okkupationen: Ein Überblick über seine Arbeit. *Forschungen zur baltischen Geschichte, 3,* 233–238.

Ahonen, H. (Ed.). (2014). *Estonia's occupations revisited. Accounts of an era.* Tallinn: The Kistler-Ritso Estonian Foundation.

Apor, P. (2012). Eurocommunism: Commemorating communism in contemporary Eastern Europe. In M. Pakier & B. Stråth (Eds.), *A European memory? Contested histories and politics of remembrance* (pp. 233–246). New York, NY: Berghahn.

Benčić-Rimay, T. (Ed.). (2006a). *Jasenovac memorial site.* Jasenovac: Jasenovac Memorial Site.

Benčić-Rimay, T. (Ed.). (2006b). *Spomen područje Jasenovac.* Jasenovac: Spomen područje Jasenovac.

Blume, R. (2007). *Das lettische Okkupationsmuseum. Das Geschichtsbild des Museums im Kontext der Diskussionen über die Okkupationszeit in der lettischen Öffentlichkeit.* Bremen: Forschungsstelle Osteuropa.

Burch, S., & Zander, U. (2010): Preoccupied by the past. The case of Estonian's Museum of Occupations. *Scandia, 74*(2), 53–73.

Bútora, M. (2007). A compelling testimony. In I. Kamenec (Ed.), *On the trail of tragedy. The Holocaust in Slovakia* (pp. 7–16). Bratislava: Hajko & Hajková.

Čulić, M. (1999). *Tuđman: anatomija neprosvijećenog apsolutizma.* Split: Feral Tribune.

Diner, D. (2007). *Gegenläufige Gedächtnisse. Über Geltung und Wirkung des Holocaust.* Göttingen: Vandenhoeck & Ruprecht.

Dunnage, J. (2010). Perpetrator memory and memories about perpetrators. *Memory Studies, 3*(2), 91–94.

Eckel, J., & Moisel, C. (Eds.). (2008). *Universalisierung des Holocaust? Erinnerungskultur und Geschichtspolitik in internationaler Perspektive.* Göttingen: Wallstein.

Goldstein, I. (2001). *Holokaust u Zagrebu.* Zagreb: Novi liber.

Haughton, T. (2003). Facilitator and impeder: The institutional framework of Slovak politics during the premiership of Vladimír Mečiar. *The Slavonic and East European Review, 81*(2), 267–290.

Horváth, Z. K. (2008). The redistribution of the memory of socialism. Identity formations of the 'survivors' in Hungary after 1989. In P. Apor & O. Sarkisova (Eds.), *Past for the eyes: East European representations of communism in cinema and museums after 1989* (pp. 249–273). Budapest: CEU Press.

Judt, T. (2005). *Postwar: A history of Europe since 1945.* London: William Heinemann.

Kaas, K. (2002, October 22). Okupatsioonimuuseum sai Merilt nurgakivi. *Postimees.* Retrieved from http://www.postimees.ee/

Katz, J. (2012). *Stamped 'Judenfrei': The Holocaust on the territory of Nazi-occupied Estonia 1941–1944.* Tallinn: Jewish Community of Estonia.

Knigge, V. (2008). Europäische Erinnerungskultur. Identitätspolitik oder kritisch-kommunikative historische Selbstvergewisserung. In Kulturpolitische Gesellschaft e. V. (Ed.), *Kultur.macht.europa – europa.macht.kultur. Begründungen und Perspektiven europäischer Kulturpolitik* (pp. 150–161). Bonn: Klartext.

Koch, T. (2003, July 5). Muuseumi rajanud Olga: eestlastel tuleb kokku hoida. *Eesti Päevaleht.* Retrieved from http://epl.delfi.ee/news/eesti/

Köhr, K. (2007). Flucht in die Moral? – Museale Darstellungen des Holocaust zwischen nationalen Fragen und universellen Zugängen. *Medaon,* p. 1. Retrieved from http://medaon.de/pdf/A-Koehr-1-2007.pdf

Lášticová, B., & Findor, A. (2008). From regime legitimation to democratic museum pedagogy? Studying Europeanization at the museum of the Slovak national uprising. In S. Wahnich, B. Lášticová, & A. Findor (Eds.), *Politics of collective memory. Cultural patterns of commemorative practices in post-war Europe* (pp. 237–257). Vienna: Lit.

Lazda, P. (2003). *Latvijas 50 gadu okupācijas muzejs: Kāpēc? Kas? Kā?* Retrieved from http://lpra.vip.lv/om.html

Leggewie, C., & Lang, A. (2011). *Der Kampf um die europäische Erinnerung. Ein Schlachtfeld wird besichtigt*. München: Beck.

Levy, D., & Sznaider, N. (2005). *The Holocaust and memory in a global Age*. Philadelphia, PA: Temple University Press.

Mark, J. (2008). Containing fascism. History in post-communist Baltic occupation and genocide museums. In S. Wahnich, B. Lášticová, & A. Findor (Eds.), *Politics of collective memory. Cultural patterns of commemorative practices in post-war Europe* (pp. 335–369). Vienna: Lit.

Michel, G., & Nollendorfs, V. (2005). Das Lettische Okkupationsmuseum, Riga. In V. Knigge & U. Mählert (Eds.), *Der Kommunismus im Museum. Formen der Auseinandersetzung in Deutschland und Ostmitteleuropa* (pp. 117–129). Köln: Böhlau.

Museum of Occupation of Latvia. (2016a, June 3). *The Iranian Foreign Minister visits the museum*. Retrieved from http://okupacijasmuzejs.lv/en/news/iranian-foreign-minister-visits-museum

Museum of Occupation of Latvia. (2016b, April 1). *Minister of Foreign Affairs of Georgia visits the museum*. Retrieved from http://okupacijasmuzejs.lv/en/news/minister-foreign-affairs-georgia-visits-museum

Museum of Slovak National Uprising. (2006). *Exposition guide*. Banská Bystrica: Múzeum Slovenského Národného Povstania.

Nollendorfs, V. (2008). Vergangenheit in die Zukunft: Das Lettische Okkupationsmuseum vor dem Umbau. *Forschungen zur Baltischen Geschichte*, *3*, 225–232.

Nollendorfs, V. (2011). Die Zukunft der Vergangenheit. Das Okkupationsmuseum in Riga wird (endlich) umgebaut. *Baltische Briefe*, *756*(10), 1–4.

Pavelić, B. (2005, May 15). Koji Ante. *Novi List*. Retrieved from http://www.novilist.hr

Radonić, L. (2010). *Krieg um die Erinnerung. Kroatische Vergangenheitspolitik zwischen Revisionismus und europäischen standards*. Frankfurt am Main: Campus.

Radonić, L. (2013). Croatia's politics of the past during the Tuđman Era (1990–1999) – old wine in new bottles? *Austrian History Yearbook*, *44*, 234–254.

Rév, I. (2008). The terror of the house. In R. Ostow (Ed.), *Politics of collective memory. Cultural patterns of commemorative practices in post-war Europe* (pp. 47–89). Toronto: University of Toronto Press.

Rousso, H. (2011). History of memory, policies of the past: What for? In: K. H. Jarausch & T. Lindenberger (Eds.), *Conflicted memories. Europeanizing contemporary histories* (pp. 23–38). New York, NY: Berghahn Books.

Rudienė, V., & Juozevičiūtė, V. (n.d.). *The museum of genocide victims. A guide to the exhibitions*. Vilnius: The Museum of Genocide Victims.

Schmider, K. (2002). *Partisanenkrieg in Jugoslawien 1941–1945*. Hamburg: E. S. Mittler und Sohn.

Schmidt, M. (2008). *House of terror. Andrássy út 60 (catalogue)*. Budapest: Public Endowment for Research in Central and East-European History and Society.

Schröder, B. (2008). *Litauen und die jüdischen Partisanen*. Retrieved from http://www.heise.de/tp/artikel/28/28708/1.html

Seewann, G., & Kovács, E. (2006a). Halbherzige Vergangenheitsbewältigung, konkurrenzfähige Erinnerungspolitik – Die Shoa in der ungarischen Erinnerungskultur. In B. Faulenbach & F.-J. Jelich (Eds.), *'Transformationen' der Erinnerungskulturen in Europa nach 1989* (pp. 189–200). Essen: Klartext.

Seewann, G., & Kovács, E. (2006b). Juden und der Holocaust in der ungarischen Erinnerungskultur seit 1945. *Südosteuropa*, *54*(1), 24–59.

Sniegon, T. (2008). *Den Försvunna Historien. Förintelsen i tjeckisk och slovakisk historiekultur*. Lund: Lund University Press.

Sommer-Sieghart, M. (2006). Historische Ausstellungen als 'contested space'. In J. Feichtinger, E. Großegger, G. Marinelli-König, P. Stachel, & Heidemarie Uhl (Eds.), *Schauplatz Kultur – Zentraleuropa* (pp. 159–166). Innsbruck: Studienverlag.

Stanislav, J., & Halaj, D. (1996). K deformáciam interpretácie protifašistického odboja na Slovensku a SNP. In D. Halaj & D. Tóth (Eds.), *Nezodpovedané otázky: K spochybňovaniu odboja a SNP v našich národných dejinách* (pp. 9–20). Bratislava: Peter Juriga.

Tenžera, M. (2004, July 27). Novi postav spomen-područja Jasenovac. *Vjesnik*. Retrieved from www.vjesnik.hr

Ungváry, K. (2010). Remembering communist crimes in Hungary: The House of Terror and the Central Cemetery (Rákoskeresztúr). *Journal of Modern European History*, *8*, 155–158.

Velmet, A. (2011). Occupied identities: National narratives in Baltic museums of occupations. *Journal of Baltic Studies*, *42*(2), 189–211.

Welzer, H. (Ed.). (2007). *Der Krieg der Erinnerung. Holocaust, Kollaboration und Widerstand im europäischen Gedächtnis*. Frankfurt am Main: Fischer.

Williams, P. (2007). *Memorial museums. The global rush to commemorate atrocities*. Oxford: Bloomsbury Academic.

Index

Note: Italic page numbers denote figures.